MW01617209

'LET US DIE THAT WE MAY LIVE'

The cult of the saints – martyrs being the most notable among them – was an important feature of the daily life of Early Christian communities. The supernatural powers believed to reside in the saints' relics attracted many visitors to their sanctuaries, and inspired a variety of devotional practices. The homily on the martyr was a culmination of the yearly feast day in and around each sanctuary.

This book presents fresh, lively translations of fourteen such homilies, the majority for the first time in English. The homilies were delivered in some of the main cities of the Greek East of the later Roman Empire, by well-known figures such as Basil of Caesarea, Gregory of Nyssa and John Chrysostom, as well as the equally gifted preachers, Asterius of Amasea and Hesychius of Jerusalem.

Each author receives a separate introduction, and each homily also has its own introduction and notes. The main introduction gives useful background information on the cult of the martyrs in Roman Asia Minor, Palestine and Syria, and on the martyr homily as a literary genre, while also presenting possible methodological approaches to the texts.

'Let Us Die That We May Live' offers an approachable, surprising and not always reverent insight into the life of the Early Church. It reveals the full importance of the martyr homily in terms of style, treatment of its subject and social and liturgical issues, in a way that will be useful across disciplines such as theology, classical studies and religion.

Johan Leemans is Postdoctoral Fellow at the Faculty of Theology, Katholieke Universiteit Leuven. **Wendy Mayer** is Research Fellow in the Centre for Early Christian Studies, Australian Catholic University. **Pauline Allen** is Professor of Early Christian Studies and Director of the Centre for Early Christian Studies, Australian Catholic University. **Boudewijn Dehandschutter** is Professor of Patrology and Ancient Church History at the Faculty of Theology, Katholieke Universiteit Leuven.

'LET US DIE THAT WE MAY LIVE'

Greek homilies on Christian martyrs from Asia Minor, Palestine and Syria (*c.* AD 350–AD 450)

Johan Leemans, Wendy Mayer, Pauline Allen and Boudewijn Dehandschutter

Routledge
Taylor & Francis Group

LONDON AND NEW YORK

First published 2003
by Routledge
11 New Fetter Lane, London EC4P 4EE

Simultaneously published in the USA and Canada
by Routledge
29 West 35th Street, New York, NY 10001

Routledge is an imprint of the Taylor & Francis Group

Typeset in Garamond by
Florence Production Ltd, Stoodleigh, Devon
Printed and bound in Great Britain by
TJ International Ltd, Padstow, Cornwall

British Library Cataloguing in Publication Data
A catalogue record for this book is available from the British
Library

Library of Congress Cataloging in Publication Data
Let us die that we may live: Greek homilies on
Christian martyrs from Asia Minor, Palestine, and Syria,
c. 350-c. 450 AD/Johan Leemans . . . [et al.].
p. cm.
Includes bibliographical references and index.
1. Christian martyrs–Turkey–Sermons. 2. Christian martyrs–
Middle East–Sermons. 3. Sermons, Greek. I. Leemans,
Johan, 1965–

BR1604.23.L48 2003
252'.9–dc21   2002036979

ISBN 0–415–24041–7 (hbk)
ISBN 0–415–24042–5 (pbk)

CONTENTS

PREFACE

Homilies constitute an exciting part of the legacy which the early Church bequeathed to posterity. While these texts suffered from neglect by scholars during the past centuries, they now enjoy a genuine and increasing interest from scholars. This may have to do with the fact that they offer the reader a 'life view', a window on a late antique ecclesial community in action. We read the same words as ordinary Christians at the time may have heard. By reading them, we become aware of both distance and nearness. The local early Christian community is both immeasurably different and yet in many respects so similar to local church communities of today. Just like today these communities gathered to meet one another and to celebrate, to sing and to pray together, to hear readings from the Scriptures, to receive instruction, moral exhortation and encouragement in the sermon. Many of the issues addressed in late antique sermons still exist today: exegesis of scriptural passages, moral issues, admonishments for the spiritual life and the like. These similarities may give the reader a justified sense of recognition but they do not of course do away with the differences: a different style of preaching, a different approach to the Scriptures, a different philosophical and theological background.

Beyond these differences, however, there are even bigger challenges in homiletical study to be confronted: of many texts or groups of texts a study of the textual transmission or a reliable text-edition does not yet exist; in many cases the question of authenticity has not yet been addressed, let alone been solved satisfactorily. In these circumstances it is no wonder that scholars have turned only fairly recently to the study of these texts. Consequently there are still large gaps to be filled, both in studying these texts as well as in making them accessible. With this volume we contribute to this enterprise by presenting English translations of and succinct commentaries on fourteen martyr homilies, all originally in Greek. These homilies, also called panegyrics on martyrs or orations in praise of martyrs, were largely delivered on the annual feast day of the martyr in question. The homilies collected in this volume were delivered by important authors such as Basil of Caesarea, Gregory of Nyssa, Asterius of Amasea, John Chrysostom and Hesychius of Jerusalem. Given the numerous studies on the cult of the saints existing to date, the importance and renown of the authors involved and the increasing scholarly interest, it is really surprising that there are very few studies that focus on these texts. That many of the homilies have no translation in English prior to this one, also bears testimony to this neglect.

Yet, for several reasons, these texts are most interesting. First, as homilies, they give us a window on an ecclesial community during a liturgical celebration. Second, we know that during martyr feasts the entire community (men and women, rich and poor, educated and illiterate) were present. This feature singles out this kind of homily in comparison to homilies on more learned theological or scriptural topics. Third, these texts constitute important elements of the hagiographical tradition of that particular saint or martyr. Thus, this volume also contributes to hagiographical studies. Fourth, they tell us something about the interaction between the preacher and his audience: what was the intention of the preacher? (e.g. to portray the martyr as an example worthy of imitation); how did he convey his message? (e.g. use of rhetorical strategies; biblical models and quotations); how did the audience react? Finally they also offer material for a 'theology of martyrdom', an important element of early Christian spirituality. The latter aspect is reflected in the main title: 'Let Us Die That We May Live', a quotation from the sixth chapter of Basil's *Homily on the Forty of Sebaste*. This adage reflects the early Christian martyrs' conviction that their true home was with God, the day of their death being their *dies natalis* (day of birth).

For all these reasons these martyr homilies deserve to be made accessible for a more thorough study and a wider audience. We intend to limit ourselves to martyr homilies in Greek, namely two by Basil of Caesarea, three by Gregory of Nyssa, three by Asterius of Amasea, four by John Chrysostom and two by Hesychius of Jerusalem. We put these texts into the public domain of scholarship by providing English translations and introductory commentaries. The latter comprise a general introductory chapter, an introduction to each individual author and to each separate homily. Where necessary for understanding the text, additional notes for clarification are added. They constitute a primary commentary on our texts.

This book is the result of a collaboration by a Belgian–Australian team: Boudewijn Dehandschutter and Johan Leemans (Leuven), Wendy Mayer and Pauline Allen (Brisbane). The first seeds were planted prior to and during the Patristic Conference of 1999 in Oxford, the project taking definitive shape at the end of that year. Though each contributor is responsible for the chapter(s) assigned to her or him, virtually all parts have benefited from being read by at least one other member of the team. Wendy Mayer's effort in checking the English translations of Boudewijn Dehandschutter and Johan Leemans, in particular, must be mentioned in this regard.

At the end of this project it is our pleasant duty to thank the persons and institutions involved. On the Australian side we would like to mention the Centre for Early Christian Studies at the Australian Catholic University (of which Pauline Allen is Director), the Australian Research Council (which generously funds the research work of Wendy Mayer) and Dinah Joesoef (Administrative Assistant of the Centre for Early Christian Studies). On the Belgian side our thanks go to the Katholieke Universiteit Leuven, to the staff of its Library of Theology, to Britt Weynants (Secretariate of the Faculty of Theology) and to the Flemish Fund of Scientific Research, which is funding the postdoctoral research project of which this volume is a part.

Johan Leemans
Wendy Mayer
Pauline Allen
Boudewijn Dehandschutter

ABBREVIATIONS

BHG	*Bibliotheca Hagiographica Graeca*
BHL	*Bibliotheca Hagiographica Latina*
CPG	*Clavis Patrum Graecorum*
DHGE	*Dictionnaire d'histoire et de géographie ecclésiastiques*
EEC	*Encyclopedia of Early Christianity*
GCS	*Die griechischen christlichen Schriftsteller der ersten Jahrhunderte*
GNO	*Gregorii Nysseni Opera*
HE	*Historia ecclesiastica*
LTK	*Lexikon für Theologie und Kirche*
PG	*Patrologia Graeca*
PL	*Patrologia Latina*
PO	*Patrologia Orientalis*
RAC	*Reallexikon für Antike und Christentum*
SC	*Sources Chrétiennes*

General Introduction

INTRODUCTION

The christianisation of the Roman Empire gained momentum spectacularly during the fourth and fifth centuries AD. In those centuries the still young religion increasingly succeeded in finding its way into the veins of the Roman Empire and in stamping its own distinctive mark on its face. Though many things remained the same, others changed, the whole being irrevocably different from a century before (Mayer and Allen 2000: 4). This process of christianisation found a poignant expression in the christianisation of place and time (Markus 1990; Perrin 1995; Hunt 1998b).

The christianisation of the space available for buildings is an obvious sign of the growing importance of the young religion. From the fourth century onwards more modest church buildings were gradually substituted by splendid basilicas. In the process pagan temples were demolished or reused for the building of places for Christian worship (Fowden 1978; Vaes 1984–86). Besides the use of the available building space the regulation of time was also increasingly christianised, the most spectacular outcome of this process being no doubt the inauguration of the Christian era *Anno Domini* in the first decades of the sixth century. Parallel to and in competition with the traditional calendar featuring pagan feasts and celebrations of the imperial cult, a full-blown Christian calendar came progressively into existence with the weekly Sundays as regular points of interval and the strong liturgical times – the feasts of Easter and Christmas, the time of preparation of Lent and (later) Advent and the other feasts such as Pentecost, Ascension and Epiphany – as culmination points.

The cult of the saints contributed greatly to this process of christianising place and time. During the first centuries this cult was celebrated more or less in hiding, venerated with celebrations situated on or in the neighbourhood of their graves in graveyards at the outskirts of the cities. When Christianity grew, and certainly from the moment it enjoyed imperial support, the cult of the martyrs was celebrated more openly and with greater splendour, reflected in that the martyrs' sanctuaries grew from modest chapels into splendidly adorned basilicas. These became visible signs of the Christian occupation of that particular part of the territory. From the fourth century onwards not only martyrs were venerated but also important and pious bishops, monks and biblical saints, thus multiplying the number of sanctuaries. It also led to an increase in feast days since the memory of a saint was especially celebrated on his or her *dies natalis*: the day of the saint's death. These feast days came to supplement the regular feast days, and certainly in big cities with many churches and sanctuaries the number of saints venerated could be considerable.

This volume concentrates on the earliest 'type' of saint: that of the martyr (including the biblical protomartyr Stephen). It presents in English translation fourteen martyr homilies (or panegyrics), delivered on the annual feast day of the martyr in question. The homilies collected here were delivered by Basil of Caesarea, Gregory of Nyssa, Asterius of Amasea, John Chrysostom and Hesychius of Jerusalem. They reflect the vitality of the martyr cult during the period AD 350–450 in the eastern part of the Roman Empire in important cities such as Antioch and Jerusalem, middle-sized cities such as Sebaste, Caesarea and Amasea as well as the modest town of Euchaïta, which boasted the most important sanctuary of the soldier-martyr Theodore the Recruit. They offer a window onto the local celebrations of the cult of the martyrs as well as specimens of the homiletical activity of the early Church.

To introduce these texts we will discuss the following topics: (1) the veneration for martyrs in the East of the Roman Empire (fourth–fifth centuries) and the panèguris as the yearly point of culmination of this veneration and *Sitz im Leben* for the homilies in praise of the martyrs; (2) the literary genre of these martyr homilies, their purpose and the influence of classical rhetoric; and (3) a sketch of several possible avenues for reading and interpreting these texts against the background sketched in this introduction.

MARTYRIUM AND RELICS: THE CENTRE
OF THE MARTYR CULT

The centre of the martyr cult was the martyrium, the sanctuary that contained the martyr's relics. In some cases martyria were already present within the city gates in the middle of the fourth century: St Demetrius in Thessaloniki and sanctuaries built by Constantine and his sons in cities such as Jerusalem (St Sepulchre) and Constantinople being some examples (Skedros 1999; Wagner-Lux and Brackmann 1996: 695–700; Grabar 1943–6: I, 212–13; 315–22). Yet, allowing for regional differences, it was not before the last decades of the fourth century that martyr's sanctuaries were gradually making their way into the city centres. Before this shift, they were mostly situated in the cemeteries, outside the city walls. On the occasion of the yearly feast of the martyr, 'cities were turned inside out as Christian bishop and clergy led their people away from the urban centre to the martyr shrines which encircled the outskirts' (Hunt 1998b: 254).

For Cappadocia there are many examples of shrines at the border of cities. In Caesarea this was certainly the case for the shrines of Gordius and Mamas, as well as for the shrine in which some indecently dressed women were dancing while drunk.[1] The Basiliade, Basil of Caesarea's great caritative project, most probably also containing a martyr's shrine, was also situated outside the city,[2] as was also the case for the sanctuary of Mamas in Nazianze.[3] For Pontic Amasea we have one testimony for a martyrium outside the city: in his *Homily in Praise of the Holy Martyrs* Asterius asks what is more beautiful than seeing a city emptying itself because its inhabitants are going to the holy place of the martyr's shrine and to celebrate the holy mysteries of true religion.[4] The great metropolis Antioch could boast a large number of sanctuaries (Maraval 1985: 337–42), among them those of Babylas, one of the city's former bishops, and of Julian, a martyred bishop of Cilicia, both situated on the outskirts of the city. The most famous Antiochean cemeteries with collective martyria, housing the relics of several martyrs, were outside the gate beside the road leading to the suburb of Daphne and outside the Romanesian gate (Pasquato 1998: 207; Mayer and Allen 2000: 19). So numerous were the tombs of martyrs in the suburbs and surrounds of the city that John Chrysostom on occasion claimed that they surrounded the city like a protective wall.[5]

But the veneration of martyrs was not only a matter of Christians living in or near the city; it was also an essential part of Christian life in small country villages. For Asia Minor in the fourth century many testimonies support the idea that the martyr cult acted as a standard-bearer for Christianity and contributed to the spread of the religion (Mitchell 1993: 68–9). An inscription from NW Cappadocia attests the veneration of a martyr Lucian (Eyice and Noret 1973). Gregory of Nazianze's *Letter 122* mentions a yearly panèguris in the village of Arianza and in a letter to Gregory of Nyssa he apologises for being unable to meet his namesake on a panèguris in Euphemiades, a village near Nazianze.[6] In his famous *Letter 1* Gregory of Nyssa narrates how he travelled on horseback in a mountainous region to meet Helladius of Caesarea who was attending a panèguris in the small village of Andaemonè.[7] In the province of Pontus there is the sanctuary of Theodore the Recruit in Euchaïta, a small town that thanks to Theodore's cult would rise to the importance of an episcopal see (Trombley 1985). In Armenia too, the martyr cult was already during the fourth century present in small villages. Basil of Caesarea's *Letter 95*, addressed to Theodotus of Nicopolis, attests the existence of a well-attended panèguris, held in the month of June, in a village with the name Phargamos.[8] From the *Passion of Athenogenes* (BHG 197b) we learn that for this martyr there existed a sanctuary in Pedachthoe, a large estate at some distance from a city[9] and the *Passion of Eustratius and his Companions*, possibly dating from the fourth century, informs us that these martyrs had at the time a sanctuary in Ararauka, a small village in the neighbourhood of Sebaste.[10]

A similar picture arises for the Syrian countryside, as is testified by some of Chrysostom's panegyrics, most notably his sermon *On the Holy Martyrs* (Pasquato 1998: 207). The text makes it abundantly clear that there were many martyrs in the countryside: the Christians there may not have many gifted preachers but they can hear many martyrs' sweet voices, since God, to compensate for their poverty of preachers, 'organised a greater number of martyrs to be buried among them'. Elsewhere in this sermon he says that there are more martyrs (and festivals) in the countryside than in the city. Moreover there is the absence of Flavian, the bishop of Antioch, who is in the countryside to attend a martyr festival (panèguris) leaving John to preach in his stead. This also indicates something of the importance attached to martyr festivals in Syria and to the importance of at least this festival in the Syrian countryside. Moreover, Flavian's journey provides an interesting parallel to the above-mentioned presence of

Helladius of Caesarea at a panèguris in an at least according to Gregory of Nyssa desolate region in the Cappadocian mountains.[11]

Now, what did these martyria look like? *Grosso modo* up to the Constantinian period above the tombs of martyrs arose commemorative monuments marking the presence of the tomb and constituting the first sanctuaries where the faithful could celebrate the martyr's memory. These relatively modest sanctuaries were mostly found in suburban cemeteries or along the roads leading to a city. From the Constantinian period onwards, together with the gradual expansion of Christianity, these monuments were replaced by more splendid buildings: both martyria proper and martyrs' sanctuaries attached to or within the walls of a church building. The same evolution happened to the sacred places in the Holy Land: there too increasingly splendid sanctuaries were built to commemorate and celebrate the events of Christ's life and death as well as those of other biblical saints, the veneration of the latter being fuelled by the discovery (invention) of their relics, starting with those of St Stephen in 415. Trying to picture what these sanctuaries looked like is of importance for getting in touch with the ambience in which the panegyrics were delivered. In addition it helps one to grasp something of the dynamics going on between the preacher and his audience (Mayer 1997).

This is most evident with regard to the basic plan according to which these martyria were built. This can be very diverse: some are built following a quadrangular or rectangular plan, others in a circular or a polygonal form, still others according to a cruciform plan (Grabar 1943–6, I). So the sanctuary of Babylas, in which Chrysostom preached his panegyric *On the Martyr Babylas*, shows a clear cruciform plan. Other martyria show a more complicated floor plan, being adorned with several absides or combining two or more floor plans. The latter is the case for the martyrium that Gregory of Nyssa had built in Nyssa. According to Gregory's detailed description of the building in a letter to his friend Amphilochius of Iconium[12] – because of the absence of archaeological remains of martyria in Cappadocia an extremely valuable source – the martyrium in Nyssa combined a cruciform plan with a circular one. The building had four rectangular halls, each measuring approximately 3.65 × 5.48 m. These four halls, the four arms of the cross, did not meet but were connected by four concave absides. The octagonal space in the middle was roofed by a complicated dome-construction (Klock 1984; Stupperich 1991). The martyrium was provided with an entrance hall and a peristylium, formed by forty pillars.

Of some other martyria, or churches also functioning as martyria, we can gather the appearance from less detailed literary testimonia. They concern sanctuaries from Nazianze (Cappadocia) and Pedachthoe (Armenia). An example of a plain octagonal-shaped church building in Cappadocia is the one built by Gregory of Nazianze's father, a description of which is given in Gregory's *Funeral Oration*. We learn from this that the church had two storeys and that it was surrounded by a peristylium.[13] Another octagonal construction with a dome was built in the fourth century in Pedachthoe (Armenia) by the martyr Athenogenes, whose own relics were buried in it. The building was nicknamed 'the cage', suggesting a rather small building of a conic form.[14]

The care spent on the building of martyria is especially revealed by the materials used and the decorations with which the buildings were adorned. Again we have only literary sources at our disposal to picture something of what a martyrium must have looked like. In his letter to Amphilochius about the martyrium in Nyssa, Gregory explicitly mentions that he cannot afford the cost to pay stone-carvers to make the stones perfectly rectangular and smooth, so that they could be placed seamlessly upon each other. Clearly such a building style was a luxury, which also is proven by the fact that Gregory of Nazianze proudly mentions that such a careful and expensive style of building was applied in the church constructed by his father in Nazianze.[15] But the martyrium in Nyssa offered work enough for the stone-carvers. They were to carve the eight monumental pillars carrying the whole construction. These had to be placed on a large base in the form of an altar and were to be crowned by carefully carved Corinthian capitals. Moreover, together with many other craftsmen, the stone-carvers were to assist in the adornment of the entrance hall, which was to consist of marble decorations and sculpture, including the frieze running along the roof. Since the main purpose of Gregory's letter was to ask Amphilochius to send craftsmen to Nyssa, the description of the building stops here. Gregory of Nazianze in his description of the church in Nazianze also mentions the same elements. The pillars were of an exceptional marble from abroad but Gregory hastens to assure his listeners that the polychromous marble, coming from inland quarries and used in the decoration of the frieze, was of the same superb quality.[16]

More details can be gathered from Gregory of Nyssa's detailed description (ecphrasis) of the sanctuary of Theodore the Recruit in the oration in praise of that martyr. We learn that for this sizeable building the mason had polished the stones until they had the smoothness of silver. The building was decorated with wooden statues of animals and with a mosaic floor. Most attention, however, the orator gives to the walls of the sanctuaries, which were covered with colourful paintings, depicting the martyr's brave deeds, his most blessed end and Christ present at the contest.[17] A similar series of paintings is described in Asterius of Amasea's *Ecphrasis on Euphemia*. These series of paintings on the walls of the sanctuaries did not only add to the beauty of these buildings but were also of great use for the religious and spiritual formation of the viewer (Leemans 2000).

All in all, these literary sources offer us a basic but colourful image, scanty as it may be, of what a martyrium was like. In any case we can imagine ourselves more or less what it must have been like. The most important element of the sanctuary, however, was not the building itself but the martyr's relics it contained. These were the guarantee of the living presence of the saint and the heart of his or her cult.

The bones and other remains were the tangible centre of the cult because they guaranteed the real presence of the martyr. This is perfectly consonant with the *Lebensgefühl* of man in antiquity, for whom the divine, the *numinosum* was almost palpably present and the martyr's tomb a place where heaven and earth met (Brown 1981: 1–22).[18] The conviction that in the relics the martyr him- or herself was present, led to many devotional practices in the martyrium. Before discussing these, the preliminary question is: where did these relics come from?

The veneration of the martyr has always been a local religious phenomenon. Originally the martyr belonged to the local community and was venerated by this local community. Such was the case with a martyr like Gordius, a centurion who as a catechumen was martyred under Licinius in Cappadocian Caesarea and was venerated there, as is testified by Basil of Caesarea's encomium about him. These cases are not rare but left relatively fewer traces in the sources than the translations, that is the transportation of relics from one place to another. The earliest attested case is the one of the relics of St Babylas. Initially buried in the common cemetery, they were on the initiative of the Caesar Gallus moved to Daphne, the famous suburb of Antioch. Later, the emperor Julian the Apostate moved them back. They found a definitive resting place in a church dedicated to him.[19] A spectacular example of the spread of a cult through translations of relics is that of the Forty of Sebaste. Despite their wish – laid down in their so-called *Testament* – that their relics should always be buried together, before the end of the fourth century they were scattered all over the Roman Empire, East and West.[20] The correspondence of Basil the Great preserved an exchange of letters showing how Basil, through the mediation of his nephew Iunius Soranus and of Vetranio, the bishop of Tomi (Scythia), gained possession of the relics of Sabas, who had died during persecutions in Scythia.[21]

Another way of founding a new martyr cult or spreading an existing cult was the invention: as a consequence of a dream or another form of revelation relics were detected. The invention under the episcopacy of Ambrose of the relics of the two Milanese martyrs Gervasius and Protasius is a well-known and fairly early example.[22] In Gregory of Nazianze's *Oration on Cyprian* one reads the story of the invention of the martyr's relics, which had been kept for a long time by a pious Christian woman.[23] A spectacular invention is described at the end of the *Passion of the Forty Martyrs of Sebaste* (BHG 1201). After the martyrs' bodies had been burned it was decided to throw the relics into the river to avoid the origin of a cult. But the relics stayed together and collected themselves at a rock in the river. After three days this was revealed to Peter, the bishop of Sebaste, and, in a passage employing direct speech, the relics ask the bishop to come to the river and take them out. When he, together with some of his clerics, arrive at the spot, they see the relics glowing like stars, assisting them in collecting them.[24]

So, these relics made of the martyrium a sanctuary, a holy place, a place where heaven and earth met. It was a place people could visit for no other reason than simply to find spiritual nourishment, to spend some time of recollection. In *On the Ascension* Chrysostom mentions that laity for a long time already used to visit the martyrium at the Romanesian gate to spend a moment of prayer there,[25] and in his *On the Holy Martyrs* he strongly encourages his audience:

> whenever the crowd of affairs and multitude of day-to-day worries . . . spreads a thick darkness over [your] mind . . . leave [your] house, exit the city, say a firm farewell to these confusions and go off to a martyrium, enjoy that spiritual breath of fresh air, forget [your] substantial preoccupation, luxuriate in the peace and quiet, be in the company of the

saints, . . . pour out much supplication and, when [you] have shed the weight from [your] conscience through all of these actions, go back home with considerable refreshment.[26]

During a visit to the martyr's sanctuary, a number of devotional actions could also be practised. Of these, the first is the invocation to the martyrs, testimony to the widespread belief that it was profitable to ask favours of them.[27] To be sure, martyrs shared this potential of being suitable intercessors with other deceased persons and asking for the support of deceased family members was not unusual (Michel and Klauser 1976: 19–21). Yet, it would seem that the martyrs were considered extremely powerful intercessors, providing influential connections with God. In any case the belief in their intercessory powers is voiced in powerful passages in some of the homilies in this volume. In his panegyric on the Forty of Sebaste Basil of Caesarea describes how the martyrs are asked for their assistance and encourages his audience to continue this:

> The one who is in trouble takes refuge in the Forty, the one who rejoices runs off to them – the former to find release from difficulties, the latter to protect his prosperity. Here a pious woman is found praying for her children, begging for the return of her husband who is away, for his safety because he is sick. Let your petitions be with the martyrs.[28]

Another example is found at the end of Gregory of Nyssa's homily on Theodore the Recruit. There, on behalf of the community of Euchaïta, the homilist asks the martyr to use his *parrèsia* with God and to provide assistance against the imminent danger of the incursions of the Scyths.[29] Reading this passage, and keeping in mind that in the homily's introduction the Recruit has already been thanked for similar assistance in the past, one has the impression that Theodore functions towards the community of Euchaïta as a kind of patron saint. Another case of a martyr functioning as patron saint is that of Phocas, the martyr of Sinope (Pontus). Concerning him Asterius narrates in his encomium how he is believed to protect the seamen: when a storm was expected, he was seen awaking the helmsman who was dropping asleep over his rudder, at another moment stretching the ropes and taking care of the sail, looking forward from the prow to the shallow waters. The seamen have turned the songs they usually sing for the relief of their labour into a eulogy for Phocas.

And every day they reserve at the table an equal part of their food for Phocas. This part is then bought by one of them and the money is distributed among the needy.[30]

But the belief in the power of the martyrs went further than invocation or a particular group or community having a particular martyr as patron saint. It was also believed that touching the relics or even only being in their neighbourhood had a supernatural and salutary effect. 'He who touches the bones of a martyr', says Basil, 'partakes in the sanctity and grace that reside in them'.[31] About the relics of the martyr Julitta he says that they sanctify both the place where they rest and the people who assemble there.[32]

According to Gregory of Nazianze, 'the bodies of the martyrs have the same power as their holy souls, whether one touches them or just venerates them. Just a few drops of their blood, the signs of their suffering, can effect the same as their bodies.' Chrysostom also expresses this belief in various places (Pasquato 1998: 212–13): 'Not just the martyr's bones, but even their tombs and chests brim with a great deal of blessing.' Therefore, it is good, he advises his audience, to take holy oil – oil that has touched the martyr's relics – and anoint the whole body with it.[33] As the salutary effect of the martyr's remains Chrysostom mentions 'the healing of fevered bodies and forgiveness of sins, removal of evil, treatment of diseases of the soul, incessant prayer, bold speech with God – everything spiritual and brimming with heavenly blessings'.[34] In the same vein, Gregory of Nazianze mentions as effects caused by the veneration or touching of the martyr's relics: the chasing away of demons, the curing of the sick, the causing of visions and predictions of the future.[35]

A combination of the second and the third element we find in the phenomenon of incubation. This is the widespread practice of people sleeping in sanctuaries, hoping to receive dreams or visions about the future or to be cured from health problems or handicaps. In paganism it was especially practised in the cult of Asclepius and of Isis and Serapis. For Christianity important centres for incubation were those of Cosmas and Damianus in Constantinople and of Cyrus and Johannes in the neighbourhood of Alexandria (Wacht 1997). But martyria also functioned as places to practise incubation, as is testified by a lengthy passage from Gregory of Nyssa's *Second Homily on the Forty of Sebaste*. There he tells his public about a limping soldier who received, while sleeping in the sanctuary of the Forty Martyrs of Sebaste in Ibora (near Nyssa), a vision and was cured.[36] Gregory then continues the homily with his own experience of an incubation by relating a dream-vision in which a group of soldiers (presumably the Forty) were threatening him and it was only thanks to the mildness of one of them that he escaped a severe beating. Gregory interprets his dream as a criticism of his reluctant attitude to attend the panèguris of the Forty inaugurating their cult in their sanctuary at Ibora.[37]

In exchange for a healing, a safe return-journey, a vision or other benefits received from the martyr, people often brought presents to the martyrium. These could be hands, feet, eyes or another part of the body in wood or silver, symbolising the part of the body that was healed thanks to the martyr.[38] According to Asterius, Phocas' sanctuary was decorated with many treasures, mainly gifts from the Christian emperors but also a diadem and a cuirass offered by the leader of the barbarian Scyths to thank the martyr and God for his power and military success.[39]

The deeply-rooted belief in the miraculous power present in the martyr's relics also led to the practice of *inhumatio ad sanctos*: people having themselves buried in the immediate vicinity of the martyr's relics.[40] The practice is well attested for late antiquity, both in the East and the West of the Roman Empire. Christians hoped that the presence of the relics would protect their own grave against demons and the more mundane dangers of tomb violation. More-over, the martyrs were expected to act as the defenders of the deceased before God. Finally it was hoped that the deceased would be resurrected together with the martyr (Duval 1988).

For Cappadocia we have several testimonies of such burials *ad sanctos* (Duval 1988: 66–73). Both Gregory of Nyssa's parents and his sister Macrina were buried in the vicinity of relics of the Forty of Sebaste. With regard to his parents, Gregory states explicitly that this burial *ad sanctos* happened 'so that at the moment of the resurrection they should be raised together with bold-speeched helpers'.[41] Gregory of Nazianze, his parents and his beloved brother Caesarius also had a burial place in the vicinity of relics,[42] as was also the case for his uncle Amphilochius and his family. They were buried in a monumental tomb consisting of two storeys: the lower one for the family and the upper one for martyrs' relics.[43] For Syria we have a number of examples of holy men, themselves 'athletes of virtue' who were buried in the neighbourhood of relics (Duval 1988: 73–83). Here we only single out the case of the ascetics Theodosius, Aphrahates and Macedonius who were buried in the sanctuary of the Julian on whom Chrysostom delivered a panegyric.[44]

As is clear from the above, the martyrium, with the tomb and the relics as its centre, was a place where the divine was present, where contact was possible with what we call today 'the transcendent'. The described devotional practices certainly took place all year and, probably depending upon their size and the importance of their location, the martyria received visitors throughout the year. Moreover, it might be surmised from several passages in martyr homilies that the martyria not only exercised a religious and liturgical function but also had social and caritative functions attached to them. Gregory of Nyssa's eloquent testimony about Theodore the Recruit's sanctuary in Euchaïta, mentioning both the great number of visitors and their non-religious expectations, is in this regard very revealing:

> He (sc. Theodore) turned this place into a hospital for the most diverse diseases, a harbour for those suffering from the storms of life, a well-filled warehouse for the needy, a convenient resting-place for those who are travelling, a never-ending feast for those who are celebrating. We celebrate this day with annual feasts and yet the stream of people arriving here because of their zeal for the martyrs never ceases.[45]

About Phocas' sanctuary in Sinope, Asterius says in a very similar passage that 'The thoroughfares from every country are full of people coming to this place of prayer. This splendid shrine is a place of relaxation for the afflicted, a resource for the needy, a surgery for the sick, an Egypt for the hungry.' The martyr indeed takes care for the poor and the hungry, who turn in great numbers to his sanctuary for assistance: 'As when in wintertime the doves through need of food fly to the recently sown land and gather there, so the host of wandering poor assembles on the Isthmus of Sinope as at a common storehouse.'[46]

Thus it seems one can conclude that the martyrium was a nexus of several functions: religious, caritative, social. Surely, as a religious centre it was a place where various kinds of devotional practice took place. But besides this religious function it was also a place to which the poor and the afflicted could turn for material assistance. Finally it performed also a social function in the sense that it was a meeting place for people. In what follows we will see that these functions were present in a more intense way in the context of the annual martyr feast, the panèguris.

THE YEARLY PANÈGURIS

While it was of course possible to visit the sanctuary of the martyrs during the entire year, the cult of each individual martyr reached its peak during the celebration by the local community of the martyr feast (panèguris). Though some very important sanctuaries, such as the ones located on the holy places of Jerusalem, continuously attracted pilgrims and therefore regularly celebrated a panèguris, in most cases it was an annual event, celebrated on the anniversary of the martyr's death or the deposition of his or her relics (Maraval 1985: 213–16). These feasts were an essential part of Christian popular devotion in late antiquity. Among the elements constituting the religious part of the event one must in the first place mention the practices described above: the veneration and touching of relics, the invocation of the martyrs, the incubation, the offering of *ex-votos* in thanks for the favours received through the intercession of the saint.[47] These took place during the entire year but were also undoubtedly executed during the panèguris. Besides these more individual ways of participation there were also communal liturgical celebrations: a vigil service, a Eucharist and a procession.

In the night before the saint's feast day the panèguris started around midnight with a vigil. This liturgical service could go on until dawn and was celebrated in the martyrium lit by lamps, hand-held candles and torches. The service mainly consisted of the singing of psalms and hymns, both alternately and responsorially to a cantor. There was also room for intercessory prayers, silent prayer and Scriptural readings. A homily was often also part of the service (Maraval 1985: 216–17; Pasquato 1998: 215; Leemans 2001d: 253–7). On the feast day itself a solemn eucharistic celebration took place.[48] In this context the local bishop or his delegate delivered the panegyric, the homily in praise of the martyr or saint. It also occurred that several preachers were featured and more than one homily was delivered.[49] Part of the solemn character of the occasion was due to the fact that the bishop invited other bishops to attend the celebration. Certainly the local clergy, priests, deacons and lower ranks of the clergy were also expected to attend (Maraval 1985: 217; Leemans 2001d: 257–63). Part of these liturgical celebrations could take place in the open air. This was the case for processions (Maraval 1985: 217; Pasquato 1998: 215–19, *passim*), a long-standing and important part of the proceedings of a martyr festival, as well as a bone of contention for pagans. The revulsion they may have felt is voiced in Julian the Apostate's horrified statement:

> The carrying of the corpses of the dead through a great assembly of people, in the midst of dense crowds, staining the eyesight of all with ill-omened sights of the dead. What day so touched with death could be lucky?[50]

For processions in Cappadocia there is the example of the relics of Mamas in Nazianze, which were solemnly carried around in the open air as part of the celebration.[51] For the Antioch of John Chrysostom we have several examples of processions, both in and outside the context of the martyr cult. On Good Friday and on Ascension Day it appears that there were processions to and from martyria in the cemeteries outside the Golden and Romanesian Gates.[52] John's homily *On Drosis* also hints at a procession and when John, in *On Julian*, suggests that they take the martyr's coffin to the Golden Gate leading to Daphne, this also might indicate this practice.[53]

Despite the solemn and undoubtedly well-organised character of vigil and Eucharist, one should not imagine that they were too formal or strict. A beautiful example of the degree of improvisation that was possible in these services is what Basil of Caesarea did during his encomium on Mamas, a martyr about whom not much more was known than that he was a shepherd. Basil solves the problem in a double way: on the one hand by keeping his homily rather short and general, on the other by asking that everybody should try to remember all they know about the martyr and the benefits received through his assistance. By sharing their knowledge with each other and joining all these pieces of information into a kind of common oration in praise of Mamas, they 'feed each other and thus meet our weakness'.[54] A second example of the relatively informal character of liturgical services is that, since the vigil went on for hours, it was not unusual that people went in and out the martyrium or attended only part of it. One can think here of Gregory of Nyssa's testimony about how he fell asleep outside while a vigil service in honour of the Forty of Sebaste, organised by his mother, was going on.[55] One should also take into account that, when the building of the sanctuary was not that large, people could be pressed unpleasantly against one another, giving rise to irritations, disputations and even fighting during the service (Maraval 1985: 217).

A final example of the unpredictable and improvised character of the liturgy is that, contrary to what one would expect, the homily during a liturgical service on the occasion of a martyr festival was not always or exclusively an oration in praise of the martyr celebrated that day. The following examples bear testimony to the homilist's freedom to choose his subject and to devote part or his entire homily to another subject (Leemans 2001d: 265–7). In his *Homily on Julitta* Basil of Caesarea keeps the first part of his homily, in which he treats the deeds and merits of Julitta, a female martyr from Caesarea, extremely short and then continues his sermon of the day before on the importance of performing acts of gratefulness.[56] At the end of his *First Homily on the Forty of Sebaste (Ib)* Gregory of Nyssa rather abruptly changes the subject and ends his homily with the discussion of an exegetical issue. Asterius of Amasea opens his *Homily on Avarice* with a reflection on the spiritual importance of panègureis but then moves quickly to the theme of avarice, the topic of the previous day to which also the lion's share of this homily is devoted.[57] John Chrysostom likewise on at least one occasion opens his homily by referring to the present panèguris but swiftly moves to another topic which he considers more compelling.[58] Finally Hesychius of Jerusalem's *Homily on Procopius* duly starts with praising the martyr but also gradually moves away from the topic to address more general issues.

Yet, to the crowds attending it, the panèguris was much more than just participating in these liturgical services. The celebration also took on social aspects: it became an opportunity to meet people, presumably including people one did not meet on ordinary occasions such as other liturgical services, markets or other usual meeting places. This was also true for the bishops themselves. As the head of the local community and as presider over the liturgical services, the panèguris provided an excellent opportunity for them to invite other bishops or civil officers to the gathering. Our sources show that this was happening very often. So, Gregory of Nazianze invited Theodorus of Tyana to attend a martyr feast in the village of Arianza and he explicitly adds that it is a good occasion to discuss some ecclesiastical business.[59] Basil of Caesarea's correspondence shows abundantly that to him martyr festivals were an excellent opportunity to build and strengthen relationships. In the year 372 he sent to Eusebius of Samosata an invitation to attend the panèguris in Caesarea for the martyr Eupsychius, a cult Basil promoted strongly. The letter explicitly mentions that Basil wants to discuss with

Eusebius the appointment of some bishops as well as some difficulties caused by Gregory of Nyssa's clumsiness.[60] Two years later he sent, for the same feast, an invitation to Amphilochius of Iconium, insisting that he come a few days earlier, so that they could spend some time together 'and exchange spiritual gifts'.[61] And in 376, again two years later, Basil sent a circular letter to all the bishops of Pontus to invite them to come to Caesarea for the feast of Eupsychius, an effort he qualifies as 'small trouble'.[62] In the same year the bishop of Caesarea was expected at a panèguris in Phargamos (Armenia), where he would meet Meletius of Antioch and Theodotus of Nicopolis, two other strongholders of the Neo-Nicene party for whom a lot was at stake at this period (Haykin 1994: 32–40).[63]

The above examples show that the panègureis were instrumental for the construction and maintaining of the social networks between bishops and played a crucial role in ecclesiastical politics. The martyr feasts also provided bishops, however, with welcome occasions for tightening relations with dignitaries from the secular realm. One telling example is Basil's short *Letter 142* to the *numerarius*, a kind of financial supervisor and assistant to the provincial governor. The bishop of Caesarea expresses his regret that the *numerarius* did not attend the great panèguris for the martyr Eupsychius. The reason for this regret is that Basil had convened all his *chorepiscopoi* (suffragan clerics) at the feast to introduce them to the official. He had hoped that this introduction would lead to the granting of fiscal immunity to some of these *chorepiscopoi* or at least for the house for the poor that one of them was administrating.[64] Another case is Gregory of Nazianze's *Homily in the Presence of the Tax Collector Julian*. This man was sent to Nazianze to revise the city's tax contribution to the treasury. Gregory was an old study-friend of his and was therefore asked to address him and to make an attempt to plead for some mildness on his part.[65] These Cappadocian situations can be easily transposed to big cities and provincial capitals like Antioch and Jerusalem. There too many high civil officials were stationed, not a few of them Christians. One can easily imagine that they attended the panèguris and were warmly invited to do so. Thus it is not surprising when Chrysostom mentions that the governor, presumably the provincial governor of Syria, is attending a martyr's festival.[66] In this way the martyr feasts were constitutive in the creation of social relations and networks that were profitable for all the parties involved. Besides the local bishop, his peers and high civil officers, all the local clergy (priests, deacons and lower ranks) of course also attended the celebration. In that sense the panègureis also contributed to strengthening a sense of unity between the various levels constituting the local ecclesiastical community.

This gathering of large crowds also generated commercial activity, which sometimes took excessive forms that could distract people's attention from the religious aspects and led to severe criticism on the part of the bishops.[67] Yet it is no surprise that the panègureis were generating commercial activity. Everywhere where a large crowd gathers, sellers of drinks, food and many other products take their chances. Furthermore, in this sense the panègureis feasts were the heirs of the pagan festive assemblies in honour of gods or organised in the context of the imperial cult. Finally it is typical of pre-industrial societies with their limited possibilities for mobility that people, out of necessity, bring together in one place several different aspects of life (De Ligt and De Neeve 1988). In the case of regularly organised events, such as the annual martyr festivals, it was profitable both for customers and salesmen to attach to the religious celebration an opportunity to buy and sell goods not readily available on a daily basis. In this way, much to the irritation of the ecclesiastical authorities, there originated in the context of panègureis markets which, in the case of big cities such as Antioch and Jerusalem, could be of considerable size and importance. One such market took place in Antioch yearly on the occasion of a festival in honour of Philogonius. It was busily attended, both by buyers and vendors, and a great variety of goods was for sale: wheat and barley, but also flocks of sheep and herds of cattle and even clothes.[68] Preachers – without any effect it seems – pointed out the contradiction between the religious aspect of the liturgical celebrations and the commercial aspects of the markets,[69] stressed the danger for the soul caused by 'the serving of mammon' and warned against attaching more importance to the market than to the liturgical service (De Ligt 1993).

Beyond this commercial activity, there were also activities of sheer pleasuremaking, equally provoking the irritation of the ecclesiastical authorities. In one of his homilies Basil voices his indignation about some inebriated women who danced in a martyr's sanctuary in a sexually provocative way.[70] One of Chrysostom's homilies is almost exclusively devoted to this topic. In *A Homily on Martyrs* he exhorts his audience to forsake their deeply entrenched habit of adding to the celebration of the panèguris a pub crawl with heavy drinking, playing dice and visiting brothels.[71] And in *On Julian* he goes even a step further. Foreseeing that part of his audience will forsake the second day of the festival and instead of participating look for the rival pleasures of Daphne and its surroundings, he suggests that, after the end of the celebrations of that second day, they should stay in the martyrium, under the martyr's watchful eye, have a picnic together and prolong the feast in a more leisurely and less harmful way. Chrysostom here clearly wants to offer an alternative of a community-building character that is less in opposition to the solemn and religious atmosphere of the panèguris than the behaviour he foresees from part of his congregation. At the same time, however, he seems to expect that his plea will not convince everybody and therefore he exhorts his audience to engage in more severe measures: 'Tomorrow let's occupy the gates ahead of time, let's keep a watch on the streets, let's pull them down from their vehicles, men [pulling] men, women [pulling] women. Let's bring them back here; let's not be ashamed.'[72]

Whatever the success of these measures may have been, from the above examples it is clear that the panèguris exhibits a combination of various aspects of the life of a local church community. This multifaceted character reflects what was earlier said about the activities in the martyrium throughout the year. The panègureis surely were busy gatherings and many martyr homilies explicitly mention the huge crowd that attended the panègureis. Our sources also allow us to draw a more detailed picture of the crowd. The picture emerging is that the panèguris was attended by a wide diversity of people: rich and poor, men and women, educated and illiterate, free people and slaves. The example of Gregory of Nazianze's *Homily Delivered in the Presence of the Tax Collector Julian* is a case in point. This homily, delivered in 374 on the occasion of a martyr feast, contains a long paraenetic part in which the homilist exhorts his audience to grow in detaching themselves from wordly goods and riches and instead sacrifice themselves spiritually to God. This exhortation is explicitly directed towards everybody: men and women, young and old, citizens and countrymen, rich and poor, lower or higher class. Gregory adds that not so much the degree of detachment reached is important but the intention and the effort. He lists and illustrates the virtues to be pursued and concretises these with examples. Moreover he encourages everybody to pursue this Christian lifestyle at their own level and with their own possibilities and limitations. In this part of the homily a number of people are addressed directly: the priests, the faithful 'in general', the educated, the soldiers, people working in the civil office and, finally, Julian, the tax collector himself. A passage such as this illustrates that the local community in all its diversity was present at the panèguris.[73]

Besides more general passages, such as the one from Gregory of Nazianze's homily, our sources also inform us of the presence of several distinct groups. The presence of higher clerics, especially bishops, both higher and lower, is well attested. Together with the bishops also priests and other lower ranks of clergy, such as deacons and country bishops, surely attended the martyr feasts. Maybe because their presence was largely taken for granted, it has left few traces in the sources. The opposite is true with regard to the presence at the martyr feasts of people belonging to the upper strata of the local community. From several lengthy passages exhorting rich people to adopt a much more modest lifestyle, we gather that members of this top layer of society were also indeed present during the panèguris. This is especially clear from a paraenetic passage in Gregory of Nazianze's *Homily on Low Sunday*, delivered on the occasion of a panèguris. Using a yesterday–today antithesis he both evokes their wrong behaviour and describes a true Christian behaviour. He exhorts them to transform themselves 'from party-animals into monks' (Bernardi 1968: 252). To Gregory this means they have to say goodbye to their love for the games, sumptuous banquets, stretching out on luxurious ivory couches, expensive perfumes and houses with gilded ceilings. The fact that he is addressing them in the second person clearly suggests that his audience contained some of these excessively rich people whose lifestyle was characterised by the excessive luxury he is describing.[74]

Another important issue is the religious adherence of those attending martyr feasts. Here I think one should keep in mind that in this period the boundaries between Christians and pagans were not so clear. Many were only Christians of the first or second generation, had bidden paganism farewell only recently and had in many cases not given up all practices associated with their old religion. On the other hand, there was within paganism a strong henotheistic current which made its distance from Christianity less great. Add to this vagueness of boundaries the fact that martyr feasts were not an exclusively religious event but also a social and economic one and one understands that many people who were not 'hardcore Christians' were attracted to the festive atmosphere of the panègureis and their opportunities, if only by simply accompanying their neighbours to the gathering. Moreover, there were special occasions. It is easily conceivable that, when Julian the tax collector visited Nazianze and was addressed by Gregory, many non-Christians were also present since they were also an interested party in the matter at hand.

All in all, the annual celebrations of the cult of the martyrs must have been very busy, noisy, gatherings of the local community; festive gatherings of enthusiastic people enjoying themselves, combining the religious with the more mundane aspects of the occasion. This is the larger context of the liturgical services during which the panegyric or homily in praise of the martyr was delivered. It is to the latter that we now turn.

MARTYR HOMILIES

The genre of biographically-oriented literature was extremely successful in late antiquity. Both in Christian and non-Christian milieux a great number of writings originated which were not structured around the elaboration of an idea or the description of a series of events but had as their backbone and content the life or lives of an individual or a group (Cameron 1998: 699–700; Hägg and Rousseau 2000: 1–5). The Christian biographical literature, which reached a quantitive and qualitive peak in the fourth and the fifth centuries, can be characterised as 'hagiobiographical'. This means that at its centre is not so much the individual, his/her life and accomplishments as such but the individual as *hagios*, as a man or a woman of God. Ultimately its purpose is not descriptive but exhortatory: portraying the saint as a model Christian, as an example worthy of imitation.

'Hagiobiographical literature' is a collective noun for a number of distinctive literary subgenres that have as their subject accounts of martyrs, biblical or historical saints (monks, ascetics, bishops) or other exemplary Christians such as emperors or pious virgins. These accounts can be vitae – biographical accounts of a more descriptive nature, though not completely free from laudatory overtones – or panegyrics, works that have as their primary goal extolling the person and virtues of their subjects. Panegyrics can be encomia (orations in praise of somebody) but also funeral orations or orations of consolation. Famous examples of this kind of literature are Athanasius' *Life of Antony*, Jerome's lives of several hermits, Gregory of Nazianze's funeral orations on his father Gregory the Elder, his brother Caesarius and his sister Gorgonia or his encomium on Athanasius of Alexandria.

The authors featured in this volume also contributed substantially to this hagiobiographical literature. One can think of Gregory of Nyssa's *Life of Macrina*, his *Oration on Basil*, his funeral oration on Meletius of Antioch and his orations of consolation pronounced on the occasion of the death of the empress Flacilla and (a bit later) their daughter Pulcheria. As for biblical saints, both Gregory of Nazianze and John Chrysostom preached in praise of the Maccabees; of the latter at least two genuine homilies on this theme are extant. Besides the ones of Hesychius of Jerusalem and Asterius of Amasea included in this volume, Gregory of Nyssa also preached a homily in praise of Stephen the Protomartyr. Asterius also delivered a homily in praise of Peter and Paul and from Chrysostom we even have a set of seven homilies in praise of Paul.

Panegyrics on historical martyrs must be seen within the context of the wider genre of hagiobiographical literature. In fact it can be said that in the panegyrics of authors such as the Cappadocians, Asterius of Amasea, and John Chrysostom we witness the flowering of a new genre of epideictic rhetoric. These texts have even been credited with having fixed the laws of this new genre for centuries to come (Delehaye 1921: 184). According to the rules of classical rhetoric, which are skilfully applied by the homilists, their primary aim is to extol the qualities and virtues of the martyr who is their subject. Before turning to examine the way they achieve this, it is good to point out that these homilies presented their audience with a multi-layered discourse that served more than just this sole purpose. For, precisely in presenting the martyr as a man or a woman of God and extolling his or her Christian way of life, the subject of a panegyric could function as a spiritual model. In the panegyrics on martyrs some homilists state this explicitly as their purpose. In the introduction to his *Homily on Phocas* Asterius deals at length with the theme of the martyr as exemplary figure. Theoretical research is important, Asterius says, but the didactic value of the practical example is much greater. Somebody wanting to study geometry, astronomy or medicine must start by working their way through theoretical handbooks but they will only master the skill by observing the example of the practice of a master. The same is true with regard to pursuing virtue and faith: then, also, one needs an example and none is better than the martyr's, who demonstrated remaining steadfast in the faith, even in the most difficult of circumstances.[75]

So, these encomia on martyrs explicitly or implicitly presented their subject as an example of Christian virtue worthy of imitation.

To that effect, the homilists' oral representations of the martyr's life and death were supplemented by visual representations on the walls of the sanctuaries. These wall paintings portrayed the martyr's life, interrogation before court, suffering and death as well as the presence of Christ comforting his martyr (Leemans 2000).

The martyr was a classic example of virtue, going back to the second century. During the fourth century other characters, who became the subject of panegyrics, joined the martyr in his role as exemplar: the pious virgin, monk, bishop. Thus it can be said that the hagiobiographical literature of the fourth century created new heroes. This was a necessity: the adherents of a successful and rapidly growing religion needed other spiritual models than the members of a persecuted religious minority. The martyr still functioned as an example of Christian virtue worthy of imitation but to suit the changed situation these new spiritual models were put forward. Through biblical quotations and allusions these characters were partly detached from their particular context and presented as ideal Christians. Biblical exempla from the Old and the New Testament transformed these historical persons into models referring to Christ, the Model par excellence. In late antiquity, when training and education were largely the result of imitation and imitation rather than innovation a virtue, such models fulfilled a powerful role (Brown 1983). They were expected to inspire Christians to lead an ethically and spiritually excellent life (Wilson 1998).

But, just like other kinds of hagiobiographical literature, panegyrics on martyrs were multilayered discourses: their effect went beyond singing the martyr's praise and presenting him or her as an example. In the course of the homily a host of other issues could be addressed explicitly or implicitly, touched upon briefly or discussed at length. The festive atmosphere of the panèguris and the occasion for social and economic activities that it offered, provided the bishop with opportunities for lengthy moral exhortation. Here too the martyr's example could be invoked.[76] Moreover, in the context of the above comment about the improvised character of the liturgy during panègureis, some examples were given of homilies which were almost entirely or partly devoted to other topics than the commemoration of the life and death of the martyr of the day. In these homilies the exhortatory purpose and presentation of the martyr as an example are much less prominently present, though not necessarily absent.[77] Another element that often comes to the surface is the dialogue with, namely, polemic against other religions and the positioning of

Christianity in the religiously varied landscape of late antiquity. Gregory of Nazianze's *Homily on the Maccabees*, preached in 362, is, besides a panegyric on the Maccabean brothers, also a reaction against Julian the Apostate's unsuccessful attempt to promote paganism to the detriment of Christianity (Vinson 1994). Gregory of Nyssa's *Homily on Theodore the Recruit* can equally be read as an implicit rejection of the Apostate's religious policy (Leemans 2001c). John Chrysostom's homily *On Babylas* does not give much attention to the martyr's story but contains an invective against Julian and asserts Christianity's superiority over Hellenism in general (Guinot 1995).

While this caveat about the presence in martyr homilies of purposes other than narrating the martyr's story and portraying his or her behaviour as exemplary, should be taken seriously, it is also true that in most cases the exhortatory aspect remains a very important key for reading and analysing the panegyrics of the fourth and early fifth centuries (as well as other types of hagiobiographical texts). Scriptural borrowings are one, evident, means by which the homilist succeeded in portraying the martyr as an exemplar of Christian virtue worthy of imitation. Another, in this regard distinctive feature of martyr encomia that must be discussed, is the influence of the principles of classical rhetoric. Charting this influence, even in an introductory way, will show the extent to which Christianity was integrated into the culture of Hellenism.

The homilists featured in this volume were all, with the exception of Hesychius of Jerusalem, bishops of important cities. John Chrysostom even occupied the see of the imperial capital, after his period as a presbyter in Antioch, another of the Empire's metropolises. As bishops they belonged to late antique society's upper class. A good education was the hallmark of this upper class as well as the *conditio sine qua non* for making a career, both in the Church and in the civil administration of the Empire. Its main goal can be summarised in the word *paideia*, an amalgam of knowledge and skills. This education introduced men to the classical culture, it taught them how to behave in the circles of the elite and provided them with a savoir-faire. The ideal of *paideia* was most notably present in the accomplished orator. He had learned how to collect the contents and arguments of his oration (*inventio*), to arrange this material in a logical and purposeful unity (*dispositio*) and compose in a refined and suitable style a text (*elocutio*) that could be memorised (*memoria*) and performed (*actio*). The training of an orator throughout antiquity comprised these five elements which were exercised over and over again over the course of many years.

The rhetoric taught in late antiquity was mainly rhetoric as it had taken shape during the imperial age in a movement that is commonly called the Second Sophistic. This term refers *stricto sensu* to the Greek orators who were active from the reign of Nero until *c.*AD 230, many of whom were catalogued and celebrated by Philostratus in his *Lives of the Sophists*. Among the most important orators of the Second Sophistic can be mentioned Polemon of Laodicea, Aelius Aristides and Herodes Atticus. The most characteristic feature of these orators, also present in Greek prose-writers of the time, is their Atticism: the attempt to write, using the forms and vocabulary of the Attic dialect as it was spoken in Athens during the Classical period, more than half a millennium earlier. The great Athenian orators (Demosthenes, Lysias, Hypereides, Aeschines) were their great examples.

In the fourth century AD the Second Sophistic had passed its peak but its profound influence on the theory and practice of rhetoric had found its way into the rhetorical handbooks, through which it continued to exert influence on the rhetoric of the fourth century and later. For it is through training based on these handbooks that great pagan orators such as Libanius and Themistius learned their profession. In consequence the rhetoric practised by these great orators was basically the rhetoric of the Second Sophistic. The same is true for Christian bishops. Since there did not exist a network of Christian schools, Christians attended the same institutions as pagans, receiving the same training in rhetoric. The influence of the Second Sophistic on Christian homiletics therefore is not surprising. Moreover, some of the most popular rhetorical handbooks of the Second Sophistic have been preserved: *On Funeral Orations* by Pseudo-Dionysius of Halicarnassus, the *Progymnasmata* of Theon (comprising a chapter on the panegyric) and Aphthonius, and the rhetorical treatises of Longinus. These handbooks make it possible to study the theory of the Second Sophistic and its application by Christian orators. In that way the influence of the Second Sophistic on Christian homilies can be assessed in some detail (survey with rich bibliography on this already well-studied subject in Kinzig 1997). With regard to panegyrics a most useful basis for comparison is *On Epideictic Speech* by Menander. In his handbook this teacher of rhetoric describes a number of models of epideictic speech in great detail. Hereby he is paying attention to the elements a particular oration should be structured around and the purpose of each of these elements, but also to the tone the orator should strike. Meanwhile, and despite the detailed character of his prescriptions, Menander also underlines the orator's freedom to omit some elements or to adapt them to the particular situation in which he finds himself.

The influence of the Second Sophistic on Christian homiletics in general and panegyrics on martyrs in particular – all in all, an already well-studied subject[78] – can be assessed on two levels: the structure of the homily and the style, especially the stylistic flowers adorning the text. The structure of the panegyric is often (however loosely) modelled after Menander's *basilikos logos*, the oration in praise of the emperor. It ideally consists of the following elements:

1 A prologue in which the relevance and importance of the subject, in this case the martyr, is stressed as well as the homilist's inability to rise to the challenge and do justice to his subject.
2 In the corpus of the text the following recurring elements or topoi may occur:
   The land, the city, the people (*patris, polis, ethnos*) that have brought forth the hero.
   His family (*genos*).
   His birth (*genèsis*), especially when this was surrounded with miraculous events or signs foreshadowing his illustrous life.
   His natural qualities (*ta peri fuseôs*).
   His education (*anatrophè*).
   His childhood (*paideia*).
   His way of life, his profession and other activities (*epitèdeumata*).
   His heroic deeds and martyrdom (*praxeis*).
   His eventual fortune and rewards in heaven (*ta tès tuchès*).
3 Each of the above topoi may be embellished by comparisons (*sunkriseis*), mostly with biblical characters. At the end of this part there often follows, by way of general assessment, a global evaluation of the martyr in the form of a *sunkrisis* with a biblical character. Of course the homily is also full of other Scriptural quotations and allusions.
4 The panegyric ends with a conclusion (*epilogos*).

The homilist had a great deal of freedom in using this basic scheme. When he considered it superfluous or didn't have any knowledge about it, he could easily drop an element. He could, on the other hand, if he felt like it, also develop an element more fully than the structure suggests. Menander had already foreseen this kind of liberty for the orator, so the freedom with which the Christian homilists used his models is not surprising. As a consequence, the basic scheme is not present in full or even easily recognisable in every panegyric. In some panegyrics on martyrs, especially those of Basil and Gregory of Nyssa, many of the items are present and their order in the development of the homily can be relatively easily followed. The brilliant rhetor John Chrysostom, on the other hand, is much more spontaneous, was less attached to the conventions and shows much greater ingenuity (Delehaye 1921: 196–203).[79]

The influence of the Second Sophistic on our homilists was not only present at the level of the homily's structure. It also had a profound influence on the style. The construction of the sentence, the building of the periods, the search for symmetry and rhythm gave these homilies a distinctive melodious sound, in some passages even coming close to the hymnic.[80] This is especially the case in the homilies of Hesychius of Jerusalem, who employs so many parallel constructions and antitheses, repetitions and sweet-flowing periods that his text often comes close to poetry and his homily must have sounded almost as if it were being chanted.

The effect achieved by our authors was the result of the carefully balanced construction of the periods as a whole. This was in its turn the result of the application of a host of stylistic ornaments which formed the stock-in-trade of the accomplished homilist. With these means at his disposal he could appeal to his audience, move his listeners, highlight part of a sentence, and keep their attention captivated. In short, these homilists did much more than convey a message: they did it in an artistic form that made homilies into works of art and that turned listening to homilies into moments of joy. The audience also experienced it that way and responded to it. Late antique church congregations could appreciate a beautiful, well-constructed homily and didn't hesitate to make their approval (or the opposite) known to the homilist by making noise or applauding him.[81]

The stylistic features and rhetorical tricks present in the homilies of the Cappadocians, John Chrysostom and Hesychius of Jerusalem betray something of the theatrical, exuberant character and the love for the stylistic relief proper to the Second Sophistic. A full survey of these here is impossible (see Rowe 1997). Because quite a number of studies on the style of our homilists exist,[82] it may be sufficient to limit the following discussion to some of the stylistic means, illustrating them by passages taken from the panegyrics in this volume.

The abundant use of *metaphors* is one of the stylistic features colouring these panegyrics.[83] The metaphor is a figure of speech whereby a word is not used in its literal meaning but in a figurative sense. The transfer from the literal to the figurative level helps to highlight or clarify an element of the contents, while on the other hand satisfying the audience's appreciation for the well-chosen stylistic ornament. When narrating how the jailer of the Forty, when seeing their courage, was struck and took the place of the one who had apostatised, Basil comments: 'Judas departed, and Matthias was substituted'. The reference to the two biblical characters gives extra meaning and vividness to the passage. A metaphor can also refer to a phenomenon of nature, as is the case at the end of Gregory of Nyssa's *First Homily on the Forty of Sebaste* (Ia) – as well as the prologue of Ib – where the metaphor of a wild sea is applied to the gathered community to reflect the tumultuous noise they were making, up to the point of forcing Gregory to abandon his homily.[84] The world that inspired most metaphors, as far as panegyrics on martyrs are concerned, is the world of the stadium. The martyr is an athlete, his martyrdom is a race (*dromos*) or a contest (*agôn*), at the end of which he receives the victor's crown (*stefanos*) and prize (*brabeion*). The contest was presided over by the president of the games (the *agônothetès*), in the martyr's case God or Christ.[85] Instances of this agonistic metaphorical language are ubiquitous in our panegyrics. Often it concerns stock-terms that through centuries of use have lost part of their metaphorical power but sometimes our authors succeed in creating original uses of agonistic metaphors. A case in point we find in Chrysostom's *On Julian*, where he uses agonistic metaphors to say that the martyr suffered in this world but receives his reward in the next:

> So, while the athletes in the civic games wrestle and win and are proclaimed winner and crowned all in the same pit of sand, it isn't the same for these athletes of piety. Rather, while they did their wrestling in the present age, they are crowned in that age that is to come.[86]

The same creativity can be witnessed with regard to our authors' use of metaphors from the military world. Though less numerous, we find metaphors of this kind also quite often used to denote the practice of martyrdom, which is then portrayed as warfare, mostly against the Devil. An example of a creative metaphor of this kind we find in Gregory of Nyssa's use of metaphors inspired on the passage about the armour of God:

O those who so marvellously transferred their experience in military warfare to the battle line against the Devil! Not with swords did they arm their hands, nor did they hold a wooden shield before them, nor did they protect themselves with a metal helmet and greaves; but they put on the armour of God, which the general of the Church, the divine Apostle, describes: shield, breastplate, helmet and dagger (Eph 6: 11–17) and so they marched against the opposing force.[87]

Our panegyrists make ample use of the *hyperbole*, the exaggerated presentation of facts clearly surpassing what is reasonably possible. In this way the merits and laudatory feats of the subjects of panegyrics can be highlighted. In particular it is used to describe the martyr's heroic deeds and his or her steadfastness in the faith. In order to make clear his firmness Theodore declares to his judges:

Because of my faith in him [Christ] and my confession of it, let he who is wounding me cut me; let he who is whipping me lacerate me; let he who is burning me bring the flame close; let he who is taking offence at these words of mine cut out my tongue, for each part of the body owes to its Creator an act of endurance.[88]

And Basil's Gordius exclaims: 'How then shall I deny my God, whom I have worshipped since childhood? Wouldn't heaven above be horrified? Wouldn't the stars darken because of me, wouldn't earth resist me completely?'[89]

A third stylistic means is that of the *comparison*. This can help to clarify something or it can underline an element in the sentence or in a part of the homily. To that end in a comparison the homilist can refer to common knowledge from nature, agriculture, astronomy, medicine, art, the world of the stadium or the theatre etc. Scripture can also offer material for a comparison to the homilist. Sometimes comparisons are rather short but it not seldom occurs that they take on an elaborated form and function as rhetorical showpieces that are no longer subservient to the content (Méridier 1906: 117–38). Our panegyrics abundantly contain examples of both kinds, the following being illustrations chosen at random. In the prooemium to the second part of his *First Homily on the Forty* Gregory of Nyssa compares the panèguris and his homily with a banquet: the day before the community had been the martyrs' guest, today the martyrs are the guests, who are treated with the leftovers of the banquet of the day before.[90] To underline the unity that is enhancing their individual beauty, the group of the Forty is compared to a necklace and to the lights in the sky[91] and their time in prison Gregory compares to training in the gymnasium, preparing the athletes for their contest.[92] The same homily also employs comparisons to biblical stories. In his narration of the rain miracle that happened to the Legio XII Fulminata, Gregory makes a comparison to an intervention of the prophet Elijah, as told in 1 Kings 18:30–45:[93] in both cases prayer and sacrifices caused highly necessary rain.[94] In *On Julian* Chrysostom is making the point that it is a good thing that the martyrs first suffered and then got their recompense: in this way one is motivated to go first through hardships which only last for a limited time while, on the other hand, the pleasure afterwards is pure and unending. To illustrate his point Chrysostom makes a negative comparison to people having lost their once luxurious lifestyle, and positive comparisons to boxers and sailors.[95] In *On Pelagia* John describes how a good shepherd catches a lion that is terrifying his lambs and makes it into a harmless being his sheep can poke fun at and then compares the shepherd to Christ, who made death so harmless that even virgins like Pelagia could poke fun at it.[96]

Another feature, typical for the somewhat strained, artificial style of the Second Sophistic, is the *periphrasis*: the use of a paraphrase where one word would be sufficient or the use of a euphemism instead of a more concrete substantive. In panegyrics on martyrs this stylistic means is especially applied to persons, including both positive and negative players in the drama that is sketched. Examples abound. Gregory of Nyssa calls Christ the Master, the common Master or the common King,[97] Paul is indicated as the general of the Church and the divine apostle[98] and Asterius calls Phocas 'our holy man', 'helper of Christians' (5.1) 'the servant of the Lord' (8.1).[99] More conspicuous are the innumerable cases in which periphrastic turns are used to indicate the martyrs' opponents. The name of the emperor during whose reign the persecutions took place is very seldom mentioned and the same is true for the civil officers who executed the persecution on the local level. Virtually never is it revealed who exactly was responsible for the martyr's execution; at best the players in the martyr's drama are indicated by their rank, but often the homilist contents himself with a vague negative notion such as 'the tyrant'.[100] By using such periphrastic turns to indicate the martyr's persecutors, the homilist robs them of their individuality, demonises them and reduces them to the morally base opponents of the hero of their story. Thus, the periphrasis leads in these cases to an effective *damnatio memoriae*. The martyrs' opponent par excellence was of course the Devil, who is the root of all evil and the ultimate instigator of the evil deeds committed against the martyr. For him too, our panegyrists have numerous periphrastic indications. He is the Enemy of human life,[101] the Enemy (*ho echthros*),[102] the bad one (*ho ponèros*)[103] or similar expressions. Ultimately, this demonising of the Devil as the source of all evil of which the martyr is the victim contributes to the heroic character of the latter's deeds. In the end the martyr did not fight badly-inspired human beings but succeeded in defeating their instigator, the source of their wicked deeds, the personification of Evil itself.

The panegyrists in this volume also shared the love the rhetors of the Second Sophistic had for *parallelism*. Examples of these so-called 'Gorgianic schemes' abound in all our authors' homilies, though the homilies of Chrysostom and Hesychius witness a more frequent use of it than the Cappadocians. The following three examples are chosen at random. In Basil's *On Gordius* a symmetrical structure and repetition is used to underline the judge's rage and prepares the ground for the ensuing demonstration of the martyr's superiority over the official:

> And he said: 'Call the executioners. Where are the sling-bullets? Where are the whips? Let him be stretched on the wheel. Let him be tortured on the rack, let the instruments of torture be brought; let the wild beasts, the fire, the sword, the cross, the pit, be made ready.'[104]

An example of an antithetical parallelism in the prologue of Chrysostom's *On the Holy Martyrs* opposes the theatre or the hippodrome to the panèguris: 'There there is devilish pageantry; here Christian festivity. There demons leap around; here angels dance. There there is loss of souls; here salvation for all who are gathered.'[105] He then continues exhorting his audience to come to the panèguris with the same enthusiasm and eagerness that they engage in those frivolous pastimes. My final example comes from Hesychius of Jerusalem, illustrating how extensive the parallelisms can be and

32

to what extent they can contribute to altering the nature of the homily from prose to poetry. The following passage from his *Homily on Procopius* can be taken for an elaborate form of the rhetorical 'Unfähigheitstopos': the homilist declaring the task at hand too heavy for him. Hesychius says:

> But who would be capable of singing the praises of
>   Procopius one after the other?
> Which of his struggles shall we take up first?
> Which shall we rank second?
> Which shall we put third?
> Where will the fourth be situated?
> What fitting spot will the fifth find?
> What sixth crown shall we fit on him?
> What seventh prize shall we devise for him?
> To what eighth step of praise shall we ascend?
> What ninth tower of encomia shall we forge?
> Which of the stories shall we be able to run through as
>   the last?[106]

Another means of making the homily more lively is to insert *direct speech* (*prosopoiia*) in the form of monologues or dialogues. Dialogues occur often in our panegyrics on martyrs, most notably in the form of (fictitious) dialogues between the martyr and his or her judges, torturers or persecutors but occasionally also with other persons. In Asterius' *On Phocas* the story of the martyr is told by the homilist. The moment supreme of the story, however, when the martyr reveals to his persecutors that he, the man who showed them hospitality, gave them food and a roof for the night, was in fact the one they were looking for, is underlined by using dialogue.[107] Such dialogues provide the homilist with the opportunity to insert some humour. A beautiful example is the witty dialogue between Theodore and a pagan soldier of his unit, in which the latter tries to ridicule the Christian belief in Jesus as the Son of God but is rebutted by the martyr who makes fun of his belief in a female god and 'his veneration for her, a mother of twelve children, a kind of very fertile demon who just like a hare or a sow effortlessly conceives and gives birth!'[108] Inserting fictitious monologues equally makes the homily more lively and provides the homilist with the opportunity to introduce another perspective into the narration, to show the events from another person's viewpoint. It can also be an opportunity to bring some emotion into play, the farewell-monologue addressed by the mother of one of the Forty to her dying son being a strong example:

> 'You are', she said, 'not my child, not the fruit of my labour during childbirth. Since you have received God, you were born in God. You received *the power to become a child of God*' (John 1:12). 'Run to your Father, so that you are not left behind by your comrades, so that you do not arrive second at the crown, so that you do not render useless my maternal prayer.'[109]

An extremely ingenious example of direct speech is found in John Chrysostom's *On Holy Martyrs* in which he has the martyrs themselves address in direct speech the audience, in this way conveying all the more forcefully the message that, however hard martyrdom may be, it is well worth it.[110]

The final stylistic feature that should be discussed here is that of the *ecphrasis*. According to the rhetorical handbook on *Progymnasmata* by Theon, one of the masters of the Second Sophistic, an ecphrasis is (part of) an oration 'that brings as it were the subject to be clarified under the eyes of the hearer through a detailed description'. The ecphrasis was one of the *progymnasmata*, a kind of finger exercise every advanced student in rhetoric had to go through. It can be a description of persons, places, buildings, works of arts, phenomena of nature, the seasons of the year. Though ecphraseis *stricto sensu* already occur in the Bible and in the earliest masterpieces of Greek literature (e.g. the description of Achilles' shield in the *Iliad*), the genre came to fruition during the Second Sophistic and reached its peak in the pagan and Christian literature of the fourth and fifth centuries (Downey 1959). The homilies in praise of martyrs in this volume also contain a number of ecphraseis. Basil of Caesarea's *Homily on Gordius* contains descriptions of the persecution in Caesarea and of the savage-looking martyr, descending from the mountains to the amphitheatre in the city.[111] Gregory of Nyssa's ecphrasis of the martyrium in Euchaïta in his *Homily on Theodore the Recruit* is justly famous.[112] And in his *First Homily on the Forty of Sebaste*, a group of martyrs who died by freezing, the same author gives a beautiful ecphrasis on the season of winter and the difficulties caused by it.[113] Chrysostom's *On Babylas*, partly an invective against Julian the Apostate, contains a description of the dreadful times when he was emperor and trying to demolish Christianity.[114] Finally, the *Ecphrasis of the Martyrdom of Euphemia* by Asterius of Amasea, a description of a painting, is even transmitted not as part of a homily but as an independent piece.

These ecphraseis were passages in which the Christian homilist could give his rhetorical talent free rein and impress his audience with these artistic masterpieces. Yet, just like the other stylistic means discussed above, the ecphraseis in our panegyrics served more than only this artistic purpose; they also contributed to conveying to the audience the homily's messages. Gregory of Nyssa's ecphrasis on Theodore the Recruit's martyrium is a case in point. The description of what the audience could see with their own eyes anyway, was aimed to let them see the reality of the martyrium with new eyes. Beyond being a beautiful building, the sanctuary showed to what extent the martyr was venerated after his death. Thus the building constituted proof that the martyr's way of life and his incarnation of Christian virtue was well worth it and therefore worthwhile to imitate.

To this point we have been sketching traces of the influence of the Second Sophistic on the basic structure and the style of martyr homilies. Hereby it was indicated that these features were not only adopted for themselves but contributed to conveying the homilist's message. Yet, this 'diagnostic approach' could lead to the much too one-sided conclusion that the Christian rhetoric as we find it in the sermons of the Cappadocians, John Chrysostom and Hesychius of Jerusalem, was no more than putting Christian content in a form borrowed from the traditional rhetoric of the Second Sophistic. And while the influence of the Second Sophistic is undeniable, it was certainly not that absolute. On the contrary, Christian rhetoric was the result of an interweaving of Christian and non-Christian elements into something irreducibly new. In many Christian authors clearly employing an Atticising style, such as Basil and John Chrysostom, one also finds syntactical structures quite unknown in Classical Attic. Moreover, on the linguistic level our authors' language is influenced by the Bible, a phenomenon also quite incompatible with Atticism. Indeed, as testified by Lampe's *Patristic Greek Lexicon*, the influence of the Bible, together with the institutions, rites and theology of early Christianity led to many linguistic innovations.

Moreover one has to take into account the genre of the homily, the purpose and the audience. There too, important differences with regard to the Second Sophistic's influence can be noted. An exegetical homily, explaining verse by verse a biblical text, shows much less dependence in that regard than a panegyric which, as we have seen, is much more likely to have been influenced by the traditional rules of epideictic rhetoric. Furthermore one shouldn't forget that the Christian rhetoric took place in a liturgical setting. The homilist was very likely influenced by this context and so was his sermon's content. The element of prayer – even if it was restricted to the concluding doxology as in most of our panegyrics – is a clear example in that regard (Kinzig 1997: 646–51).

From the above it is clear that, whereas in the panegyrics of our authors a notable influence of the Second Sophistic can be detected, this influence was not absolute. The texts present themselves as inseparable unities of Christian and non-Christian elements on all levels. While this is surely not illogical – after all pagans and Christians enjoyed the same education and joined in the same culture at large – this synthesis came about not without difficulty. During the first five centuries of its existence the issue of to what extent Christianity should adopt the non-Christian culture was a burning one (Klock 1987: 47–122). Traces of this discussion and its unsettled character are found in the panegyrics on martyrs of Basil of Caesarea and Gregory of Nyssa. This is a bit surprising: in his *Letter to Young Men* Basil espoused a clear vision of how the non-Christian culture should serve Christianity and his younger brother's works are a clear demonstration of that principle. Yet, in his *Homily on the Forty Martyrs of Sebaste*, Basil says:

> In this very way let us too remind those present of the men's virtue, and as it were by bringing their deeds to their gaze, let us motivate them to imitate those who are nobler and closer to them with respect to their course of life. I mean that this is the encomium of the martyrs: the exhortation of the congregation to virtue. For not even sermons about the saints permit accommodation to the rules of encomia. This is why those who applaud them take the starting-point of their applause from worldly materials. How could anything worldly provide material to make conspicuous those for whom the world is crucified?[115]

Despite his negative evaluation of the rules of encomia as inappropriate for talking about the martyrs' achievement and its significance for his audience, in the remainder of his homily Basil goes on applying the rules of rhetoric. The same rejection and simultaneous application of the rhetorical rules for panegyrics can be found in Gregory of Nyssa's *First Homily on the Forty Martyrs of Sebaste*. This homily was delivered in Armenian Sebaste. When treating the topos of the martyrs' fatherland and city Gregory rejects the necessity of singing the praise of the land's fertility, the advantages offered by the rivers in the city's neighbourhood and other causes of the region's reputation. If others really want it, Gregory says, they can sing the praise of these traditional elements. For Christians though, these wordly things are not important. What really matters and constitutes the city's reputation is the deeds and the memory of the Forty:

> Let a man of the world, who in this life is knowledgeable in judging splendours, add to these praises, if he wants to, also the other river. I am speaking about the river that is the neighbour of the first . . . If one really must give the catalogue of the founders of the city, must extoll beyond measure the most distinguished families of the dwelling from its foundation onwards or include some of the military successes in accounts about us . . . let these subjects remain far from our gathering here. For Christian discourse is ashamed to attach to friends of Christ praise to subjects external to the faith, which is like extolling the shadow of a hero instead of his trophies. Therefore the homily must turn towards what is at hand and bring under our eyes the fruit that is yours. Let the splendours of the world remain unmentioned, even if they abound in material for rhetoric, as well as all such subject matter of orations of praise.[116]

These two explicit examples[117] of a rejection of the influence of the classical rhetoric in homilies which abound in illustrations of the reverse, is remarkable. One could say that they are only examples of what Delehaye called 'a feigned independence' (Delehaye 1921: 193). This might be the case, but we would say that passages such as these document the ongoing debate about the precise relationship and the allowed degree of Christianity's intertwining with the culture of Hellenism. At least it shows that these homilists took the trouble to take into account the possible sensitivity their audience might have in that regard.

APPROACHING THE HOMILIES:
POSSIBILITIES AND LIMITS

The term 'panegyrics on martyrs' covers a group of homilies which have a lot in common and are yet very diverse. Not all of them are devoted to the martyr; many other topics are brought to the fore and sometimes the theme of martyrdom and the martyr's story are barely touched upon. And when the martyr's story is at the centre of a homily the homilist still develops other subthemes along the way. Moreover, the homilists' concern is not with the presentation of historical facts about the martyr but with the edification and moral exhortation of their audience, one of their main endeavours – though not the sole one – being to show the martyr's importance as an example of virtue. All this means that panegyrics on martyrs are examples of a multilayered discourse that serves more than one purpose and consequently can and should be assessed from many different viewpoints. Finally, the panegyrics collected in this volume were delivered by different homilists and bear their respective stamp in terms of style and the development of their subject. To end this general introduction it is, therefore, not without relevance to sketch the main lines of a methodology for approaching these texts. Given the diversity of the homiletic material it is undesirable to offer a strict step-by-step methodology that could be applied successfully to every separate homily. Instead, I will suggest a number of possible, partially overlapping, approaches each highlighting a particular aspect of homiletical texts. Depending on the personal preference of the reader/scholar and the possibilities offered by each separate text, they can be applied to each homily.

The first approach considers homilies *as historical sources*. Homilies contain a wealth of information on a great diversity of topics pertaining to the political, economic, social, cultural and religious history. They inform us about daily life (especially in the cities), about the history of theology, liturgy and exegesis, about norms and values, about clothes, fauna and flora, about the military life, the world of the theatre and the stadium, human anatomy, astronomy, cosmology, topography and many other themes. The possibilities of a systematic application of this approach and its rich harvest, is demonstrated by Drobner's analysis of Gregory of Nyssa's *Homilies on Ecclesiastes* (Drobner 1996). A similar, larger project, mining the information of Constantinopolitan sources, is going on at the Australian Catholic University (Allen and Mayer 1993), and dovetails with an even larger project, undertaken by Mayer in 2001, in which the entire homiletic corpus of John Chrysostom is being analysed for historical information. The advantages and possibilities of this approach are obvious. The biggest disadvantage is the fragmentary character of our homiletical source material, meaning that for many homilies we cannot be completely sure about their date and/or location of delivery. For data pertaining to fields without quick evolutions in late antiquity (e.g. the sciences) this is not that important, but when using homiletical material for the history of theology the lack of a sure and precise date can be very annoying. Moreover, in general the homilists take for granted a very concrete background and ambience that for their audience was self-evident but that to us is only partially accessible. The end of the first part of Gregory of Nyssa's *First Homily on the Forty of Sebaste* is a case in point: Gregory has to abandon his homily because of the noise made by his audience and it is only in the second part (Mart Ib) that we hear that it was the noise of approving applause, not of booing and showing disapproval.

It goes without saying that the panegyrics in this volume, as well as the other examples of the genre, are an important source about the martyr and the celebration of his or her cult. Many other nuggets of historical information on a host of other topics can, however, also be gleaned from them, as is shown by the following examples, chosen at random.

As for the late antique knowledge of biology (in particular entomology) it is revealing that Basil mentions in the prologue of *On Gordius* that the leader of a colony of bees is their king, a misconception he shared with all his contemporaries.[118] In the context of the rhetorical topos of Sebaste as the city that produced the Forty, Gregory of Nyssa gives a detailed description of its two rivers, their position and what they mean for the inhabitants, thus being a source for late antique topography and agriculture.[119] With regard to the social life in late antiquity our panegyrics contain some, to us, still very recognisable customs. With regard to the 'laws of the symposium' we learn from Gregory of Nyssa that, when being invited to a banquet, it was customary to issue a counter-invitation to one's host. In Chrysostom's *Homily on the Holy Martyrs* we read how, in the public baths, people are hesitant to go into the pool with hot water and how it is not a long-winded speech that convinces people to go into the water but the example of somebody who actually puts a toe or a hand in it and then the rest of their body.[120] And in his panegyric *On Julian* we hear about the doctor's behaviour when visiting somebody on his sickbed: he says little to the sick person himself but summons that person's relatives and enjoins upon them all the instructions for the treatment.[121]

For socio-economic history a passage in John Chrysostom's *On Babylas* is of interest. In this homily John includes an invective against Julian, informing us that in the years that he was emperor, Antioch and its surroundings were struck by famines, caused by drought and by inflation and economic distress. He describes market-places that were empty due to the low adduction of goods and scenes of people fighting in shops for the scarce goods when some had arrived. This low adduction of goods was partly the result of a lower production caused by the drought and partly of the pressure put on the market by the moving of troops through Antioch towards the eastern frontier.[122]

Finally, our panegyrics also contain valuable nuggets of information regarding the pagan cults in late antiquity. Basil informs us that Gordius died the martyr's death in Caesarea on the occasion of the celebration of the cult of 'a war-loving god'.[123] Given the date of Gordius' death in early March,[124] this homily can be taken as evidence for the existence in Caesarea the cult of Mars, the celebration of which traditionally occurred in the very beginning of the month that is named after him. In the same vein Gregory of Nyssa, in narrating how Theodore the Recruit burnt the temple of the Great Mother in Amasea, preserved for us the valuable information that this goddess was venerated in Amasea as was also the case in many other cities in Pontus and Asia Minor.[125]

A second way of approaching panegyrics on martyrs is that of focusing on their genesis. This diachronic or *historical–critical approach* tries to define the sources from which the author drew his inspiration and considers the text as the final result of a more or less gradual development. Especially the method of *redactional criticism*, which is often used in New Testament exegesis, can also be applied fruitfully to many of our panegyrics. In reconstructing the development of which the final text as we have it is the result, this approach focuses on the activity of the author, addressing questions such as: which sources did the author use? How did he handle them? And with what purpose? Perrin formulates it as follows: redactional criticism 'is concerned with the theological motivation of an author as revealed in the collection, arrangement, editing, and modification of traditional material and in the composition of new material or the creation of new forms within the traditions of early Christianity'.[126]

Our homilist's 'theological motivation' can be described as presenting the martyr as a worthy example of Christian virtue, putting
the audience on guard against deviant theological opinions and the
attraction of other religions as well as giving edification, teaching and
moral exhortation to his congregation.

Reconstructing the genesis of a panegyric and tracing the
homilist's contribution to the process is an approach that can bear
rich fruits. It can only be successfully executed, however, on condition that one has a fair idea of the sources the homilist had at his
disposal. Only then is it possible to see glimpses of his input. For
panegyrics on martyrs it means that this approach is most likely to
be successful when the panegyric is part of a larger hagiographical
tradition about the martyr or saint in question. With regard to the
panegyrics in this volume this is the case for Basil and Gregory of
Nyssa's panegyrics on the Forty Martyrs of Sebaste. Together with
the Passion of the Forty, their Testament and the panegyric of the
'Greek Ephrem' we have sufficient and coherent material to grasp
the development of this tradition and hence to study how Basil and
Gregory handled their sources (Karlin-Hayter 1991). Something
similar is possible with regard to Gregory's panegyric *On Theodore*.
With the Passion of Theodore, a document which originated inde-
pendently from Gregory but largely reflects the same traditional
elements of the martyr's story, we are in a good position to see
Gregory's handling of these traditional elements and his using them
within the framework of his own 'theological motivation'. With
regard to Asterius of Amasea's and Hesychius of Jerusalem's panegyrics on Stephen we are in an equally favourable position since
Stephen's story as it is narrated in Acts is their main source. The
same is true for Gregory of Nyssa's *First Homily on Stephen*. As an
illustration of a case in which it is virtually impossible to apply the
redaction-critical method one can mention the *Ecphrasis of Euphemia's
Martyrdom* by Asterius of Amasea. About this martyr we have but
two sources: Asterius' ecphrasis and a Greek Passio (BHG 619).
The problem is that what these sources tell about Euphemia differs
to such an extent that it is not even completely sure that they concern
the same person. Add to that the different literary genre (passio
vs ecphrasis) and the fact that Asterius' describes the events only
from her trial and one understands that the basis for a full-blown
redaction-critical approach is too small indeed.

The third method of studying homiletical material does not consider the text as the result of a genesis but on the contrary mainly

41

reads it in its final version, as a literary product on its own. This *synchronic approach* can include questions that bring in the actual reader: e.g. what do these texts mean to me? To what extent is the idea of sanctity and Christian virtue that they contain still appealing? Do these texts for somebody on the verge of the twenty-first century *mutatis mutandis* offer models for speaking about martyrdom and sanctity? Especially to Christians living in the many regions on the globe where martyrdom is still a reality, these texts from a distant past might still resonate with surprising force.

In patristic studies, however, the focus mostly is on what can be conveniently indicated as a literary analysis of the texts. Then, the study limits itself to the texts as they functioned in the fourth and fifth centuries; it tries to place and understand them within the parameters of the time in which they originated. Many issues that have already come to the fore above, can be incorporated in such an analysis: the influence of classical rhetoric; the homily as literature (e.g. style and rhythm); the identification of traditional agonistic metaphors used to speak about the martyr and martyrdom.

A feature that in the context of a literary analysis also must be addressed is the presence of hagiographical topoi in the text. This can include basic schemes, e.g. the judge trying to win the martyr over by a friendly attitude and/or promises – the martyr's refusal – the rage of the judge or the presentation of martyrdom and the events preceding it as a contest with Satan. Recurrent topoi can also concern more abstract concepts, such as the idea of the persecutor bringing himself down by condemning and killing the martyr. Other, more detailed topoi are the frequent playing on the *double entendre* under the name Stephen, *stefanos* being both a proper name and the substantive for crown, the recurrent presentation of Christ as the *agônothetès* (president of the games) or the angels as the supporters of the martyr.

A final important feature is the use of Scriptural quotations and allusions. This is an important element in all homiletical literature and it is also of great relevance when making a literary analysis of panegyrics. The Scriptures, both Old and New Testament, were for patristic authors and homilists the most important horizon of inspiration as well as a source of arguments, metaphors, images and stock-phrases on which they were drawing freely and seemingly effortlessly for a variety of purposes. A verse that for evident reasons occurs several times in our panegyrics is Ps 115:6: 'in the eyes of the Lord the death of His saints is precious'.[127] Several Scriptural characters are presented as exempla, the imitation of which was incarnated by the martyrs. So, in the tradition around the Forty a recurring element is the courageous attitude of the mother of one of them, a clear adaptation of the biblical theme of the mother of the Maccabean brothers (Karlin-Hayter 1991: 285–6). Job is another obvious example, evidently for his courage in suffering but also for his obedience towards God and the jealousy he awaked in Satan. Often a Scriptural verse is put into the saint's mouth, voicing their triumphant courage and confidence towards their persecutors and their willingness to endure torture and eventually die.

Reading a panegyric while paying special attention to the biblical quotations and allusions can be very fruitful. In each case a closer look to discover what the borrowing in question contributes to the argument or the homiletical power is a rewarding exercise and will certainly lead to a richer understanding. Once this question has been addressed, a second, though more time-consuming, step can be to see whether this author uses this specific verse(s) also in other homilies or writings and, if so, whether he does so in the same way and with the same purpose or not. This sheds light on the role of the Scriptures in homiletical works and often brings to light interesting parallels and observations. So, a closer study of the use of Ps 115:6 – to take this example – in Gregory of Nyssa reveals that he does not quote this verse very often. In his funeral orations *On Meletius* and *On Flacilla* he quotes it to argue that, because they lived exemplary Christian lives, one can be sure that God will look mercifully upon them and grant them also after death a happy life.[128] In *On Theodore* he quotes it to close his argumentation that the present status of the martyr's body, as venerated and preserved in a magnificent martyrium, bears testimony to God's looking benevolently upon him.[129] In some other Greek patristic writings from the first four centuries the verse is also used in a context which connects it with martyrdom: Origen,[130] Eusebius of Caesarea[131] and the *Apostolic Constitutions*[132] being mentioned as examples.

The final approach to homiletical literature that must be mentioned here is the *preacher–audience analysis*. This method of analysis studies a homily as an ongoing process of communication between the preacher and his audience. For that purpose it tries to define as precisely as possible the actors engaging themselves in this process. For the knowledge about the homilist as a man of culture (*paideia*) one can build on insights gained from the study of style and rhetoric. More particular questions are: is the homily as we have it the text which was actually delivered? And, was the homily the result of a thorough preparation, the result of improvisation or a mixture of both? (Hammerstaedt and Terbuycken 1996: 1257–84). With regard to the audience, among others, the following questions can be addressed: what is the social make-up of the audience? Are men and women present? Is this sermon maybe only preached for monks and virgins or, on the contrary, on a big feast day for the complete congregation, who have showed up in great numbers? Moreover, with regard to the years AD 350–450, from which the homilies in this volume date, one should keep in mind that the audience showed a varying intensity in their adherence to Christianity: some were recent converts, others were Christians of the second generation, still others belonged to a family whose allegiance to Christianity went back several generations. Ultimately, when both actors are studied as carefully as possible, one is ready to assess how in a particular sermon an ongoing process of communication between these two actors is going on. Elements which should be taken into account here are the location where the homily was delivered, the occasion for which it was held, the liturgical context, the duration of the sermon (see for all these elements the basic work of Olivar 1991: 487–902).

A survey of what is possible with this method, when applied to the *œuvre* of Chrysostom, is outlined by Mayer 1998 (see also Allen 1996, 1997). Without neglecting the difficulties, it must be admitted that with the *œuvre* of Chrysostom one is indeed in the most favourable of circumstances to apply the preacher–audience analysis: an extensive corpus of texts, containing a considerable number of relevant indications, reflecting the homiletical and pastoral activity of a priest and bishop in Antioch and Constantinople, cities the history of which is illuminated by a host of other sources, both literary and archaeological. With regard to the other authors in this volume, the situation is somewhat less favourable, though certainly not as difficult as in the case of most later Byzantine authors, as is illustrated by the studies collected in Allen and Cunningham 1998. For the Cappadocian Fathers a moderate positive assessment with regard to the applicability of the preacher–audience analysis can be made. About the Christian Church in fourth-century Cappadocia and the surrounding regions we are relatively well informed, largely through the correspondence of Basil and the two Gregories. This provides us with a background against which to read their homiletical *œuvre*. Moreover, these homilies contain some quite useful indications about their audiences and the verbal and non-verbal communication between preacher and congregation (thorough analysis in Bernardi

1968). For Asterius of Amasea and Hesychius of Jerusalem the situation is less favourable, though certainly in the former's case, one feels how he is trying to connect with his audience.

Thus, all in all our knowledge of the background of our authors and their homiletical *œuvre* is relatively satisfactory. Moreover, with regard to the martyr festivals – the concrete context in which panegyrics on martyrs were delivered – we are really well informed. We know that they were busy gatherings, assembling a substantial part of the local Christian community in all its social diversity, joining in a celebration that combined religious, social and economic activities and provided room for devotional practices (see pp. 15–22). From all these elements taken together one can conclude that most of the homilies in this volume offer possibilities for the application of the preacher–audience analysis, albeit not in all cases to the same extent.

It is unavoidable that, in reading a panegyric, we read with the eyes of the homilist and perceive the reality of preaching from his vantage point. This has the advantage of enabling us to analyse the kind of discourse the homilist addressed to his audience and to gauge which goals – both implicit and explicit ones – he was pursuing. It also means, however, that we are not in the most favourable position to consider a homily from the audience's perspective. Yet, homilies from the fourth and fifth centuries contain sufficient evidence – albeit from the preacher's perspective – about the involvement of the audience. In particular we learn that the congregation was seldom listening passively but, on the contrary, was responding in an active way to what the preacher was saying. These reactions took various forms: applause or booing to voice approval or disapproval, comments on what the preacher was saying, signs (e.g. nodding) showing agreement or disagreement, expressions of horror or commotion, laughter and tears, or sighing (Olivar 1991: 786–815). The noise made by the audience could be as loud as to drown out the homilist's voice. The already mentioned example of Gregory of Nyssa's having to abandon his sermon on the Forty in their martyrium in Sebaste is a very strong example but there are many other instances of preachers asking for silence and the audience's attention (Olivar 1991: 815–33; 868–79).

In other instances one also witnesses the preacher reacting directly to his audience, even to the extent of changing the course of his sermon. Basil of Caesarea's *Eighth Homily on the Six Days of Creation* contains a beautiful example: some attentive listeners had caught Basil on an obscurity and made that clear, first to each other and then to the preacher using some gestures of their heads. Basil understood what was happening and stopped his sermon to explain it to the rest of the audience.[133] His homily *On Not Attaching to Wordly Goods*, delivered in Satala (Armenia), offers another example. Basil had spent most of his homily on encouraging the rich people present in the audience to give more alms and also to show more concern to the miserable situation of the poor. Right when he wants to pronounce the doxology, some people in the audience protest and require that he should also address the problems caused by a disaster that had occurred the day before, when a fire had turned into ashes the houses of some people present in church. Basil honours their request and goes on for a considerable time about this topic.[134] The homilies in this volume do not contain such unusually informative passages. A less spectacular example one finds in Chrysostom's *On Babylas*. Making the transition to telling the martyr's story, he acquiesces to his audience, which seemingly started showing signs of impatience, saying: 'Wait, don't get rowdy if we take the story back a little. After all, those who want to show off their paintings to advantage, position the viewers back a little from the tablet. In this fashion they uncover the paintings, making the view clearer for them by means of the distance. For this reason, then, be indulgent too as the storyline draws you back.'[135]

On the basis of such examples it can be safely concluded that delivering a homily was a two-way communication. This communication happened, evidently, with words but was also supported by non-verbal ways of communicating. As is clear from the above-mentioned example from Basil's *Eighth Homily on the Six Days of Creation*, the audience communicated in a non-verbal way with the preacher. The non-verbal communication, however, also went in the reverse direction: according to the handbooks of rhetoric gestures formed an essential part of a good rhetorical performance and Christian rhetoric, it seems, did not reject this habit, though some preachers were using more explicit gestures than others (Steinbrink 1992; Quacquarelli 1970). Unfortunately this part of the delivery of sermons is largely lost to us. One cannot do much more than imagine the homilist pointing to something or somebody or under-lining with gestures of arms and hands an important sentence or indicating with his fingers a number he mentions.

This preacher–audience approach can certainly be applied success-fully to the homilies collected in this volume. In addition to noticing the passages which explicitly reveal something of the dynamic between preacher and audience, one can bring in this perspective in the following ways. First of all one should keep in the back of one's mind the context of the homilies: that of the panèguris. Second, it helps to be attentive to all the ways the homilist is using to get his message across: referring to well-known Scriptural passages, making comparisons to the daily lives of his audience or to other things they were well acquainted with, most notably the features of the local cult of the saints itself. Finally, while doing a close reading of the text, it is also advisable to chart in as much detail as possible the flow of communication between preacher and audience. Besides the elements mentioned above, one should be particularly attentive to the alternation between passages in which the homilist addresses his audience directly, by using the second person, and passages in which he uses discursive speech. In doing so, one gets a clear picture of the extent to which this particular homily generated a real communication between the preacher and his audience.

Notes

1 Basil of Caesarea, *On Gordius* 1 (PG 31, 489C, 4); *On Mamas* 2 (PG 31, 592B, 10–14); *On Drunk People* 1 (PG 31, 445C, 13–14).
2 Basil, *Letter 150.3* (Courtonne 1957–66: II, 74–5).
3 As is strongly suggested by the bucolic context and the mentioning of a procession towards the sanctuary in Gregory of Nazianze's *Homily on Low Sunday*, which was pronounced in the context of a martyr feast. Cf. PG 36, 620C, 2–5.
4 Asterius, *On the Holy Martyrs* 1.2 (Datema 1970: 135).
5 John Chrysostom, *On the Egyptian Martyrs* (PG 50, 694, 4–21).
6 Gregory of Nazianze, *Letters 122* and *197* (Gallay 1964–67: II, 13–14; 88).
7 Gregory of Nyssa, *Letter 1* (Maraval 1990a: 84–91).
8 Basil, *Letter 95* (Courtonne 1957–66: I, 207).
9 *Passion of Athenogenes* (BHG 197b) 25 (Maraval 1990b: 54–5).
10 *Passion of Eustratius and his Companions* 29; 33 (PG 116, 501; 505).
11 John Chrysostom, *On the Holy Martyrs* (PG 50, 647). See below also Mayer's general introduction on the martyr cult in Antiochia and Constantinople.
12 Gregory of Nyssa, *Letter 25* (Maraval 1990a: 288–301).
13 Gregory of Nazianze, *Funeral Oration for his Father* 39 (PG 35, 1037A, 9-B, 6).
14 *Passion of Athenogenes* (BHG 197b) 13; 37; 39 (Maraval 1990b: 40–1 and 76–81).
15 Gregory of Nazianze, *Funeral Oration for his Father* 39 (PG 35, 1037B, 6–13).
16 Gregory of Nazianze, *Funeral Oration for his Father* 39 (PG 35, 1037B, 8–11).

17 Gregory of Nyssa, *On Theodore* (GNO X, 1/2, 62, 25–63, 15).
18 Cf. e.g. 'Seeing the gods', ch. 4 of Fox 1986: 102–68.
19 Cf. the introduction to the translation of John Chrysostom's *On Babylas* in this volume.
20 *Testament of the Forty Martyrs of Sebaste* 1 (Musurillo 1972: 354–7). For the dispersion of their relics, see e.g. Amore 1968.
21 Basil, *Letters 155, 164* and *165* (Courtonne 1957–66: II, 80–1 and 97–101) with Pouchet 1992: 457–65.
22 Ambrose, *Letter 77* (Zelzer 1982: 126–40) with Amat 1985: 214–16 and den Boeft 1988.
23 Gregory of Nazianze, *On Cyprian 17* (Mossay and Lafontaine 1981: 74–7).
24 *Passion of the Forty Martyrs of Sebaste* 13 (Gebhardt 1902: 180–1).
25 John Chrysostom, *On the Ascension* (PG 50, 443, 10–15).
26 John Chrysostom, *On the Holy Martyrs* (PG 50, 649, 4–18).
27 Some examples in panegyrics: Basil, *On the Forty Martyrs of Sebaste* 8 (PG 31, 523); Gregory of Nazianze, *On Cyprian* 19 (Mossay and Lafontaine 1981: 84–5); Gregory of Nyssa, *On Theodore* (GNO X, 1/2, 70–1); *On Stephen II* (ibid., 104–5). Asterius, *On the Holy Martyrs* 4 (Datema 1970: 136–7).
28 Basil, *On the Forty Martyrs of Sebaste* 8 (PG 31, 524A, 4–13).
29 Gregory of Nyssa, *On Theodore* (GNO X, 1/2, 70, 6–71, 17).
30 Asterius, *On Phocas* 11 (Datema 1970: 125–6).
31 Basil, *Homily on Psalm 115* (PG 30, 112).
32 Basil, *On Julitta* (PG 31, 241).
33 John Chrysostom, *A Homily on Martyrs* (PG 50, 664). ET: Mayer and Allen 2000: 94–7, at 96.
34 John Chrysostom, *On Julian* (PG 50, 673).
35 Gregory of Nazianze, *Against Julian* I, 69 (Bernardi 1983: 178–9).
36 Gregory of Nyssa, *On the Forty Martyrs of Sebaste II* (GNO X, 1/2, 166–7).
37 Gregory of Nyssa, *On the Forty Martyrs of Sebaste II* (GNO X, 1/2, 167, 11–168, 5). Other, briefer testimonies of incubation in the context of the martyr cult are Basil of Caesarea's testimony that the shepherd-martyr Mamas appeared to people in dream-visions (Basil, *On Mamas* 1; PG 31, 589C, 7–8) and the passage at the end of Asterius of Amasea's *Homily on Phocas* which mentions the countless and unceasing effects of the dream-visions and healings achieved by the martyr's intermediation; cf. Asterius, *On Phocas* 13 (Datema 1970: 127).
38 Theodoret of Cyrrhus, *Graecarum affectionum curatio* VIII, 63 (Canivet 1958: 333–4).
39 Asterius, *On Phocas* 12 (Datema 1970: 125–7).
40 Gregory of Nyssa, *On the Forty Martyrs of Sebaste II* (GNO X, 1/2, 166); Gregory of Nazianze, *Carmina* II, 20 and II, 76 (PG 38, 20 and 50). For a discussion of these passages and for the *inhumatio ad sanctos* in general, see Duval 1988 (for Cappadocia and surroundings, esp. 66–73).

41 Gregory of Nyssa, *On the Forty Martyrs of Sebaste II* (G X, 1/2, 166, 9–12); Gregory of Nyssa, *Life of Macrina* 13; 34 (Marav 971: 186–7; 250–3).

42 Gregory of Nazianze, *Carmina* II, 20 and II, 76 (PG 38, nd 50).

43 Gregory of Nazianze, *Epigram* 118.

44 Theodoret of Cyrrhus, *Historia religiosa* 10.8; 13.19.

45 Gregory of Nyssa, *On Theodore* (GNO X, 1/2, 69, 24–70, 3).

46 Asterius, *On Phocas* 9.2–3 (Datema 1970: 123).

47 A good survey of these and other activities going on in and around the martyrium, both during the year and on the occasion of the panguris, can be found in Maraval 1985. For incubation, see Wacht 1997.

48 The evidence is rather scanty. The following passages can be mentioned: Basil, *Homily on Psalm 114*, 1 (PG 29, 484); Gregory of Nyssa, *Life of Macrina* 33, 6–7 (Maraval 1971: 248–9); Gregory of Nyssa, *On Theodore* (GNO X, 1/2, 69, 12–14). See Maraval 1985: 214–18.

49 This was the case on a festival for Philogonius, during which first Chrysostom delivered a panegyric and indicates that he will be followed by Flavian, his bishop (*On Philogonius*; PG 48, 752, 35–50). He adds that Flavian will cover partly the same material but will provide more detail (Mayer and Allen 2000: 184). This seems to suggest that they briefly exchanged the contents of their respective sermons or that John knew from earlier experiences what approach Flavian was likely to choose. A second instance is provided by Chrysostom's *On Babylas*, at the outset of which he announces that he will leave the narration of biographical events about the martyr to 'the more senior preachers and our common father' (*On Babylas* 2; SC 362, 296, 5–7).

50 Translation from Brown 1981: 7.

51 Gregory of Nazianze, *Homily on Low Sunday* 12 (PG 36, 620C, 1–4).

52 John Chrysostom, *On the Cemetery and the Cross* (PG 50, 393 1–11); *On Ascension* (PG 50, 441, 1–442, 10).

53 John Chrysostom, *On Drosis* (PG 50, 685 12–16); *On Julian* (PG 50, 674 17–45).

54 Basil, *On Mamas* 1 (PG 31, 589C-D, 5).

55 Gregory of Nyssa, *Second Homily on the Forty of Sebaste* (GNO X, 1/2, 167, 19–22).

56 The sermon is edited in PG 31, 237–62. The part about Julitta runs only from cols 237 to 241 (chs 1 and 2).

57 Cf. the edition in Datema 1970: 27–37. Only the prooemium (op.cit., 27) considers the occasion of the panèguris.

58 E.g. John Chrysostom, *On: 'I have seen the Lord' hom.* 3 (SC 277, 104, 10–11), where he says that he will leave discussion of the martyrs to the bishop, Flavian, while himself focusing on the topic on which he has recently been preaching.

59 Gregory of Nazianze, *Letter 122* (Gallay 1964–67: II, 13–14).

60 Basil, *Letter 100* (Courtonne 1957–66: I, 219).

61 Basil, *r 167* (Courtonne 1957–66: II, 112–13).

62 Basil, *er 252* (Courtonne 1957–66: III, 93).

63 Basil, *ter 95* (Courtonne 1957–66: I, 207–8).

64 Basil, *tter 142* (Courtonne 1957–66: II, 64–5).

65 For t's homily, see Bernardi 1968: 131–9.

66 John Chrysostom, *A Homily on Martyrs* (PG 50, 663).

67 Bas' *Homily on Riches* (PG 31, 281C); Basil, '*Long Rules*' (PG 31, 1020B-D)

68 Jo'n Chrysostom, *On Philogonius* (PG 48, 749).

69 Femplary passages: Basil, '*Long Rules*', quaestio 40 (PG 31, 1020–1); Asterius, *On Avarice* 1.3 (Datema 1970: 27, 16–21).

7(' Basil, *Homily on Drunk People* 1 (PG 31, 445).

71 PG 50, 661–6. ET: Mayer and Allen 2000: 94–7.

72 John Chrysostom, *On Julian* (PG 50, 672–6). The picnic is mentioned in col. 673; the passage quoted in ET is in col. 674.

73 Gregory of Nazianze, *Homily Delivered in the Presence of Julian the Tax Collector* 5–11 (PG 35, 1049–57) with Bernardi 1968: 131–9. A similar general passage in John Chrysostom, *A Homily on Martyrs* (PG 50, 663); ET: Mayer and Allen 2000: 94, 24–31.

74 Gregory of Nazianze, *Homily on Low Sunday* 9 (PG 36, 617A, 10-B, 10).

75 Asterius, *On Phocas* 1 (Datema 1970: 115). Other texts in panegyrics on martyrs in which this imitation idea can be found: Basil, *On Gordius* 1 (PG 31, 492A, 7–12); Basil, *On the Forty Martyrs of Sebaste* 1–2 (PG 31, 508B, 4–6; 509A, 4–17); Gregory of Nyssa, *On Theodore* (ed. Lendle, GNO X, 1/2, 62, 3–9); Gregory of Nyssa, *Second Homily on the Forty of Sebaste* (GNO X, 1/2, 159, 10–160, 3); Asterius, *On Avarice* 1.2 (Datema 1970: 27); John Chrysostom, *On the Egyptian Martyrs* (PG 50, 697–8); John Chrysostom, *On the Holy Martyrs* (PG 50, 709–12). Cf. Leemans 2000.

76 One example: when Chrysostom reacts against people taking off to Daphne, even before the festival is over, he argues that imitation of martyrs and striving after emulating their virtue is the ground of the moral exhortation he is about to give (*On Julian*; PG 50, 672).

77 Asterius of Amasea's *Homily on Avarice*, delivered during a panèguris, explicitly mentions the imitation theme and the pedagogic function of the panègureis, which he calls 'schoolrooms for our souls' (*On Avarice* 1.2; Datema 1970: 27).

78 Rich bibliography in Kinzig 1997.

79 'Chez lui [Chrysostom] le flot de l'éloquence franchit plus aisément les digues et la convention et l'adaptation est plus entière et plus géniale' (Delehaye 1921: 202). See, however, also Mitchell 2000, esp. 22–8, who argues in relation to the seven *Homilies in Praise of St Paul* that Chrysostom adhered to rhetorical conventions more closely than has previously been acknowledged.

80 For an analysis of Gregory of Nyssa's homilies from this perspective, see Klock 1987.

81 This kind of interaction between preacher and audience has been studied in depth by Olivar 1991: 761–879.

82 For Chrysostom, see Mitchell 2000: chs 2–6; Mayer and Allen 2000: 27–9. Other examples and references can be found in Méridier 1906; Ameringer 1921; Campbell 1922; Bretz 1914: 85–105.

83 For Gregory of Nyssa, see Méridier 1906: 96–115.

84 Gregory of Nyssa, GNO X, 1/2, 142, 10–13 and 145, 14–21.

85 About this image, see Leemans, forthcoming. For this motif in the writings of Chrysostom, see Sawhill 1928: 31–4.

86 John Chrysostom, *On Julian* (PG 50, 667).

87 Gregory of Nyssa, *First Homily on the Forty of Sebaste (Ib)* (GNO X, 1/2, 149, 11–17).

88 Gregory of Nyssa, *On Theodore* (GNO X, 1/2, 66, 8–12).

89 Basil, *On Gordius* (PG 31, 148A).

90 Gregory of Nyssa, *Mart Ib* (GNO X, 1/2, 145, 5–13).

91 Gregory of Nyssa, *Mart Ib* (GNO X, 1/2, 148, 13–21).

92 Gregory of Nyssa, *Mart Ib* (GNO X, 1/2, 152, 3–9).

93 All references to the Old Testament throughout this volume conform to the Septuagint, the Greek translation used by our homilists.

94 Gregory of Nyssa, *Mart Ib* (GNO X, 1/2, 146, 26–147, 2).

95 John Chrysostom, *On Julian* (PG 50, 667–8).

96 John Chrysostom, *On Pelagia* (PG 50, 579).

97 Gregory of Nyssa, *On Theodore* (GNO X, 1/2, 70, 12; l.8 and l.20 resp.).

98 Gregory of Nyssa, *Mart Ib* (GNO X, 1/2, 149, 15–16).

99 Asterius, *On Phocas* 5.1 and 8.1 (Datema 1970: 119 and 121).

100 Gregory of Nyssa, *On Theodore* (GNO X, 1/2, 66, 12 and 67, 4); *Mart Ib* (GNO X, 1/2, 153, 6).

101 Gregory of Nyssa, *Mart Ib* (GNO X, 1/2, 147, 18).

102 Gregory of Nyssa, *Mart Ib* (GNO X, 1/2, 148, 8; 150, 1, 4 and 17).

103 Gregory of Nyssa, *Mart Ib* (GNO X, 1/2, 150, 14–15).

104 Basil, *On Gordius* 4 (PG 31, 500B).

105 John Chrysostom, *On the Holy Martyrs* (PG 50, 645).

106 Hesychius of Jerusalem, *On Procopius* 4 (Aubineau 1978–80: II, 550).

107 Asterius, *On Phocas* 8.1–2 (Datema 1970: 121).

108 Gregory of Nyssa, *On Theodore* (GNO X, 1/2, 66, 16–67, 2).

109 Gregory of Nyssa, *Mart Ib* (GNO X, 1/2, 155, 5–10).

110 John Chrysostom, *On the Holy Martyrs* (PG 50, 647).

111 Basil, *On Gordius* 2 (PG 31, 493C-496C) and *On Gordius* 4 (PG 31, 497A).

112 Gregory of Nyssa, *On Theodore* (GNO X, 1/2, 62, 25–64, 3).

113 Gregory of Nyssa, *Mart Ib* (GNO X, 1/2, 152, 18–29). An even longer ecphrasis on the same topic may be found in Gregory's *Second Homily on the Forty of Sebaste* (GNO X, 1/2, 162, 13–27).

114 John Chrysostom, *On Babylas* 4 (SC 362, 300–3).

115 Basil, *On the Forty Martyrs of Sebaste* 2 (PG 31, 509A).

116 Gregory of Nyssa, *Mart Ib* (GNO X, 1/2, 139, 27–140, 13).

117 Other examples: Basil, *On Gordius* 1–2 (PG 31, 489–93); Asterius, *On Peter and Paul* 2 (Datema 1970: 86).

118 Basil, *On Gordius* 1 (PG 31, 489) with Koep 1951.

119 Gregory of Nyssa, *Mart Ia* (GNO X, 1/2, 139, 18–140, 6).

120 John Chrysostom, *On the Holy Martyrs* (PG 50, 647, 62–648, 8).

121 John Chrysostom, *On Julian* (PG 50, 674, 10–16).

122 John Chrysostom, *On Babylas* (SC 362, 302, 21–4).

123 Basil, *On Gordius* 3 (PG 31, 496D–497A).

124 Giving preference to the early testimonies of the *Martyrologium Syriacum* (or 'Martyrologium of Wright') and the *Martyrologium Hieronymianum*, both dating Gordius' feast day on 2 March. This is also in agreement with the testimony of Basil, who clearly delivered his homily *On Gordius* in spring. These, our three earliest testimonies, differ from an Armenian Passio (2 January), the Synaxarium of Constantinople (3 January) and some later Byzantine liturgical texts (4 January), all dating Gordius' *dies natalis* in early January. The difference in date might be explained by ascribing it to the influence of a *Passio Gordii* (BHG 703b) which is in fact nothing more than a Passion for the Antiochene martyr Hesychius in which the name Hesychius is systematically substituted by the name Gordius. Hesychius' *dies natalis*, which is on 3 January, might in this way have become associated with Gordius.

125 Gregory of Nyssa, *On Theodore* (GNO X, 1/2, 67, 11–25). For the cult of the Great Mother (Cybele) in Anatolia, see Mitchell 1993: 19–22. Amasea as a place of her cult is seldom mentioned in encyclopedia-articles and other literature on the city, Ireland *et al.* 2000 being an exception.

126 N. Perrin, *What is Redaction Criticism?*, London 1970, p. 1, quoted in Biddle 1999 and Donahue 1999.

127 Gregory of Nyssa, *On Theodore* (GNO X, 1/2, 64, 3–4); Asterius of Amasea, *On Phocas* 9.4; *On the Holy Martyrs* 18.5; Hesychius of Jerusalem, *On Procopius*, titulus and ch. 6.

128 Gregory of Nyssa, *On Meletius* (GNO IX, 455, 2–5); *On Flacilla* (GNO IX, 482, 18–19).

129 Gregory of Nyssa, *On Theodore* (GNO X, 1/2, 64, 3–4).

130 Origen, *Against Celsus* VIII.54 (SC 150, 296, 42–5); *Exhortation to Martyrdom* 29 (GCS 2, 26, 15–19); *Commentary on Matthew* XVI.6 (GCS 40.1, 481–6, esp. 483, 14–27).

131 Eusebius of Caesarea, *Commentary on the Psalms* (PG 23, 812C and 1360D).

132 *Apostolic Constitutions* V.8.2 and VI.30.2–3 (SC, 329, 238–41 and 388–91).

133 Basil, *Eighth Homily on Hexaemeron* 2 (SC 26bis, 436–8).

134 Basil, *On Not Attaching to Wordly Goods* 9 (PG 31, 556C).

135 John Chrysostom, *On Babylas* 2 (SC 362, 298, 34–40).

Texts

I

BASIL OF CAESAREA

GENERAL INTRODUCTION

Basil, bishop of Caesarea in Cappadocia, is not known in the first instance for his martyr homilies. His name is more usually associated with his brother Gregory of Nyssa and his friend Gregory of Nazianzen, with the later phases of the Arian controversy, with the development of a theology of the Spirit, or with the reordering of the monastic life.[1]

In stark contrast to Asterius of Amasea or Hesychius of Jerusalem, we are remarkably well informed about Basil. Born around 330 in Pontus, Basil was educated in Caesarea, Antioch and Athens (where his Cappadocian friend Gregory of Nazianzen was also a student). He was baptised in 357 and shortly afterwards made a tour of the monasteries in Egypt. Subsequently he returned to Pontus and led an ascetic life with friends and relatives. At a synod in Constantinople in 360 Basil appeared in the company of Eustathius of Sebaste and Basil of Ancyra as a member of the semi-Arian or Homoiousian party, which tried to find the middle ground between the extreme Arian position of Eunomius and the pro-Nicene stance of Athanasius and others. Basil was, however, later to become a staunch supporter of the Nicene Creed, although he died before its vindication at the Council of Constantinople in 381. In 365 Basil returned to Caesarea, and on 14 June 370 he was consecrated bishop there. Despite his involvement in ecclesiastical politics and in the ascetic life, he was committed to the welfare of his congregations, and established hospitals for the poor. He died on 1 January 379.

Basil was also a prolific writer, composing homilies on biblical books, five books against Eunomius, treatises on the Holy Spirit, ascetical works and homilies, and liturgical works. We also have nearly 370 of his letters.

The enormous influence which Basil had as a homilist can be judged by the extent to which his homilies survive in translations. The series of nine homilies *On the Six Days of Creation* (CPG 2835), for example, was translated not only into Latin but also into Syriac, Georgian, Armenian, and Arabic. The same is true of the fourteen homilies on the Psalms (CPG 2836) and of many of his individual homilies. Severus of Antioch (*c.*465–538), in his Homily 18 *On the Forty Martyrs*, which was preached on 9 March 513, used Basil's homily on the same topic.

We have four extant Greek homilies of Basil on martyrs,[2] all apparently delivered within a span of four years (372–76). However, the cult of the martyrs in Caesarea was developed to such an extent, as attested by the variety of martyrs' sanctuaries in the city and its vicinity,[3] that we can assume that the bishop preached on other martyr feasts homilies which have not come down to us.[4] Basil's homily on the local martyr Julitta (CPG 2849), a rich resident of Caesarea whose remains rested in one of the most beautiful monuments of the city and whose feast had been established by Basil himself, was probably delivered in 372.[5] The homily on the Forty Martyrs of Sebaste (Armenia) was delivered in 373,[6] as was the homily on the local martyr Gordius (CPG 2862).[7] The homily on the obscure local martyr Mamas, a shepherd, whose feast was held on 2 September, was probably delivered in 376 (CPG 2868).[8] On these feastdays of martyrs the communal and public liturgical act, of which the homily was an integral part, resulted in what Philip Rousseau calls a 'sense of collusion between preacher and audience, of shared engagement in a common experience' (Rousseau 1994: 47 with n. 87), which is particularly vivid in Basil's preaching.

TEXTS

A homily on the martyr Gordius

Introduction

Basil's homily on the local martyr Gordius, a centurion who as a catechumen was martyred during the reign of Licinius, was delivered in Caesarea in 373.[9] Establishing the day on which it was delivered is a matter of discussion. Bernardi believes that the homily was delivered in spring (Bernardi 1968: 80), an impression that can be gained from the opening lines, mentioning that the martyr 'changes winter depression into spring brightness'. The text, however, can also be taken to mean that it is winter and that the swarming behaviour of the crowd and the martyrs, who attract the crowd like flowers, lead him to claim that winter has been (miraculously) converted into spring. Both a day in January and a day in spring conform with the data in the various calendars of saints' feasts, some of which mention it for early January, others on 2 March.[10]

We are told at the beginning of the homily that the place of delivery was a martyrium outside the city, and that this monument was dedicated to more than one martyr. The audience is said to be in attendance in great numbers, and Gordius is vaunted as being particularly popular with them because he is a native of Caesarea. However, Basil himself admits that he is short on facts about the martyr's exploits, speaking of 'some vague story which has been transmitted to us'. However, the general veracity of his account of the martyr's death is guaranteed by the fact that in the audience there are some who remember the event. The breakdown in civic order caused by the persecution is said to have forced Gordius to turn his back on city life in order to withdraw to the mountains. Yet in time he returned to Caesarea, precisely to the hippodrome – a symbolic location in urban living. When his martyrdom took place, the entire population of Caesarea went out of the city to see it, just as Basil's audience has left the city behind to celebrate the feast of Gordius, only to return to it afterwards, 'vividly aware of what it once had wrongly represented, and of what it might now become' (Rousseau 1994: 187).

Basil's homily was translated into Armenian and Old Church Slavonic, and was used in Byzantine hagiographical collections and menologia for 3 January (Halkin 1961: 6). An Armenian Passion of Gordius also survives (Esbroeck 1976: 357–86). The St Gordius of Antioch whose Passion survives in Greek is a doublet of St Gordius of Caesarea (Halkin 1961: 6–8), and a camouflage for the martyr Hesychius of Antioch (Lackner 1970).

Translated from the edition by Garnier; PG 31, 489–508.

Text

1. The rule of nature for bees is not to leave the beehives before their king (*sic*) leads the way in flight. And so, since I have just now seen the Lord's people going out to the heavenly flowers –

the martyrs, I look for their leader. Who is it who stirs up this great swarm? Who is it who changes winter depression into spring brightness? For pouring forth just now out of the city, as if from beehives, in a crowd the people have reached the ornate shrine outside the city, this revered and very beautiful stadium of the martyrs.[11] And so, since the wonder of the martyr has brought us [here] too, excited, having forgotten our feebleness, come let us too with a forceful voice hum around the man's works like around a flower, performing deeds that are both holy and at the same time a source of grace for those present. For *when the just man is praised, the people will rejoice* (Prov 29:2), the wise Solomon has just told us.[12]

And yet I have been at a loss within myself about what the enigmatic saying of the author of the Book of Proverbs could possibly mean. Does he mean that when an orator or a clever speech-writer composes a speech to stun his audience, deafening his hearers with elegant resonance, the people rejoice, receiving favourably both the breadth of the ideas and the arrangement [of the speech], and the solemnity of the diction and the harmony he has wrought? But he certainly wouldn't ever have said that, because nowhere does he use such a figure of speech. Nor would he have encouraged us to show off eulogistically by praising the blessed ones, because he preferred pedestrian diction and plain expression throughout his work. So what do his words mean? [They mean] that people rejoice with spiritual rejoicing at the very remembrance of the exploits of the just, urged on by what they hear to energetic imitation of good persons. I mean that the account of men who have lived a good life produces as it were a light for those who are being kept safe with regard to the road of life. This is why, as soon as we have heard the Spirit recounting the life of Moses, we are immediately energised to emulate the man's virtue, and the gentleness of their way of life (cf. Num 13:3) obviously becomes a matter of emulation and blessing to each person.

I mean that whereas the encomia of other human beings are composed out of the multiplication of words, the truth of the exploits performed by the just is enough to demonstrate the superiority of their virtue. The upshot is that when we set out in detail the lives of those who have been eminent in piety, in the first instance we are glorifying the Master through his servants; we are praising the just through their witness, with which we are familiar; we are making the people rejoice through hearing fine deeds. I mean that the life of Joseph is an encouragment to chastity (cf. Gen 39:8), and the tales of Samson [are an encouragement] to bravery (cf. Judg 14:5–9).

2.   Divine teaching, therefore, does not recognise the rule of encomia, but counts the witness of the exploits rather than encomia, on the grounds that it is quite sufficient in order to praise the saints, and enough to profit those striving for virtue. For the rule of encomia is to examine the fatherland, and investigate pedigree, and discourse on education, but our rule, silencing mention of the people around them, fills the witness of each from their individual deeds. For why am I more august on this account, if the city which once bore the burden of grievous and huge struggles sets up glorious trophies over its enemies? Why [am I more august] if it enjoys a favourable location such that it is comfortable in both winter and summer? But if it both produces men, and is suitable for raising cattle, what benefit do I have from that? But also with regard to herds of horses it outdoes any city under the sun. How, then, can these facts make us better with regard to human virtue? Or even if we were to discourse on the peaks of the neighbouring mountain, [saying] both how they are above the clouds and how much they protrude into the sky, shall we deceive ourselves, on the grounds that we have piled up praise for these men on account of these facts? Most ridiculous of all, when the entire world was disdained by the just, is that we should pile up encomia to them from the paltry objects which they despised.

Well then, remembering them is enough to profit us continually. For indeed they do not need a supplement to their good repute, but remembrance of them by imitating them is essential to us in this life in order to imitate them. For just as light automatically accompanies fire, and a sweet smell accompanies unguent, so too does benefit necessarily follow on the heels of good works. And yet this is no small task – to arrive accurately at the truth of what happened in those days. I mean that there is some vague story which has been transmitted to us preserving the manly feats of the man in his struggles. And in some way it is reasonable that we compare ourselves to painters. For when they translate images out of images, mostly, as is likely, they fall short of the model. And there is no small danger that we, who have lost sight of the events, will diminish the truth. But since the day has dawned which brings remembrance of the martyr who struggled notably in making acts of witness for Christ, let us say what we know.

He was born in this city, which is why we love him more, because he is our own ornament. I mean that just as fruitful trees provide the fruit which they grow for their own land, so too Gordius, running up from our womb and raised to the greatest height of fame, gives the enjoyment of his own fruit of piety to the land which produced and reared him. Beautiful indeed are the exotic fruits when they are both sweet and nutritious, but much sweeter than foreign fruits are the native and home-grown, which, as well as being enjoyable, have an added attraction in our eyes because they are our own.

After enlisting as a soldier in the army he occupied a prominent position such that he was entrusted with the leadership of one hundred soldiers, and he was conspicuous among the military ranks for the strength of his body and the bravery of his spirit. When the tyrant of the time[13] extended his bitterness and savagery of spirit to war with the church, and lifted against piety his hand which fought against God, there were proclamations everywhere and edicts were spread in every marketplace and every place of note, not to worship Christ or the penalty for worshippers would be death. And there was a command for everybody to bow down before idols, and to regard as gods stones and wood fashioned with the mark of craft, or for the disobedient to suffer unbearable punishments. There was confusion and disturbance through the whole city, and booty was taken from pious people. Money was seized, the bodies of those who loved Christ were torn to shreds with beatings, women were dragged through the middle of the city, there was no pity for youth, no respect for age. Instead, those who did no wrong underwent the punishment of criminals; prisons were crowded, those who had prosperous houses were bereft, whereas lonely places were full of people seeking refuge. The complaint made against those who suffered these things was piety, and father betrayed child, and son informed against father, brothers raged against each other, and slaves rose up against their masters. As a result of madness induced by the Devil everyone did not recognise each other, and a frightful night descended on human life. Houses of prayer were demolished by unholy hands; altars were overturned; there was no offering, no incense, no place for sacrifice. Instead, a terrible depression, like a cloud, encompassed everything. The worshippers of the divine were driven out, every pious group was scared away, while the demons danced in triumph, defiling everything with the odour of fat and with blood. Then that noble man, averting the necessity of the law courts, threw off his commission, was banished, despising authorities, despising glory, all kinds of wealth, family, friends, household members, the enjoyment of life, everything that is much desired by human beings, and ran off to the deepest desolate places that are inaccessible to human beings. He considered life with wild beasts to be more civilised than mixing with idol-worshippers, in the manner of the zealot Elias, who, when he saw that idol-worship was prevailing over Sidon, ran off to Mt Horeb and lived in a cave, seeking out God until he saw the object of his great desire – as much as it is possible for a human being to see God (cf. 1 Kings 19:1–18).

3.   So Gordius was like that too, turning his back on political turmoils, the crowd in the marketplace, the vanity of magistrates, the law courts, the back-biters, the vendors, the buyers, the swearers, the liars, the foul language, the frivolous talk, all the rest, [which] like burdensome appendages, populous cities drag after them. Purifying his ears, purifying his eyes, and above all having purified his heart, so that he would be able to see God and become blessed, he saw through revelations, he learnt the mysteries, not from human beings nor through human beings but because he had the Spirit of truth as his great teacher. This is why, when he reflected on how unprofitable and vain life was, how it was more feeble than every dream and shadow, he was aroused more keenly to the desire of the heavenly calling. And he was like an athlete, realising that he is sufficiently trained and oiled for the contest by means of fasting, vigils, prayers, the continuous and incessant meditation of the sayings of the Spirit, with his eyes fixed on that day on which the entire city in a body, celebrating a feast in honour of the demon who is fond of war, occupied the theatre to view the horse-race.

And so, when the entire people was gathered in a high spot, there was no Jew absent,[14] no Greek. And a not inconsiderable crowd of Christians was mixed with them, those who were living unguardedly, and sitting with the council of vanity, not avoiding the gatherings of corrupt people, those who even at the time were present as spectators of galloping horses and experienced charioteers. Rather, masters even dismissed their slaves, and children ran from schools to the spectacle, and every common and insignificant woman was present. The stadium was full, and everyone was already intent on watching the horse race. Then that man, noble and great in spirit, great in purpose, coming down from the mountains to the theatre, was not terrified by the people. He did not consider how many hostile hands would betray him, but with intrepid heart and majestic purpose, ran past those sitting around the stadium as if they were a row of stones or many trees, and he took his stand in the middle, confirming the saying that *the just man is confident like a lion* (Prov 28:1). And he was so undaunted in his spirit that, when he was in a conspicuous place in the theatre, with unhesitating confidence he shouted out these words, which some people hear up to today: '*I was found by those not looking for me; I appeared plainly to those not enquiring about me*' (Isa 65:1). He showed through these words that he was not driven to danger out of necessity but that he surrendered himself willingly to the struggle. He imitated the Master who, when he was not recognised by the Jews in the darkness of the night, pointed himself out to them.[15]

4.   So he immediately turned the theatre upside down by the unexpected sight, being a savage-looking man with squalid hair because of his long sojourn in the mountains, with a long beard, filthy clothes, his entire body hardened, carrying a stick and fitted with a pouch. A certain grace became conspicuous to all as it shone around him from the inside. As, then, his identity became known, a mixed cry was immediately raised by all. The slaves applauded out of excessive delight at his faith, those who fought against truth urged on the judiciary to kill him and condemned him to death in advance. So everything was filled with shouting and confusion. Horses were neglected, charioteers were neglected, the display of the chariots was an idle sound. Nobody's eye had time to look at anything except Gordius, nor could anybody's ear bear to hear anything except his words. And an indistinguishable rumour, like air, went through the whole theatre, and rose above the horse race. When the heralds signalled for the people to be silent, the flutes died down, and the many-pitched instruments stopped playing. Gordius was listened to, Gordius was looked at.

And immediately he was carried off to the magistrate sitting there who was organising the race. So for a while he interrogated him closely in a mild and gentle voice about his identity and his provenance. When Gordius said his country, his race, the nature of his rank, the cause of his flight, his return, he said: 'I am here, demonstrating by my action both my contempt of your orders and my faith in God, in whom I have placed my hope. Indeed, I have heard', he said, 'that you outdo many with your cruelty, so I have chosen this opportunity as a suitable one for me to fulfil my desire.' Inflaming the official's temper like fire by these words, he incited the total fury of the man against himself. And he said: 'Call the executioners. Where are the sling-bullets? Where are the whips? Let him be stretched on the wheel. Let him be tortured on the rack, let the instruments of torture be brought; let the wild beasts, the fire, the sword, the cross, the pit, be made ready. But what's the advantage', he asked, 'in having the wicked fellow simply die once?'

'What a punishment for me', interrupted Gordius, 'not to be able to die over and over again for Christ!' The official, in addition to his natural cruelty, became even harsher when he regarded the quality of the man, thinking that his mighty loftiness of purpose was his own disgrace. And the more he saw his undaunted heart, the more he became increasingly cruel, and he became more eager to overcome the man's resolution by the thought of acts of torture. So much for the official.

5.   Gordius, for his part, looking to God, enchanted his soul with the holy Psalms as he recited: *'The Lord is my help, and I shall not be afraid of what a human being will do to me'* (Ps 117:6), and *'I shall not be afraid of evil, because you are with me'* (Ps 22:4). Every saying similar to these that encouraged bravery he had learnt from the divine utterances. He was so far removed from yielding to the threats and succumbing to them that he even invited the punishment on his head.

'Why are you hesitating?', he asked. 'Why have you stopped in your tracks? Let my body be mangled, let my limbs be pulled apart, let there be whatever torture you wish. Don't disparage my hope of happiness. The more you increase my punishments, the more you procure for me greater recompense. This is our contract with the Master. Instead of weals, which swell on the body, a bright garment will shine for us at the resurrection. Instead of disgrace there will be crowns; instead of prison, paradise; instead of being condemned with criminals, I will live with angels. Sow many seeds in me, so that I may reap many times more.'

Since they were unable to overcome him by terror and the situation was impossible, they changed tack and began to flatter him. Such is the wiliness of the Devil: he will thoroughly terrify the cowardly person; he will appease the brave person. And the tricks of the scoundrel on that occasion were like that. I mean that when he saw that Gordius was not giving in to the threats, he tried to get around him by means of acts of deceit and seduction. He promised him presents; some he gave, and others he guaranteed would come from the emperor – a prominent position in the army, ways of getting money, whatever he wanted.

6.   But when he failed in his attempt (for when the blessed man heard the promises, he derided his foolishness, if he thought that he would give anything that was the equivalent of the kingdom of heaven), then his temper became unbearable and he bared his sword and stationed the executioner beside him, and defiling his hand and tongue with blood he condemned the blessed man to death. The whole theatre transferred to this spot too, and whoever of the inhabitants was left poured out in front of the wall, and watched that great and competitive spectacle, which was wondrous both for angels and all creation, painful for the Devil, and terrifying for demons. The city was emptied of its inhabitants, the multitude in a body flowing together to this spot like a river. There was not a woman who agreed to be left out of the spectacle, no man common or distinguished. The house-guards deserted their posts, merchants' shops were unlocked, market-wares were strewn through the marketplace. The security and safety of everyone was one – the exit of all *en masse* – and there was not even one criminal left behind in the city. Slaves deserted the service of their masters, and every foreigner in the population and every native was present in that place to see the man. Then even a young girl dared to be looked at by men, and the old and infirm, having overcome their feebleness, were outside the wall. Already standing around the blessed man as he rushed through death to life, his friends put their arms around him, lamenting loudly and embracing him for the last time. And weeping hot tears over him they begged him not to give himself up to the fire, not to squander his youth, not to abandon this pleasant sun. Others tried to talk him out of it by means of clever advice: 'Simply make your denial orally, but keep the faith as you wish in your soul. God does not pay any attention at all to the tongue of the speaker but to their intention. In this way it is permissible for you to appease the judge completely and to propitiate God completely.'

7.   But Gordius was unbending and inflexible, and invulnerable to every attempted attack. You could compare the steadiness of

his intention to the house of the wise man, which neither the unbearable buffeting of winds, nor a furious torrent of water from clouds, nor torrents breaking around it, are able to ruin because of the steadfastness of stone (cf. Matt 7:24–5). The man was like that, keeping safe the foundation of his faith in Christ. Seeing with his spiritual eyes the Devil running around, inciting one person to tears, conducing another to speciousness, he spoke to the people who lamented the words of the Lord: '*Don't lament over me* (Luke 23:28), but lament over the enemies of God, those who commit such acts of outrage against the pious, those who by means of this flame which they are kindling against us are storing up the fire of gehenna for themselves. Stop lamenting and crushing my heart. For I am ready *to die* not just once *for the name of the Lord Jesus* (Acts 21:13), but also many times, if it is possible.'

To those who advised him to make a denial with his tongue, he answered this much: 'The tongue, which is created by Christ, cannot bear to say anything against the Creator. For with the heart we believe for justice, but with the mouth we confess for our salvation (cf. Rom 10:10). Surely the military order hasn't despaired of being saved? Surely no pious centurion has? I remember the first centurion who, standing by Christ's cross, recognising his might from his miracles when the insolence of the Jews was still hot, did not take fright at their anger, nor even shrank from proclaiming the truth, but confessed and did not deny that he was *truly the Son of God* (Matt 27:54). I know another centurion too, who recognised the Lord when he was still in the flesh as being God and king of the powers, and capable by his command alone of sending out help to the needy by means of his ministering spirits. And the Lord declared that his faith was greater than all Israel (cf. Matt 8:8–10). Wasn't Cornelius, though a centurion, deemed worthy of the vision of an angel, and at the end found salvation through Peter? For his acts of almsgiving and his prayers were heard by God (cf. Acts 10:4–6). I want to be a disciple of these men. How then shall I deny my God, whom I have worshipped since childhood? Wouldn't heaven above be horrified? Wouldn't the stars darken because of me, wouldn't earth resist me completely? *Do not go astray; God is not mocked* (Gal 6:7). He passes judgement on us *out of our mouth* (Luke 19:22), he justifies us by our words, and he condemns us by our words (cf. Matt 12:37). Haven't you read the terrible threat of the Lord?

"Whoever denies me before human beings, I will deny him too before my Father, who is in heaven" (Matt 10:33).'

8.   'Why do you conspire to play these subtle tricks on me? So that I might achieve something for myself from a similar act of cleverness? So that I might gain a few days? But I would forfeit eternal life as a punishment. So that I might avoid the pains of the flesh? But I won't see the beautiful deeds of the just. It is obvious madness to die by an act of cleverness, by an act of knavery and deceit to bring eternal punishment on myself. But I want to give you advice too. If you think bad thoughts, you will unlearn piety, if you dissemble at the critical moment, *having put off false-hood you will speak truth* (Eph 4:25). Say: *"Because the Lord is Jesus Christ in the glory of God the Father"* (Phil 2:11). Every tongue will utter this sentence, when *in the name of Jesus every knee bends, of things in heaven, and on earth, and under the earth* (Phil 2:10). All human beings are mortal, but there are few martyrs. Let us not wait to be corpses, but let us go over from life to life. Why do you wait for a natural death? It is fruitless, without profit, common to beasts and human beings. I mean that either time kills the person who is coming into life through birth, or sickness destroys them, or quite powerful unfortunate circumstances cause them to perish utterly. Since, then, one has to die in any case, let us bring life on ourselves by means of death. You must do the unavoidable willingly. Do not spare life; being deprived of it is unavoidable. Yet even if earthly things were similar in respect to permanence, one would have to spend effort to change them into heavenly ones. But if in fact they last for a short time, and are lacking to such a degree in worth, it is a terrible madness to lose the blessings that reside in what we hope for by spending effort on them.'

Saying this, and tracing the sign of the cross on himself, he went to be killed, changing his colour in no way, altering nothing in the brightness of his face. He did not behave as if he were going to meet the executioner but as if he were delivering himself into the hands of angels, who, immediately receiving him as a fresh corpse, transferred him to the blessed life just like Lazarus. Who will relate in detail the cry of that crowd? What thunder ever released as great an echo to earth from the clouds, as ascended into heaven from below at that moment? This is the stadium of that crowned man. This is the day which viewed that amazing sight, which time has not obscured, nor habit destroyed. The magnitude of later events has not prevailed. I mean that just as we are always amazed when we always observe the sun, so too do we always keep fresh the memory of that man. *The just man will always be remembered* (Ps 111:6), both among those on earth, for as long as earth exists, and in heaven, and with the just judge. To whom be the glory and the power forever and ever. Amen.

A homily on the Forty Martyrs of Sebaste

Introduction

Basil's homily on the Forty Martyrs of Sebaste was delivered in 373,[16] most probably on 9 March, their annual feast day. It was preached in the martyrium of the Forty in Caesarea. Bernardi speculates that this sanctuary was only recently erected on the occasion of the arrival of the martyrs' relics in the city (Bernardi 1968: 84).

Basil touches several times upon the unity of the group of Forty Martyrs – although born in different places, they all suffered together as servants of Christ. Another theme present in the homily is that of the martyrs as examples of Christian virtue (*aretè*). By this Basil hopes to encourage his audience to imitate the martyrs' virtue in their own lives. The bulk of the homily, however, is of course devoted to the detailed narration of the martyrs' story. 'When that godless and impious edict' was promulgated, they declared themselves publicly to be Christians. Not giving in to all kinds of promises, tortures and threats, they remained steadfast and declared their allegiance to Christ. Then, 'that boastful and barbarous man' decided to freeze them to death. One of the Forty could not bear the torture of freezing and deserted; he was replaced by their jailer and in this way the complete group of the Forty died the martyrs' death. Then the story of the mother of one of the martyrs is told: when she saw that her son, because he wasn't yet completely dead, was not taken away with the others to be burnt, she herself put him on the wagon, encouraging him 'to appear before the Master together with the others'.

Basil's material has much in common with the narration of their martyrdom in an anonymous document, the *Passion of the Forty of Sebaste* (BHG 1201), which might have been one of his sources. The stress on the unity of the group of martyrs might be inspired by another document, the so-called *Testament* of the Forty, in which they stipulated that they wanted to be buried together. The imitation motif and the presentation of the martyrs as examples of virtue, on the other hand, appear to originate with Basil. Many of the narrative elements present in Basil's homily were taken up in the later hagiographical tradition about the Forty, in the very first place in his brother Gregory's panegyric on the Forty (cf. below). As stated above, Basil's homily was also used by Severus of Antioch in Homily 18, preached in Lent on Saturday, 9 March 513.[17]

Translated from the edition by Garnier; PG 31, 508–26.

Text

1.   What satiety could there be in remembering the martyrs for one who loves martyrs? After all, the honour paid to fine fellow-servants is a proof of goodwill towards the common Master. For it is clear that the one who welcomes noble men will not fall short of imitating them in similar circumstances. Bless the martyred sincerely, so that you become a martyr by choice, and end up being worthy of the same rewards as theirs, without persecution, without fire, without blows. But we have not one to venerate, nor only two, nor does the number of those to be blessed extend to ten; but forty men, because they had one soul in different bodies, in one simultaneous breath and thought of faith, demonstrated one endurance too in the face of terrible circumstances, and one constancy on behalf of the truth. They were all similar to each other, equal in conviction, equal in suffering. This is why they were deemed worthy of the crowns of glory of equal value. What sermon, then, could hit on their worth? Not even forty tongues could suffice to hymn the virtue of so many men. In fact, if just one were to be praised, he would be sufficient to overthrow the force of our words, let alone such a great crowd, a phalanx of soldiers, a corps hard to struggle against, as much unconquerable in battle as inaccessible by praise.

2.   Come then, let us bring them into prominence by remembering them, let us present to those who are here the common benefit deriving from them, demonstrating to everyone, as if it were in writing, the acts of the men's prowess. When often both historians and painters express manly deeds of war, the one embellishing them with words, the other engraving them onto tablets, they both arouse many too to bravery. The facts which the historical account presents by being listened to, the painting silently portrays by imitation. In this very way let us too remind

those present of the men's virtue, and as it were by bringing their deeds to their gaze, let us motivate them to imitate those who are nobler and closer to them with respect to their course of life. I mean that this is the encomium of the martyrs: the exhortation of the congregation to virtue. For not even sermons about the saints permit accommodation to the rules of encomia. This is why those who applaud them take the starting-point of their applause from worldly materials. How could anything worldly provide material to make conspicuous those for whom the world is crucified?

The saints didn't have one native land, for they all came from different places. What does that mean? Let us say that they were without a city, or that they were citizens of the world. For just as in the joint contributions at festivals what is brought in by individuals becomes the common property of the participants, so too the native land of all of these blessed men was common property, and all of them from wherever they came gave to each other what they had brought. Indeed, why should one investigate the native lands that lie on earth when it is possible to form a notion of the nature of their city now? After all, the city of martyrs is the *city of God* (Heb 12:22). *The craftsman and the workman was God* (Heb 11:10), the Jerusalem above was free, the mother of Paul, and of those similar to him. But their human pedigree differed one from the other. Their spiritual pedigree was one between all of them. I mean that their common father was God, and that they were all brothers, not born from one father and one mother, but that as a result of their adoption by the Spirit they were joined to each other in a one-mindedness through love. The chorus was ready, a huge supplement to those who praised the Lord from ages, not gathered together one by one, but translated as a group. What was the manner of their translation? With their bodily size and at the best time of their life, and their might surpassing those of all their equals, they were appointed to serve in the military ranks; and through their experience of war, and their bravery of spirit, they already obtained the first rewards from the emperors, being universally renowned on account of their virtue.

3.　　When that godless and impious edict was promulgated,[18] to not confess Christ or to expect danger, every kind of punishment was threatened, and great and savage was the wrath aroused by the judges of iniquity against the pious. Plots and tricks were stitched together against them, and various kinds of torments were practised, and the torturers were implacable, the fire was prepared, the sword sharpened, the cross put together, the pit, the wheel, the whips. Some fled, others gave in, others vascillated. Some were terrified before their ordeal by the threat of it alone; others, having come close to the torture, became dizzy; others, having embarked on their struggles, then were unable to hold out until the end of their pains, shrinking from exhaustion in the middle of their suffering, like people tossed on the sea, and the wares of patience they already possessed were shipwrecked. Then those men, the invincible and noble soldiers of Christ, came into the public eye, while the official was displaying the emperor's instructions and demanding obedience. With forthright voice, they boldly and courageously declared themselves to be Christians, in no way cowering before what they saw, nor panic-stricken at what was threatened. O blessed tongues, which uttered that holy sound, by which the air was sanctified when it received it. Angels applauded when they heard it, the Devil with the demons was traumatised by it, while the Lord registered it in heaven.

4.   So each of them, coming into the public eye, said: 'I am a Christian'. And just as in the stadiums those proceeding to the contest at the same moment say their own names and pass on to the place of competition, so too on that occasion these men cast off the appellations assigned to them from birth, and each proclaimed themselves to be from their common Saviour. And all of them did this, one after the other following the one before him. The upshot was one appellation for all. For there was no longer this fellow or that fellow, but all were proclaimed as Christians. Who then was the one who prevailed on that occasion? For he was clever and flexible, now fawning with flattering remarks, now turning aside with insults. First he tricked them with flattering remarks, trying to break the intensity of their piety. 'Don't betray your youth. Don't exchange an untimely death for this sweet life. For it is absurd for those who have gained the prize for valour in war to die the death of criminals.' He promised money in addition to this. He gave this: honours from the emperor, and the distribution of offices, and tried to outwit them by countless devices. But when they did not give in to this attempt, he changed to the other type of wile. He threatened them with blows, and death, and the experience of intolerable punishments.

And while he did such things, what kind of reaction did the martyrs have? 'Why', they said, 'do you entice us, you enemy of God, to withdraw from the living God and to serve destructive demons, while holding out to us your rewards? Why do you give as much as you are keen to take away? I hate a gift which causes damage. I will not accept an honour which is the mother of dishonour. You give money which stays behind, glory which fades. You make me known to the emperor, but you alienate me from the one who is really emperor. Why with your hair-splitting do you hold out a few worldly rewards? The entire world is despised by us. Visible objects are not worth as much to us as the hope we desire. Do you see this sky, how beautiful it is to behold, and how great? And the earth, how big it is? And the wonderful things in it? None of these things equals the blessedness of the just. For these things pass away, but ours remain. I desire one gift – the crown of righteousness. I am excited by one form of honour, the one in the kingdom of heaven. I am ambitious for heavenly honour. I fear the punishment of gehenna. That fire is fearful for me: it is the fellow servant of your threats. It knows how to revere those who despise idols. I count your blows as children's arrows. For you hit the body, which, if it can hold out for a long time, will receive a more brilliant crown. But if it gives in more quickly, it will depart, having been delivered from you judges who are so violent [that], once you have taken over the service of our bodies, you will strive to control our souls as well. If you do not put our God first too, when you have been abused by us you will suffer as it were the extreme penalty, and you will be threatened by these fearful punishments, adding for us a complaint with respect to piety. But you have not met with cowardly people, nor with those who love life, nor with those who are easily scared, because of their love for God. *We* are ready to accept torture on the wheel, and torture by screws, and being burnt to ashes, and every kind of torment.'

5. When that boastful and barbarous man heard this, not being able to bear the forthrightness of the men, he boiled over with rage, and considered finding some device to kill them both slowly and painfully at the same time. Finally he had an idea, and consider how cruel it was. For after looking around at the nature of the country, that it was icy-cold, and the season of the year, which was winter, and keeping a watch for the night on which the most harm could be extended, especially then when the north wind was blowing on it, he gave orders that everybody was to be stripped and made to freeze to death in the open air in the middle of the city. But of course you know, having experience of winter,

that this kind of ordeal is unbearable.[19] Nor indeed is it possible to demonstrate [this] to others unless they have stored up examples from the actual experience of what we are saying. For when a body is exposed to frost it first becomes livid all over, once the blood has frozen. Next it becomes agitated and jumps, teeth chatter, nerves become taut, and the bulk of the body involuntarily becomes contracted. Piercing pain, and unspeakable suffering pervading the very marrow, produces an intolerable feeling for those who are freezing. After that it becomes mutilated, the extremities being burnt as if by fire. For the heat has been driven out of the extremities of the body and has fled into the centre, the parts from which it has retreated it leaves dead, the parts into which it is compressed it surrenders to pain; death occurs shortly after as a result of freezing.[20] So on that occasion they were condemned to spend the night in the open air when the lake, around which the city had been built, on which the holy men were engaged in this suffering, was like a plain for chariots, because the ice had changed it. And becoming mainland as a result of the ice, it provided for the inhabitants a safe pedestrian crossing over its surface. Rivers which had flowed everlastingly, constricted by ice stopped flowing, and the gentle nature of water was changed to the resistance of stone. Piercing blasts of the north wind rushed every living thing to its death.

6.   So then, when they heard the order (and please consider at this point the invincibility of the men), with great joy each of them threw off even the last tunic, and went to their death by cold, encouraging each other as if they were seizing spoils. 'Let us not take off a garment', they said, 'but let us *put off the old man who has been corrupted through his desire for error* (Eph 4:22). Let us give thanks to you, Lord, as we cast off sin together with this garment. Since we put on clothes because of the snake (cf. Gen 3:21), let us take them off because of Christ. Let us not hold on to clothes because of the paradise which we have lost. *What shall we give back to the Lord* (Ps 115:3)? Our Lord also took his clothes off. What greater suffering can a slave have [than to] suffer what his Master did? I should say that we were the ones who took off the clothes of the Master himself (cf. Matt 27:28). I mean that this was that shameless act of soldiers – they took off his clothes and *divided his garments* (Matt 27:35). So let us delete the written charge against us by our own efforts. Winter is piercing, but paradise is sweet. Freezing is painful, but rest is pleasing. Let us wait for a

little while, and the bosom of the patriarch will comfort us. Let us exchange a single night for all eternity. Let our foot burn, so that it may continually dance with angels; let our hand fall off, so that it may be able to achieve access to the Master. How many of our soldiers have fallen in the battle-line, while keeping faith with a mortal emperor? But shall we not let go this life for the sake of our belief in the true emperor? How many criminals have undergone death, after being caught in the act? And are we not going to endure death for the sake of righteousness? Let us not yield, o fellow soldiers, lest we give support to the Devil. There is flesh – let us not spare it. Since it is of course necessary to die, let us die that we may live. *May our sacrifice come before you, Lord* (Dan 3:40), and may we be received as a *living sacrifice acceptable* (Rom 12:1) to you, burnt up completely by this cold, a beautiful oblation, a new burnt offering, a complete offering, not through fire but through cold.'

Providing these encouraging words to each other, and each of them enjoining the other, as if they were fulfilling a guard's role in war, they passed the night, bearing the present circumstances nobly, rejoicing in what they hoped for, ridiculing the enemy. There was one prayer from all of them. 'The forty of us went into the stadium; let the forty of us be crowned, Master. Let not even one person be missing from that number. It is an honourable [number], which you honoured in your fast of forty days (cf. Matt 4:2), through which law-giving came into the world (cf. Exod 34:28). After a forty-day fast seeking the Lord, Elias had a vision (cf. 1 Kings 19:8).' And their prayer went like this.

One of the number, sinking in the face of the terrible events, deserted and left, to the unspeakable grief of the saints. However, the Lord did not allow their prayers to be ineffectual. I mean that the man who had been entrusted with guarding the martyrs, while he was getting warm in a gymnasium nearby, observed what was going to happen and was prepared to welcome the fugitive soldiers. And in turn he thought of this too, that he was near the bath, which promised a swift assistance for those changing sides. However, the maliciously devised plans of the enemies to seek out such a place for the suffering, in which the readiness of consolation was going to make faint the constancy of those suffering,[21] demonstrated more clearly the martyrs' endurance. I mean that it is not the person who lacks essentials who is capable of endurance, but the person who endures horrible events while abounding in pleasure.

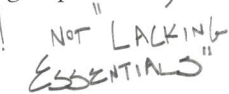

"NOT LACKING"
"ESSENTIALS"

7. While they were suffering, he observed what was about to happen. He saw a strange sight – powers coming down from the sky, and distributing huge gifts to the soldiers, as if from an emperor. They distributed the gifts to all the others, but they left just one man without a present, judging him unworthy of heavenly honours. He immediately gave up the fight in the face of trouble, and went over to the enemy. It was a pitiful sight for the just – the soldier turned fugitive, the valorous man taken prisoner, the sheep of Christ caught by wild beasts. And the most pitiful thing was that he missed out entirely on eternal life and could not even enjoy this life, because immediately his flesh was consumed by the wave of heat. And the one who loved life fell, having transgressed in vain, while the public executioner, as he saw him give way and run to the baths, put himself in the place of the deserter, threw off his clothes and joined in with the naked men, shouting the same cry as the saints: 'I am a Christian'. And astounding those present with the swiftness of the change, he both filled the number, and by adding himself he softened the grief concerning the one who had lost his nerve, imitating those in the line of battle, who, when one man falls in the front line, immediately fill up the phalanx, so that the close battle order is not broken by the man's departure. He too did something similar. He saw the heavenly miracles, he recognised the truth, he sought refuge with the Master, he was numbered with the martyrs. He renewed the deeds of the disciples. Judas departed, and Matthias was substituted (cf. Acts 1:26). He became an imitator of Paul, the persecutor yesterday, today the evangelist (cf. Acts 9:1–30). He too had a call from above, *not from human beings, nor through a human being* (Gal 1:1). He believed in the name of our Lord Jesus Christ; he was baptised into him, not by another, but by his own faith, not in water, but in his own blood.

8. And so, as the day began, while they were still breathing they were delivered over to the fire, and the remains of the fire were scattered on the river. As a result, the suffering of the blessed ones went completely through all creation. They suffered on earth, they remained steadfast in the air; they were delivered over to the fire; the water received them. Theirs was the saying: *We went through fire and water, and you have led us out into relief* (Ps 65:12). They were the ones who took possession of our land, like a continuous succession of towers, proffering security against the attack of the enemy, not confining themselves to one spot but being already

entertained as a guest in many places, and adorning many native lands. And the amazing thing is that they did not go to those who received them separated one by one, but joined to each other they danced together. What a miracle! They were neither short in number, nor did they admit of excess. If you divided them into a hundred, they do not exceed their own number; if you subsume them into one, they still remain forty like that, according to the nature of the fire. I mean that it goes over to the one that kindles, and is completely with the one who has it; and the forty are all [forty] at once, and all of them are single.

Bounteous benevolence, unsquandered grace, ready help for Christians, a church of martyrs, an army of trophy-bearers, a chorus of those giving praise. How much effort would you expend in order to find one who would importune the Lord on your behalf? They were forty, sending up a unanimous prayer. *Where there are two or three gathered together in the name of the Lord, there* he is *in the midst of them* (Matt 18:20). But where there are forty, who doubts the presence of God? The one who is in trouble takes refuge in the forty, the one who rejoices runs off to them – the former to find release from difficulties, the latter to protect his prosperity. Here a pious woman is found praying for her children, begging for the return of her husband who is away, for his safety because he is sick. Let your petitions be with the martyrs. Let boys imitate those of their own age; let fathers pray to be fathers of such children; let mothers learn the story of a good mother.

The mother of one of those blessed men, observing that the others were already dead from the cold, whereas her own son was still breathing because of both his strength and his endurance in the face of danger (the executioners had left him on the grounds that he was capable of changing his mind), lifted him with her own hands and put him on the wagon on which the remains which were lying together were being led to the fire, since she was truly the mother of a martyr. I mean that she did not shed an unbecoming tear; she did not say anything shabby and unworthy of the moment. Instead, she said: 'Off with you, boy, on the good journey with your comrades, with your fellows. Don't be separated from the chorus. Don't appear before the Master later than the others. [Be] truly a good shoot from a good root.' The noble mother showed that she had brought him up on the teachings of piety rather than on milk. And the man who had been brought up in this way was sent forth in this way by his pious mother, whereas the Devil went off dishonoured. For having set all creation against them, he found that everything was inferior to the men's virtue, the stormy night, the wintery country, the season of year, the nakedness of the bodies.

O holy chorus! O hallowed battalion! O unbroken fighting order! O common guards of the human race! Good companions in times of anxiety, helpers in prayer, most powerful ambassadors, stars of the world, flowers of the churches. The earth does not hide you; instead, heaven accepts you. The gates of paradise have opened for you. The sight is worthy of the army of angels, worthy of patriarchs, prophets, the just – men in the very flower of youth, despising life, loving the Lord above parents, above children. Having the vitality of their age, they looked down on the temporary life in order to glorify God with their limbs. Becoming a *spectacle for the world and for angels and human beings* (1 Cor 4:9), they raised the fallen, they strengthened the ambivalent, they doubled the desire of the pious. All of them raised the one trophy on behalf of piety and were crowned with the one crown of justice too, in Christ Jesus our Lord, to whom be the glory and the power forever and ever. Amen.

Notes

1 On Basil's life and works see Fedwick 1981; Gain 1985; Rousseau 1994; Meredith 1995: 19–38.
2 This does not include the homiles *On Barlaam* (CPG 2861) and *On all the Martyrs* (CPG 2941), which, although attributed to Basil, are spurious; see Girardi 1988: 451 n. 3. Two martyr homilies survive in Armenian: one on Thomas, which is unedited and not in CPG (see Gain 1985: 217 n. 274); another on Stephen (CPG 2981). On the tenor of the Greek martyr homilies see Rousseau 1994: 184–8.
3 See Gain 1985: 220–4 for the evidence.
4 Gain 1985: 219 speculates that Basil would also have preached on the feasts of the Cappadocian martyrs Eupsychius, Mercurius, George, and Hieron.
5 PG 31, 237–61. See Gain 1985: 218. On the contents of the homily see Girardi 1988: 455–60.
6 PG 31, 508–25 (CPG 2863). On the date see Fedwick 1981: I, 10 n. 48; Rousseau 1994: 46 n. 86. On the contents see Girardi 1988: 471–9.
7 PG 31, 489–508. On the date see Fedwick 1981: I, 10 n. 40; Rousseau 1994: 46 n. 86. On the contents see Girardi 1988: 460–71.
8 PG 31, 589–600. On the date see Fedwick 1981: I, 10 n. 47; Rousseau 1994: 47. Cf. Troiano 1987: 147–57, who deduces that the homily was

delivered before 373. On the contents of the homily see Girardi 1988: 479–83.

9 On the date see Fedwick 1981: I, 10 n. 40; Rousseau 1994: 46 n. 85. Cf. Bernardi 1968: 80–3.

10 See also in the general introduction at note 124.

11 This is the indication of the place in which the homily was delivered, apparently a martyrium dedicated to more than one martyr.

12 In other words, this pericope had been read out before the homily in the course of the liturgy.

13 As usual in martyr homilies, the name of the persecuting emperor is suppressed. Gordius is thought to have been martyred at the beginning of the fourth century under Licinius. See Gain 1985: 219 n. 280.

14 While this may be partly an exaggeration or a topos, there were large numbers of Jewish colonies in Cappadocia at the time. See Gain 1985: 263.

15 Cf. Matt 26:47–56; Mark 14:43–52; Luke 22:47–53; John 18:2–12.

16 On the date see Fedwick 1981: I, 10 n. 48; Rousseau 1994: 46 n. 86.

17 Severus also composed five hymns on the Forty, nos 155–9 in the collection of Jacob of Edessa's Syriac translations of hymns by Severus and others: Brooks 1911: 614–20.

18 Again, in keeping with the protocol of the martyr homily, the name of the persecutor is suppressed. The emperor at the time, according to the Byzantine synaxaria, was Licinius. See Gain 1985: 219 with n. 280.

19 On the geography and harsh climate of Cappadocia see Gain 1985: 1–10.

20 This theoretical account of death by freezing is taken over by Severus of Antioch, Homily 18; PO 37 (1975) 14, 5–13. I am indebted to Iain Torrance and Anna Wilson for allowing me to use their unpublished annotated translation of this homily.

21 This idea is expanded on by Severus, PO 37 (1975) 18, 15–20.

II

GREGORY OF NYSSA

GENERAL INTRODUCTION

Gregory's life and writings

Our knowledge of Gregory's life is surprisingly lacunose, especially when compared to that of Basil of Caesarea, his elder brother. What we know of his biography can be summarised as follows (May 1971; Dörrie 1983; Balas 1985; Maraval 1988a and 1997; Meredith 1999).

Gregory of Nyssa was born during the second half of the 330s as one of the youngest in a rich, prominent, cultivated Cappadocian family of nine children. Besides Macrina, Basil, Gregory himself and four other children about whom nothing is known, there were Naucratius, who was killed in a hunting accident, and Gregory's younger brother Peter, who was to become bishop of Sebaste (Armenia). Gregory's family was Christian and played a leading role in Cappadocian Christianity. It was also through them, especially his mother and grandmother, that Gregory was introduced into the Christian faith. Another essential part of his education, philosophy and rhetoric, he mainly received from his brother Basil, whom he calls 'father and teacher'. In 371 or early 372 Gregory became bishop of Nyssa, a small town in Cappadocia (Turkey) on the road from Ancyra to Caesarea. About the years before we do not know much. Probably he was first a lector and then a deacon (Maraval 1997: 384). It is highly likely that he was married, probably to a woman named Theosebia, who died in 371.

Gregory became bishop of the newly created see of Nyssa on the instigation of his elder brother, for whom it was important that as many sees as possible were occupied by adherents of the Neo-Nicene party. Thus Gregory became involved in ecclesiastical politics in a period during which those opposing the Neo-Nicenes enjoyed the support of the Arian-minded emperor Valens. This led in 376 to Gregory's deposition from his see, to which he was only able to return after Valens' death in the summer of 378.

Though Gregory was already active outside his diocese before then (Maraval 1997: 390), it is especially from this period onwards that Gregory makes his appearance on the stage of international ecclesiastical politics. He played an important role during the Council of Constantinople (381) and increasingly made his mark as a theologian, involved in the controversies surrounding the Trinity, the divinity of the Son and the Spirit. Many of his writings, most notably *Against Eunomius* in twelve books but also a host of shorter works, bear witness to that involvement. In 385–6 he was again in the capital. In these years – we do not know exactly when, he pronounced the funeral oration for Pulcheria, the emperor Theodosius' daughter. A few months later, Aelia Flacilla, the emperor's wife, also died and Gregory was again invited to hold the oration of consolation. In 394, he was for a last time in Constantinople, this time to attend a synod about the ecclesiastical situation in Arabia. The gathering sent Gregory to the region. His journey to Arabia and the visit he made to Jerusalem on that occasion therefore can best be situated in these years, at the eve of his life. Gregory probably died before the end of the fourth century.

Gregory of Nyssa left a large literary heritage (Balas 1985: 175–6). Part of his writings was devoted to philosophical and theological issues, such as *On the Soul and the Resurrection*, *On the Making of Men* or *On Infants' Early Deaths*. A systematic survey of his theology he laid down in his *Great Catechetical Oration*. In line with his family's engagement in the ascetic movement of the day, Gregory wrote a number of ascetical treatises of which can be mentioned *On Virginity*, his earliest work, *On Perfection* and *On the Christian Mode of Life*. As works of a more exegetical nature there are his treatise *On the Inscriptions of the Psalms* and his Scriptural homilies: on Ecclesiastes, the Song of Songs, the Beatitudes and the Lord's Prayer. Gregory's *Life of Moses or On Perfection in Virtue*, a brief presentation and allegorical reading of the passages about Moses in Exodus, is probably his best-known work of spiritual theology.

Gregory as a homilist

As a bishop Gregory preached hundreds of homilies. Only a small portion of these has actually been preserved. Most of them were delivered in Nyssa but it is beyond doubt that he preached in other cities as well. If we set aside the above-mentioned exegetical tracts, which in all likelihood are rewritten versions of homilies, the following succinct picture of Gregory of Nyssa's homiletical corpus in all its diversity can be presented (Bernardi 1968: 261–332; Moshammer 2001).

The first category of homilies addresses issues of social justice. The man who left us in his *Fourth Homily on Ecclesiastes* one of the most virulent attacks against slavery from the entire period of antiquity did not shrink from pointing the finger at unjust situations. This led to a strong condemnation of the very common practice of usury in his *Homily Against Those who Practice Usury*. Neither was he afraid to point mercilessly to unjust or not very clement behaviour towards the poor. In his two *Homilies on the Love for the Poor* he urged the rich to share their wealth and be concerned about the miserable situation in which many of their fellow citizens lived. Other homilies are of a more disciplinarian nature and have to do with his activities as a bishop. Here one can think of *Against Those who Do not Take Criticism Well*, in which he rebuked those of his community who did not accept their bishop's criticism on their extravagant ways of celebrating the New Year and their absence from the eucharist. Other sermons of a disciplinarian kind were his sermon *Against Those who Postpone Baptism* and one *Against Those who Commit Adultery*. It is typical that in this last sermon, Gregory devotes a third of the homily to explaining that it is the extreme wealth and luxury of the rich that is the ultimate root of this misconduct.

As a bishop, Gregory also had to deliver homilies on the liturgical feasts of the ecclesiastical year. A sample of these sermons has been preserved. We have three homilies delivered during the Easter triduum, a homily delivered on the day of Ascension and one on Pentecost. As for the Christmas-period there is one homily delivered on the day of Christmas, one on St Stephen (26 December – the *First Homily on St Stephen*) and one on the Holy Apostles (27 December). The latter is mistakenly called the *Second Homily on St Stephen*, because it opens with a rather long treatment of Stephen, before addressing the topic of the day, the Holy Apostles (especially James, John and Peter). Of the homily held on Epiphany an example has also been preserved (*On the Day of Lights*). Finally, the above-mentioned homily *Against Those who Postpone Baptism* was probably also delivered in the period between Christmas and Epiphany.

Besides homilies on these recurring yearly feasts, Gregory also delivered occasional sermons. In this category one can mention the *Oration in Praise of Gregory the Miracle Worker*, a panegyric he was invited to deliver when he was by coincidence in Neocaesarea, on the day when the saint was annually celebrated. Later, Gregory reworked the text of the homily into a full-blown *Vita* of the man who was allegedly responsible for the christianisation of the region of Pontus during the third century. A similar case is the *Oration in Praise of Basil*, delivered on the occasion of the celebration of one of the very first anniversaries of the great bishop's death. Other occasional homilies are the *Funeral Oration for Meletius of Antioch*, the first president of the Ecumenical Council of Constantinople (381), as well as those he held (in the same city) for Pulcheria and Flacilla. Furthermore, Gregory's involvement in ecclesiastical politics also resulted in occasional addresses to many a gathering, two of which have been preserved. The first is entitled in Greek *eis tèn heautou cheirotonian*, which can best be interpreted as *On His Vote*. It is a rather short oration, addressed to the participants of the Ecumenical Council of 381, in which he explains his position with regard to the issue of the divinity of the Spirit. Two years later Gregory pronounced in the same city an oration *On the Divinity of the Son and the Spirit*. The occasion was a synod of the important spokesmen of all involved parties, convened by the emperor Theodosius in a vain effort to deal with the situation that, two years after the 'universal agreement' of Constantinople 381, the doctrinal separation between 'Arians', Pneumatomachians and 'orthodox' had failed to disappear.

Finally there are Gregory of Nyssa's homilies in praise of martyrs. If we include the two above-mentioned *Homilies in Praise of St Stephen the Protomartyr* because in both texts the typical agonistic terminology is present and it concerns followers of Jesus who died for their faith, then Gregory's homiletical *œuvre* contains six panegyrics on martyrs. Besides the two on Stephen, there is Gregory's *Homily in Praise of Theodore the Recruit*, delivered in the martyr's sanctuary in Euchaïta (Pontus) and three *Homilies in Praise of the Forty Martyrs of Sebaste* (usually Mart Ia, Ib and Mart II). In fact the first of these consists of two parts (Ia and Ib) delivered on consecutive days in Armenian Sebaste. The *Second Homily on the Forty of Sebaste* was pronounced, probably in 379, in Caesarea, where this famous group of martyrs also had a martyrium. In what follows we present translations of the *Homily on Theodore* and of the *First Homily on the Forty of Sebaste* (Ia and Ib).

TEXTS

A homily on Theodore the Recruit

Introduction

Theodore, a soldier in the Roman army, died a martyr's death on a pyre in Amasea (Pontus; today NW Turkey) during the early fourth century. Yet, it was the small Pontic village of Euchaïta that in subsequent centuries became the most important centre of his cult. The sanctuary was equipped with a monastery and lodgings for pilgrims and in the sixth century even acquired an episcopal see (Delehaye 1923; Mango and Sevčenko 1972: 379–84). In these first centuries Theodore's cult spread widely: for this period his veneration is attested in places as far apart as Jerusalem, Constantinople and Rome (Amore 1969; Walter 1999). Its vitality in later centuries is shown by a 'twin saint': probably during the ninth century the cult of Theodore the General came into existence (Oikonomides 1986). Around both saints a large tradition of homilies, passions and miracle stories developed (BHG 1760–773; Walter 1999).

Gregory of Nyssa's homily in praise of Theodore is the earliest document of this tradition. The homily was delivered in the martyr's sanctuary at Euchaïta (Amasea is referred to as 'the metropolis'). The homily was held on the occasion of Theodore's annual panèguris which was celebrated on 17 February, as is ascertained by the *Passion of Theodore* (BHG 1761), the second oldest source about the Recruit. In which year Gregory delivered this homily is more difficult to establish. The introduction mentions that during the previous year Theodore had been instrumental in quieting down barbarian attacks and that he brought to an end the war with the Scyths. The reference is rather vague but most scholars connect it with events at the end of the 370s and date the homily between 379 and 381 (e.g. Daniélou 1955: 355–6; Zuckerman 1991). Though this is a period when Gregory of Nyssa's whereabouts are relatively well known, it is not possible to arrive on that basis at a secure date. The reason is that the traditional date of Basil of Caesarea's death (1 January 379), which is the linchpin for the reconstruction of this part of Gregory's biography, has been called into question and moved to August 377 (Maraval 1988b) and the end of September 378 (Pouchet 1992). Since then, however, other scholars (e.g. Barnes 1997 and Vaggione 2000: 305–11) have defended the traditional date. According to the traditional chronology Gregory was in Euchaïta in 380 (Zuckerman 1991); following Maraval (1990: 22–32) he was there one year earlier.

Apart from the introduction and the peroration, the homily can roughly be divided in two parts. The first part stresses that the martyr's example of Christian faith should inspire the audience. Gregory shows that this is a rewarding way of life, as is illustrated by the martyr's fate after his death: his soul is in heaven and his body is a venerated object in a beautiful building, which he describes at length. The Christian way of life yields much more and greater rewards than worldly careers. In the second part, Gregory moves from what Theodore shares with the other saints to what is specific to him by telling in great detail the Recruit's story. Gregory ends his homily with a request to Theodore that he would continue to lend his support to the community of Euchaïta, especially given the imminent danger for the Christian faith caused by the barbarian Scyths, the heretics and the pagans alike.

A distinctive feature of the homily is the anti-pagan tone. Probably the most outstanding example is Theodore's witty dialogue with a pagan fellow-soldier about the way their respective gods beget. But his burning down of a pagan temple, his sarcastic refusal of an offer to become high priest and his mockery of the sacrifical role of the emperor are equally clear rejections of paganism. Moreover, these passages are implicitly directed against Julian the Apostate's ill-fated attempt, two decades before, to reinvigorate paganism (Leemans 2001c). To that end the emperor tried to provide it with a structure in which provincial high-priests played a crucial role. The cult of the Great Mother was one of the cults Julian favoured and he also was an ardent participant in sacrifices (Hunt 1998a; Bland-Simmons 2000). Thus Gregory's *On Theodore* can be added to the group of texts denouncing Julian and his religious policies long after his death.

Translated from the edition by J.P. Cavarnos; GNO X, 1/2, 61–71.

Text

(61,4) You people of Christ, the holy flock, *the royal priesthood* (1 Pet 2:9), inhabitants of cities and villages, who have streamed together from everywhere, whence did you undertake the journey and come to this holy place? Who provided you with such a pressing and useful urge as to arrive precisely at this time? And this in the season of winter, when also the war quietens down, the soldier takes off his armour, the seaman hangs the oar above the fire and the farmer gives rest to his plough-oxen and takes care of them at their trough? Isn't it clear that, when the holy martyr from the ranks of the soldiers had issued the trumpet-call, he urged many people from different countries and called them to this usual place of rest and hearth, not with the intention of making them ready for war but to bring them together towards the sweet and, to Christians, so fitting peace? For it was he, as we believe, who last year stilled the barbarian storm and who brought to an end the horrible war with the savage Scyths by shaking, against those who were coming nearer in a menacing way while looking terrifying, not a helmet with three crests nor a sharp sword sparkling in the sunlight but the evil-barring and almighty cross of Christ, for whom he suffered and obtained this glory.

(62,3) You *servants of this pure worship* (cf. Jas 1:27) and friends of the martyr, observe by paying attention to me how great in size and number the rewards are that the just is deigned worthy of. By 'rewards' I mean for now only those of this world, those in our domain, for of the invisible ones nobody is able to estimate the splendour. And once you know the fruit of piety you must emulate the judgment of those who have been honoured in this way before you. Yes, you must set your hearts upon the prizes which Christ divides according to merit among the athletes. Meanwhile, since it seems that the enjoyment of these future good things, which the good hope preserves for the just, has been postponed until the Judge of our lives arrives, let us behold how very beautiful and magnificent the actual situation of the saints is. For his soul, after it went upward, resides on its own inheritance and without the body lives together with its equals. His body, on the other hand, the soul's holy and pure instrument, having in no way harmed with its passions the immortality of the soul who inhabits it, was buried with much honour and care and now lies solemnely in this holy place; just like a highly valued treasure it is preserved for the moment of its rebirth. The martyr's body is in many respects different from other bodies: it was not dissolved by the death that happens to everybody, though it is composed from similar matter. Indeed, to most people the remnants of the other bodies are disgusting and nobody gladly passes a grave. And if somebody encounters by chance a grave that is open and their eye catches the formless remnants in it, they are filled with all kinds of unpleasant emotions, sigh because of the gravity of the human condition, and run along.

(62,25)   But somebody coming to a place like this one, where we are gathering today, where the memory of the just is kept alive and his holy remains preserved, is in the first place attracted by the magnificence of what they see. They see a house that, like a temple of God, is splendidly adorned by the size of the building and the beauty of its ornamentation. The carpenter shaped the wood until it had the form of animals and the mason polished the stones until they had the smoothness of silver. The painter coloured the blooms of his art, having depicted on an image the martyr's brave deeds, his opposition, his continuous pain, the beastly appearance of the tyrants, the insults, the blazing furnace that was the athlete's most blessed end, the representation of the human form of Christ, who was the president of the games – having fashioned all these things for us by his use of colours, he portrayed, as if in a book that uttered speech, in great detail the martyr's contest and at the same time he also adorned the church as a beautiful meadow. For even though it remains silent, painting can speak on the wall and be of the greatest profit. And the mosaicist, for his part, made a floor to tread on that was worthy of the martyr's story.

Taking delight in the seeing of such works of art that can be observed, one longs for the rest, in particular to approach the tomb, trusting that touching it results in sanctification and blessing. And if somebody gives permission to take away the dust that lies upon the surface of the resting place, then the soil is taken away as a gift and the earth is preserved as a treasure. But to touch the relics themselves, as chance on occasion provides the opportunity, that is much-desired and the gift for prayers to the Most High, as is known to those who have had this experience and have fulfilled this kind of longing. For as if it is the same body, still alive and flourishing, those beholding it embrace it with the eyes, the mouth, the ears. And when they have approached it with all the senses, they pour tears out over it from piety and emotion. And as if he was intact and appearing, they address to the martyr a plea that he would intercede on their behalf, in a way as if they were asking God's bodyguard for a favour and he, called upon, receives presents and provides them whenever he likes.[1]

(64,3)   From all this, o pious people, you must learn that *in the eyes of the Lord the death of His saints is precious* (Ps 115:6). Every person has one and the same body that is composed from the same paste. The body of someone who died in a simple way is thrown away as usual, whereas the body that has been graced by the suffering of martyrdom is beloved, cherished and undisputed, as the previous part of the homily taught. Therefore, on the basis of what we can perceive, we believe in invisible things and because of what we experience in this world, we believe in the promise of the future things. Many give preference to their belly, vainglory (cf. Phil 3:19) and these kinds of trivialities above all possible beautiful things. These people do not care about the future and they are convinced that with the end of life everything is finished. But you who think this way, learn from the small things the great, get from its shadows an understanding of the archetype. Which emperor receives such an honour? Who of those who clearly excel are extolled by a remembrance of this kind? Who of the generals who have razed the walls of cities and have enslaved countless nations is as famous as this soldier, a poor man, a recruit, who had received his weapons from Paul (cf. Eph 6:11–13), who was anointed for the contest by angels and who, after his victory, was crowned by Christ (cf. 2 Tim 4:8)?

But, now that we have arrived in the homily at the martyr's contests, I would propose that we leave behind the general and focus on the holy man himself, because what is specific for him is precious for everyone here.

(64,23)   The fatherland of this noble man was the region where the sun rises. He was of noble birth; just like Job he was from the East (cf. Job 1:3) and with the latter he had not only his fatherland in common but neither did he omit the imitation of his character. Now, he is a martyr to the whole world, a fellow citizen to everybody under the sun. In his region of origin he was recruited for the infantry. Thus, he came with his unit to our region.[2] There winter quarters were arranged for the soldiers by their officers. All at once a war broke out, not because of an attack by the barbarians but because of a satanic law and a decree inimical to God: as a consequence of this impious edict every Christian was persecuted and carried away to be put to death. Precisely at that time the thrice-blesssed was well known for his faith and was spreading the belief in Christ everywhere: only on his brow his confession was not written. As for courage he was no longer a recruit nor was he inexperienced in war and combat. On the contrary, this noble man had strengthened his resistance to danger, he wasn't a scaredy-cat, a coward or somebody who doesn't dare to speak up freely. This became clear when their demon had constituted an evil tribunal in which his general and the leader of his unit came together, just like once Herod and Pilate did (cf. Luke 23:12). These people organised a trial for the servant of the Crucified similar to that which the latter had organised for his Master. 'Tell us', they said, 'from where do you get that over-boldness and recklessness so that you violate the imperial law, you don't bow trembling for the emperors' edicts, you don't kneel when it suits the mighty?' The group around Maximian was then enjoying imperial power.[3] With a stubborn expression on his face and undaunted purposefulness he gave them the following witty answer: 'I cannot call them gods, because in truth they are not. In honouring deceiving demons with the name god you are wrong. To me Christ is God, the Only-begotten Son of God. Because of my faith in him and my confession of it, let he who is wounding me cut me; let he who is whipping me lacerate me; let he who is burning me bring the flame close; let he who is taking offence at these words of mine cut out my tongue, for each part of the body owes to its Creator an act of endurance.'

The tyrants were beaten by these words and couldn't bear the first attack of the hero because they were seeing a young man, swollen with pride because of his suffering and attracted to his death as to a sweet drink. While they were holding back for a moment indecisively, deliberating on what should be done, one of the soldiers in his unit, who thought to be witty, said, in order to ridicule the martyr's answer: 'Theodore, has your God a Son? Does he beget, just like man, with passion?' 'With passion', he said, 'my God did not beget but I do confess the Son and I call his begetting fitting for God. You, however, o pitiable man with the intellect of a child, don't you blush or hide due to your confession in a female god and your veneration for her, a mother of twelve children, a kind of very fertile goddess[4] who just like a hare or a sow effortlessly conceives and gives birth!'

(67,3)   After the saint had in this way twice reproved on the basis of his idolatry the soldier who ridiculed him, the tyrants feigned an appearance of benevolence. They said: 'We must give this mad man some time to think it over. Maybe, when he's given some time for moderation, he might himself change his opinion for the better.' For the fools called madness temperance and, conversely, they gave the name piety to being out of one's mind and to madness, just like drunk people who reproach their own condition to sober persons. But the pious man, a soldier of Christ, used the moment of leisure that was given to him to carry out a courageous deed.[5]

How did he do that? Now for you the moment has come to hear with joy the account of what happened. There was a temple for the much talked of Mother of the Gods in the metropolis Amasea.[6] In their purposelessness the fools of that time erected the temple somewhere on the bank of the river. During the period of amnesty that was granted to him, the noble man burnt down this temple. Having kept a watch for the right moment, when there was a light breeze, he set the temple on fire. By this deed he gave the sinners the answer that they had certainly only expected after his time for reflection. Since the fire was started in a conspicuous way, it soon became clear to everybody in the heart of the city what was going on. Moreover, he didn't conceal his undertaking nor did he make any effort to hide it. On the contrary: it was crystal-clear and, on top of that, he boasted of his success and was very glad for the commotion within the ranks of the pagans, who were confused because of the temple and hurt because of the statue. He was pointed out to the authorities as the one who had started the fire. Again he had to appear before a tribunal, a more terrifying one than the previous, as is logical given the degree of irritation that had been added.

(67,25) The authorities went up to the throne of the judge. Theodore, with his great freedom of speech[7] stood in their middle in the position of the defendant. While he was questioned he showed the confidence of a magistrate and he cut off the interrogation by the readiness of his confession. Because he wasn't struck at all by terror and clearly didn't withdraw from the terrors that were threatening him, they changed their attitude to the reverse. They tried to drag down the just by talking in a friendly way to him and by making promises. They said: 'Do you realise that, if you would be willing to look favourably upon our counsel, we will very soon raise you from anonymity to a well-known person, from one of those without glory to an honoured man? Moreover, we promise you the dignity of high priest.'[8]

When he heard the dignity of high priest mentioned, the thrice-blessed bursted out in laughter and said: 'I consider even the *priests* of the idols pitiable and commiserate with the servants of such vain practices. Therefore, I pity and detest the high priests even more; of wicked persons the greater and more important is also the more pitiable. Such is also the case with the more unjust among the unjust, with the more cruel among the murderers or with the more brutal among the intemperate persons. Therefore, one is only degraded by your disgusting promises. O you, without noticing, you promised me the pinnacle of bad things. For somebody who chooses a life of piety and righteousness *it is better to be an outcast in God's house than to dwell in the tents of the wicked* (Ps 83:11). I also pity those emperors, whose unlawful edict you continuously proclaim, because on their own authority they arrogated to themselves the title of high priest, on the basis of the fact that, vested with imperial power, they had sufficient power in the eyes of the people to do so. I also pity them because, consequently, they are putting on that mourning and dark purple and are, in imitation of the demon-inspired high priests, carrying around this dreadful robe with a beaming countenance. It also occurs that they approach the impure altar and become cooks instead of emperors, sacrificing birds, scrutinising the entrails of pitiable cattle and having their clothes soiled with bloodstains as if they were ordinary butchers.'

(69,3)   After these words from the just, the magistrates no longer showed their feigned and pretended philanthropy but called him irreverent towards the gods and rude and insulting towards the emperors. Therefore they first hung his body on a stake and tore it in pieces. But, though the executioners were using excessive force, he was valiant and steadfast and he even sang during his torture a verse of a psalm: '*I will praise the Lord on every occasion, his praise is always in my mouth*' (Ps 33:2). They tore most of his flesh in pieces, he was singing psalms as if somebody else was undergoing the torture. This torture was followed by a stay in prison. There again miraculous things happened around the saint: at night the sound of a group singing psalms was heard by those outside and the light of burning torches, such as during a vigil service, was seen. But when the jailer, confused by the unusual sight and sound, leapt into the little house, he didn't find anything except the resting martyr and the other prisoners who were lying asleep.

Since, after the many things that had happened, he flourished even more in his confession and faith, he was condemned and, after it was ordered that he should end his life by the fire, he embarked upon the beautiful and blessed journey towards God. To us he left the instructive memory of his contest, he who brings people together, who teaches the Church, who chases the demons, leads the peaceful angels, looks out for our interests in the presence of God. He turned this place into a hospital for the most diverse diseases, a harbour for those suffering from the storms of life, a well-filled warehouse for the needy, a convenient resting-place for those who are travelling, a never-ending feast for those who are celebrating. We celebrate this day with annual feasts and yet the stream of people arriving here because of their zeal for the martyrs never ceases. In that regard the thoroughfare that leads to this place preserves a resemblance to a group of ants: among those who are moving along it are both those who are arriving and those who are leaving.

(70,6) So, blessed man, now that another year is gone, thanks to the Creator's philanthropy we are gathered together with you for this feast, for this holy assembly of people that love the martyrs, in order to worship our common Master and to keep alive the victorious remembrance of your contests. Come nearer to us, wherever you are, you president of this feast. You have called us; now we call you. Whether you are residing in the lofty heavens, or serving somewhere on the vault of heaven, or standing together with the choir of angels in the Master's neighbourhood or are worshipping Him as a faithful servant together with the mights and the powers, obtain leave from your occupations there and come to the people who honour you, o invisible friend. Come and see what is going on here, in order that you may double the gratitude towards God, who gave you so many rewards in exchange for one passion and one pious confession, in order also that you may rejoice because of the blood that you shed and the pain that you suffered in the fire. Because, as many spectators as you had then for your torture, as many people you have now to bring you honour. We are craving for many benefactions from you: intercede on behalf of your fatherland with our common King. After all, the fatherland of a martyr is the region where he suffered, where the citizens, yes, his brothers and relatives, buried him and are keeping him and are bringing him honour. We view with suspicion the afflictions, we expect danger: it will not take long before the sinful Scyths are plunging us into the pains of war. As a soldier, fight for us; as a martyr, use your freedom of speech on behalf of your fellow-servants. I know, you already left this life; but, on the other hand, you know the sufferings and needs of humankind. Ask God for peace, so that these feasts do not have to stop, so that the furious and lawless barbarian does not attack churches and altars nor that the profane trample upon the holy.

(70,29) All the times that we have been preserved unharmed in the past we consider a benefaction from you; we are asking this safety also for the future. And if the need for a greater number of entreaties would arise, then assemble the choir of your brother-martyrs and ask for it all together. Because the prayers of many just men can undo the sins of many peoples. Remind Peter, arouse Paul, as well as John the Theologian and beloved disciple, in order that they show care for the churches which they organised themselves (cf. 2 Cor 11:28), for whom they bore chains, for whom they endured dangers and died (cf. 2 Cor 11:26) and in order to avoid that idolatry stirs up its head against us, that heresies overgrow like thorns the vineyard, that overgrown weeds suffocate wheat (cf. Matt 13:25, 13:7), that the soil should become a rock that to our disadvantage is left without the wealth of the true dew[9] and that this shows that the power of the fruitfulness of the word is without roots.[10] On the contrary: thanks to the power of your intercession and that of those who are with you, marvellous and most bright among the martyrs, may the community of Christians prove to be a young shoot that remains forever and that in the fat and fruitful soil of faith in Christ always bears the fruit of eternal life which is in Christ Jesus our Lord. To him be, together with the Father and the Holy Spirit, the glory, the power and the honour, now and always and forever and ever. Amen.

First homily on the Forty Martyrs of Sebaste (Ia and Ib)

Introduction

The Forty Martyrs of Sebaste were a group of soldiers who died freezing on a lake near the city in the Armenian mountains. Their cult was one of the most 'successful' in late antiquity. Having originated in Sebaste, where it is attested until the sixth century, it quickly spread over the entire Roman Empire (Maraval 1999). During the fourth century the cult of the Forty is also attested for Cappadocian Caesarea (where Basil delivered a homily in praise of them) and for the village of Ibora in Pontus (a sanctuary on the estates of Gregory of Nyssa's family). For the first decades of the fifth century there is evidence for a cult of the Forty in Jerusalem and even in Brescia (Italy). Still in the first half of the fifth century their cult reached Jerusalem and Constantinople. Though remaining present in the West, it was especially in the East that the Forty were one of the most loved group of saints throughout the Byzantine period until today. This popularity is demonstrated by the fact that they were a favourite theme in art (Rice 1963; Kaster 1976; Gavrilovic 1980) while also a large hagiographical tradition, consisting of Passions, homilies and poems, written in Latin, Greek, Syriac and Armenian, was created around their memory (BHG 1201–2; BHL 7542; BHO 712–13; Amore 1968). The latter included authors such as Romanos Melodos and Jacob of Serugh but also a remarkable seventh-century Egyptian papyrus with (most of) their names, probably used as an amulet (Hagedorn 1984).

The earliest layer of this tradition contains no less than six documents going back to the fourth century and is therefore unusually rich. The oldest document is the *Passion* of the Forty that, in one form or another, seems to have influenced the homily of Basil of Caesarea delivered on the Forty. Both these texts can be taken to have inspired Gregory of Nyssa's *First and Second Homily on the Forty* (Karlin-Hayter 1991). Further there is the homily of Ephrem Graecus and last but not least the *Testament*, which may represent the earliest tradition about the Forty. The *Testament* is a peculiar document: purportedly the will of the Forty, it states where they wanted to be buried while also explicitly expressing their wish to be buried together. It is highly likely that this clause in the *Testament* was a source of the theme of the unity of the group of the Forty, a typical element present in many texts, including Gregory of Nyssa's homilies (Vinel 1997).

The most striking aspect of Gregory of Nyssa's *First Homily on the Forty of Sebaste* is that it consists of two separate homilies (Ia and Ib). It is no surprise that they are traditionally considered as one homily: the end of Ia was caused by the audience's noise that forced the homilist to break off his sermon and Ib takes up the thread where Gregory had to leave it at the end of Ia, thus clearly presenting itself as its continuation. Moreover the homilies were delivered on two consecutive days in Sebaste: Ia during the Forty's yearly panèguris on 9 March in the martyrium in the city, Ib the day after in a church. As for the year in which these homilies must be dated, Ia contains an important clue in the passage of the introduction in which Gregory says that he will save the treatment of 'the inscriptions of the Psalms that were read aloud to us' for another time. He does not make clear for which occasion exactly, but it seems beyond doubt that the final result of his exegetical endeavour was laid down in his treatise *On the Inscriptions of the Psalms*. This means that Ia and Ib must antedate this treatise, the composition of which can be plausibly placed in the years 376–78. Thus a date before this *terminus ante quem* seems assured (Leemans 2001a).

Translated from the edition by O. Lendle; GNO X, 1/2, 137–42 and 145–56.

Texts

Homily Ia

(137,5)   What, I guess, is to many a source of irritation, is to me a reason for intense joy. Indeed, being crowded against each other appears to be for many an unpleasant thing; to me, however, it is the summit of joy. Yes, the shepherd's eye rejoices at the sight of his flock that due to its large number is straitened and overflows its pen. And yet the sheep's fold isn't small but it is the thriving flock that by its large number makes the large space constricted. Surely it was a similar crowd that Peter had seen near the Lord when he reacted: '*Master, the multitudes surround you and press upon you*' (Luke 8:45). Truly, it is as the divine Apostle says somewhere, 'being pressed upon' but not 'straitened'. Yes, he says: '*We are pressed on every side, but not being straitened*' (2 Cor 4:8).

(137,15)   And I, what kind of homily am I to deliver before an audience such as this? Who will give me a voice that sounds like a trumpet, so that my words overcome the noise of the multitude and reach the ears of those who have gathered? To which of the readings shall I turn my attention in order to find a fitting homily for those present here? Job is of great use in this regard because he teaches the virtue of courage through examples from his own life; the author of Proverbs because he does the same through riddles. And what should one say about the Holy Apostle? He who, from those unutterable words, about which he says that they are beyond human understanding (2 Cor 12:4), through his teaching to the Ephesians whispers perhaps also to us the unutterable word upon the Cross, unveiling it with the help of riddles (cf. Eph 3:18). Other similar instances are the mysteries of the Psalms: the remembrance, the inscription on a stone, the wine-press.[11] Indeed, in the reflection on these expressions in the inscriptions of the Psalms which were read aloud to us, because of the riddles we see given no small resource for the homily. But I think it is better to come back to these words at a more opportune moment and to store them up for a second time. Because now I want to find a text that is fitting and appropriate for the present celebration.

(138,10) What is this then? I know a natural law that was inscribed on divine tablets by the lawgiver of nature. It orders one to pay back one's parents a full and good recompence (cf. Exod 20:12), in so far as it is in one's power. *Honour your father and your mother*, the law says, *(this is the first commandment in the promises), so that it may be well with you* (Eph 6:2–3). Since this law comes first according to the promises and its fulfilment itself becomes the profit of the one who keeps it (the honour bestowed on one's parents turns back upon the one who fulfilled the law), it would be well if every sensible human being would observe this commandment, the goal of which is the benefaction and grace of the one who observes it. Now, our parents in the flesh, who served during their own generation from the beginning during the entire time measured out for them, do not need these honours from us, since they have died long ago. Consequently it is not possible to fulfil this particular law since those who are to receive the beneficence are no longer there. But the law orders us to reach the promise through our deeds. For it cannot be that those who don't do anything should gain the rewards of those who exert themselves. What, then, should a person do when their parents are dead and they long for the promise but are in the situation of being unable to reach what they want?

(138,26) Well, what I have seen here, in my case completely solves this problem. Now that I see you, I do not need at all to take much trouble to find other parents. For, you are to me parents as well as parents of these parents. For the fatherland of those who give me life also includes in itself the dignity of parents. What, then, should we do to fulfil the commandment to honour you? Well, an understanding and loving child revives by his care his father's old age. He supports his weakness and becomes everything to his father. Thus one can see a father regaining his youth again thanks to his child. So it may be that the old and shaky hand, resting upon the force of youth, enjoys the fruit of the young man's strength or that the movement of the feet, which now succumbs to the limbs' stiffness, regains vigour thanks to the child's dedication and is secured by his support. And when in the course of time the eye-sight grows dim, it is again thanks to the child that the old man becomes sharp-sighted, in the sense that he is led by the hand towards the necessities of life. But you, my fatherland, are not in the kind of situation that you would be in want of any of the aforementioned things.

(139,13)   What then, should we do to enjoy the fruit of the commandment's blessing? What favour will we bring you as a gift, when already no advantages fail you? Or, could the narration itself of the splendours available to you possibly contribute to the honour we owe you? For in that case this could be an opportunity to speak about them, about the extent and the way they adorn your life. Or better yet, we will not speak about them but, since it is possible to show them, we will show them. Maybe you are thinking now that I will speak about everything that is common and at hand: the fertility of the earth, the abundance of fruits and the river that divides your settlement. About the latter I say the following. As a consequence of the circular form of the river-plain, it is shut up in itself and becomes a pond. Before it becomes marshy as well as after that, it is divided for the use of each of the inhabitants and delightful groves and meadows are produced. It provides the inhabitants with thousands of advantages and through splitting itself up, it accomodates every wish of the city's inhabitants. Let other men speak about these subjects. Men, whose rhetoric is at the service of their weighty character and adds a certain distinction to them, by increasing the praise to their fatherland on the basis of such kind of subjects. Let a man of the world, who in this life is knowledgeable in judging splendours, add to these praises, if he wants to, also the other river. I am speaking about the river that is the neighbour of the first. This river because of its magnitude is counted among the best-known of the world. It finds its origin in our region, then flows by the city and thereby contributes no small advantage to the increase of its beauty and life-support.[12] If one really must give the catalogue of the founders of the city, must extoll beyond measure the most distinguished families of the dwelling from its foundation onwards or include some of the military successes in accounts about us – trophies, battles, miraculous deeds of courage – such as these mini-historians set down in their books, let then these subjects remain far from our gathering here. For Christian discourse is ashamed to attach to friends of Christ praise to subjects external to the faith, which is like extolling the shadow of a hero instead of his trophies.

Therefore the homily must turn towards what is at hand and bring under our eyes the fruit that is yours. Let the splendours of the world remain unmentioned, even if they abound in material for rhetoric, as well as all such subject matter of orations of praise. For not the whole heaven, though the most beautiful and greatest of everything in creation, nor the rays of the lights of the sky, nor the surface of the earth, nor something else of the material elements that constitute the universe, does the divinely inspired homily recognise as something great or worthy of marvel. For I have learnt from the divine command to treat nothing with marvel that will pass away (cf. Matt 5:18; Mark 13:31; Luke 21:33).

(140,22)   If all of heaven and earth will pass away and, as the Apostle says it, *the whole constellation of the world passes away* (1 Cor 7:31), how could somebody deem it plausible to propose the abundance with which the earth and the water provide us as a starting-point for an oration of praise? And even if such advantages of the earth would be more numerous in your region than in that of others, still the homily knows that these are to be passed by as they are worth nothing in comparison to your own splendours.

Therefore, let us turn now to subjects that because of their nature are more worthy of praise. These I will no longer show to us through words since it is possible to see the summit of your wealth on this very spot.[13] For who doesn't know your fruit, who doesn't know that you brought forth this abundantly rich ear of corn of martyrs, one that split up into a group of more than thirty fruits? You see that holy acre; thence come the martyrs' sheaves. If you want to know which acre I mean, do not look around further than the one nearby. At which location does this gathering take place? What does the progression of the cycle of the year say to you? What narratives does the arrival of this day's commemoration bring to you? Aren't there *some conversations*, as the Prophet says, *and words, the sounds of which are not just heard* (Ps 18:4) but which narrate marvels much more vigorously than any kind of speech? When you look at the place, it tells that it is the martyr's stadium; when you consider the day, like a herald with a stentorian voice it proclaims the martyr's crown. For it seems that this

96

is what I hear the day shouting out: one day is proud because of the fabrication of the lights in the sky, another because of heaven, still another rejoices because of the construction of the earth. To me, however, suffice as ornamentation the martyrs' marvels; it is sufficient to take pride in the beauty of the crowns; it is enough to be proud of the trophies won against the Devil. What narrations originated in me! What an addition [of glory] happened through me to the angels! What fruit of her own did the earth offer to God (cf. Ps 84:13b)! What a planting did the Lord set out in me! From there almost the entire earth was planted by offshoots of the twigs of these plants, just as a thriving vine produces from itself other vines while remaining itself inexhaustible. These and similar things the grace of this day seems to me to proclaim, and the place of this gathering does other things of the same kind.

(141,27)   But what should I do, now that I am speaking to such a large crowd, having only a thin voice and being a slow speaker, so that I am hardly able to reach those standing within earshot and my speech is drowned out by the noise?[14] For normally I would have gone on for some time with the virtuous stories, of how the beautiful team of the Forty have gone through a common contest, how they have made everywhere a common settlement, divided themselves over the whole world and claimed everywhere a place for themselves. Thus, nobody who received the grace of part of the relics, did not receive the presence of the complete group of the martyrs. For all became one in Christ and through any one of them all take their dwelling place with the complete group.[15]

But how can I avoid doing justice to my homily when I keep silent about the beginning of the stories about them? What, then, is that beginning? Virtuous youth, looked upon with admiration, all of them chosen because of their skilfulness, conspicuous by their beauty, in size resembling young shoots in the flower of the season. Do you notice how my voice is disordered by the crowd's noise and how my homily is cut short by the tumult so that we, tempest-tossed on the sound of the people like on a swelling sea, are forced to seek refuge in the waveless harbour of silence? But if, thanks to God's grace, a second occasion for a homily before a quiet audience would be given to me, then, what is now left behind, will be completed with the help of God, to whom it is fitting that there be glory forever and ever. Amen.

97

Homily Ib

(145,5)   Yesterday the martyrs called the people to them; now, on their own invitation, they are entertained as guests in the inn of the Church. In hospitality it is customary that these banquets circulate in the sense that the guests give them in return to each other in a rotating order. Accordingly we must give the martyrs the same banquet in exchange for their feast. But since our supply of words falls short, it is best that we receive those who were yesterday our hosts and are today our guests with the remains of their own reception. For even a small share of a richly-laden table is enough to prepare a great feast, when the remains are of this kind. What, now, are these remains? Surely you remember at which point in the homily we were when this noise from the gathered crowd – [a noise] wholeheartedly wished and sweet to us – drowned out the hearing of my words, when this living sea of the church, overflowing due to the mass of people flowing in, through its flood, ever-swelling in waves, exceeded the critical point. By its noise it was imitating the real sea in that the hubbub of its waves beat against the seashore of our ears. In this situation we left behind our noise-tossed homily, which was – as you surely remember – directed towards those whose purpose it is to keep the martyrs' memory alive.

I believe the sermon's train of thought was as follows. The men chosen for this contest were not chosen at random, nor were they a mixed and obscure band that, starting from low pursuits in life, was lifted up to this dignity. No, at first, because of their well-shaped body, distinguishing themselves from others in beauty, might and a surplus of physical strength, they were enrolled in the ranks of the soldiers. Thereafter they excelled through a virtuous life and wise conduct and at the end of their lives they received as a reward the grace of martyrdom. And if you think that it would be a pleasure to you, let us then narrate everything about the martyrs step by step, in a way that brings their contest under your eyes on this very stage.

(146,9)   Of old there was a unit of soldiers present in the vicinity of a neighbouring city, in order to provide protection against the attacks of the barbarians for the whole population. Because of an earlier divine apparition the faith was to them of greater concern than military tactics. Maybe this is not a bad moment to narrate in passing one success of these men's faith. Once, when they were entangled in a war with the barbarians, all the key positions had been occupied by the army of their adversaries and the control of the water supplies were also in enemy hands. They were in the greatest of dangers, either because of the lack of experience of their officers, or because of a stronger and more divine dispensation, meaning that because of this the difference of the Christians vis-à-vis non-Christians would become blatantly clear. At the time they had nothing that they needed in their situation; they were helpless because in the place where they were, there was no well nor a source of flowing water and the danger existed that, through being successfully besieged by thirst, they would have to bow to their adversaries. At that moment the noble men abandoned the help of weapons and decided to seek in their terrifying situation an unconquered and invincible ally. They left behind in the camp those who had not yet received the faith and separated them from themselves. Then they imitated the miracle that happened to the prophet Elijah (cf. 1 Kings 18:30–45), asking in unison with a common voice that they should be liberated from their extremely infelicitous situation. So, they prayed, and their prayer became reality immediately. For while they persevered in kneeling, a cloud, that had been taken away from elsewhere by a strong wind, took up position in the sky high above the camp of the enemies. Then it produced an enormous thunderbolt, it threw fiery flashes of light on those beneath it and poured forth water in greater quantities than rivers, with the result that for our enemies the combination of the continuous thunderbolts and the abundant rain was the cause of their complete destruction. But to those who formed a line of battle through their prayers it served both purposes: victory against their opponents and alleviation of their thirst – the water that was abundantly pouring down in torrents provided them with drink.[16]

Now, with these men our band of soldiers was joined. Strengthened in their faith by these stories and trained in pursuits of their kind, they were stimulated to such a degree of greatness of nature that, because of their excelling in virtue, they aroused jealousy against themselves. For it was the same as what we learnt from the story about Job that was just read aloud to us, namely that the Enemy of human life considered Job's good fame an injustice to himself. Hence he sought to torture him, because Job was hurting him *by being truthful and just and without blemish* (Job 1:1; cf. 1:6–12 and 2:1–8). In exactly the same way he who clings to good men looked with a malicious eye upon these great champions and couldn't bear to see in people so youthful of age the serenity of the mature. He saw the flower of their bodies, adorned with chastity; he saw an armed chorus of men, [he saw] that they were celebrating God through their military service, that they were beautiful to look upon, with determination in their look and exulting in what they were up to. [He saw] the speed of their feet, the superiority of their strength, the symmetry of their limbs, in all of the advantages that befell them the virtue of their soul surpassing in brilliance the good fortune they had with their body. *He that walked about the entire world* (Job 1:7) because of his jealousy also walked about among these men. He did not only see one truthful man, but a divine group of such men, all of them truthful, just and God-fearing. These too he demanded for his own plans. First of all he suggested to the leader of the army, who was idol-mad, that he would never gain victory over the barbarians unless he sacrificed those who worshipped the name of Christ.

(148,6)   They were quickly pointed out, then, because of their good confession of faith and thus turned themselves to their perfection through suffering. But the Enemy refrained from passing at once to their death by the sword, which he considered as too gentle. Instead he put them into iron chains and made that the start of their torture. To them even the chain was an adornment and to the eyes of Christians it was an elegant and sweet sight: young men, selected in such a great number, more conspicuous than the others in beauty and youth. By the chain all of them were joined together with each other, like a crown or a necklace of equally-sized pearls evenly divided along a circle. Such were the saints, united by their faith and tied to each other by the chains. And because they were all individually beautiful, they effected for each other a surplus of beauty. It was like what can occur with regard to the heavenly wonders, when in a clear sky the grace of the stars is mutually embellished because each of them contributes its usual glance to the common adornment of heaven. Such was also the sight of the saints, verily, as the prophet Ezechiel says somewhere, *a vision of combined lamps* (Ezek 1:13). My sermon is dwelling on the topic of their youth. The reason is that it knows how, as Wisdom says, *to know from the greatness and the beauty of creatures by analogy also the beauty of what is hidden* (Wis 13:5), because the soul's purity shone through what could be seen and their outward appearance as man was a worthy dwelling for the invisible.

But how beautiful then was the sight for the spectators! Beautiful, that is, for those who wanted to behold beauty. Beautiful to the angels, beautiful to the powers above the world but hateful to the demons and those who clung to the demons' interests, were these men. If they really were men, who to such a degree lived up to the greatness of their nature, soldiers of Christ, foot soldiers of the Holy Spirit, champions of the faith, towers of the divine city. Men who scoffed, as if it were some children's senseless idea, at every torture and maltreatment, at every upsurge of fear, at every attempt to threaten them, as if they did not expose their bodies to the tortures but only the shadows of their bodies. Men who subdued the flesh by their flesh and looked down with disdain on the tyrant's threats because of their contempt for death, showing in this way that they were elevated above human standards. O you who so marvellously exercised in turning your bodies into trophies! O you who so marvellously transferred your experience in military warfare to the battle line against the Devil! Not with swords did they arm their hands, nor did they hold a wooden shield before them, nor did they protect themselves with a metal helmet and greaves; but they put on the armour of God, which the general of the Church, the divine Apostle, describes: shield, breastplate, helmet and dagger (Eph 6:11–17) and so they marched against the opposing force. Their leader was heavenly grace; that of the Devil's army was the one who had power over death. The place of their confrontation was the tribunal of men with blood on their hands. There both parties met and fought out their battle: one side was throwing threats and the other was defending itself by practising endurance.

(149,22)   Their enemies proposed that they forswear their faith in the Lord or pay for it with their lives. The noble men answered that they would remain faithful to their word until their death. Then they were threatened with the fire, the sword, the precipice and other such names of punishments. In reaction to all of this only one word was heard, namely 'Christ', as he was confessed in the saints' mouths. This was a blow to their opponents, this was a spear-point aimed at the Enemy, with this word the Adversary was wounded in the middle of his heart, this was the stone, slung by David's hand (cf. 1 Sam 17:49–51), that hit the helmet of the Adversary. For in the hands of the good soldier the confession of Christ becomes a sling; the Enemy falls on the ground and is decapitated.

But my sermon has broken loose from its reins, it has been carried away and transgressed its boundaries. It boldly broaches what cannot be caught in words and, continuing to speak about these things, it describes – as if it was a spectator of things invisible – that because of such a voice, boldly confessing Christ, there was applause above, and praise; there was joyful approval on the part of the citizens of the heavenly city because of their achievement, there was delight with the complete festive assembly in heaven. For indeed, what a spectacle was on that occasion displayed for the angels in the world of men! What a wrestling-match between the Devil and men the spectators of our life watched! How opposite was this confrontation in comparison to the first round, when the serpent floored Adam (cf. Gen 3)! At the time man didn't withstand one attack of the Evil One, which happened by offering him an attractive bait; rather, at once the Devil assaulted him and man was overturned by the Fall. Against these men, however, all the Enemy's tricks remained idle and without result. He stretched his hopes, they trampled them down; he threatened them with fearsome things, they laughed at him. They had only one fear: to be separated from Christ, and one good: to be with Christ only. All the rest was to them a reason for laughter, shadows, idle talk and illusory dreams. It is for this reason that my sermon boldly broaches things not to be seen and that it says that the complete celestial power rejoices because of the athletes' achievement.

Still more my sermon boldly goes on with things not to be dared, still more does it dare to describe celestial things: how, after these men had been successful in their wrestling with the enemies, the just President of the games stretched out crowns of victory, the General of the divine power prepared prizes for the winners and the Holy Spirit received them with gifts of every kind. For since they confessed their faith in the Trinity, for that reason on the part of the Trinity grace was in exchange measured out to them. What was this grace? It surely was that they were shown to be loftier than the first contestants – I mean, than Adam and Eve. These two by their sin brought down upright human nature; the martyrs' by their endurance erected it again from where it lay as a consequence of the Fall of those who came before them. The first were chased from Paradise to the earth, the latter transferred their dwelling place from there to Paradise. The first armed death against themselves – for Scripture says that *sin is the weapon of death* (cf. 1 Cor 15:56), the latter rendered death that was armed with sin ineffective through their courage; by their endurance of sufferings they blunted the point of the sting, in agreement with what is beautifully said: '*Death, where is your sting? Hades, where is your victory?*' (cf. 1 Cor 15:55). What is more wretched than the fruit of the tree? What is meaner than the tree itself? Its fruit, while looking attractive because of its colour and sweetness of taste, caused men to dishonour the grace of Paradise.

(151,16) To these, the greatest of contestants, however, not even the sun appeared sweet: they voluntarily estranged themselves from it, so that they should not apostatise from the true light. What does Scripture say about Eve? (for I am led beyond what is due to attack their ancestors). It says: '*She saw that it was attractive to see and good to taste*' (Gen 3:6). Then they exchanged Paradise for the attractiveness of these things. But to the martyrs the visible things also carried with them the sweetness of temptation: heaven, the sun, the earth, people, one's country, mothers, brothers, friends, relatives, comrades. What is sweeter to observe than these things? What is more valuable than coming to enjoy these? Children, you know your love for your parents. Fathers, you know your loving disposition towards your children. You, who see it, know the sweetness that is in the sun. You, who love your brothers, are not unfamiliar with the natural inclination towards brotherhood. Young man, you know the joy that comes from your comrades and how much this improves the quality of your life. But for them, all this was hateful, all this was strange. Only one thing was good: Christ. They renounced everything in order to gain him. The time they spent in chains wasn't short and to the saints the longing for their consummation grew together with the prolongation of their punishment. And just like those who are training their physical condition, when they have acquired sufficient strength in the sporting school, advance to the games full of confidence, in the same way the martyrs, who through the chains and their stay in prison received sufficient training towards piety, were led forward to the crown of the contests.

The sermons' course comes at its end, or better, at the culmination of the martyrs' whole achievement. This was the occasion, these were the days of their contest; this the prelude to Easter; this the mystery of the Holy Forty. Forty are to us the days of our atonement, of the same number were the crowns of their contests. But don't you deem me superfluous or a prating fellow because I am narrating your own wonders to you and am filling your ears with it? So, unless it would be without profit to you that the sermon continues, let's run together with the saints to the end of their contests.

It was icy cold that day. It is absolutely unnecessary that I explain to you what kind of cold precisely. You can guess it from today: it was the kind of cold that even permeates the walls. With its intensity you are all familiar – both those from outside the region and the natives – so you don't need to learn it from my sermon. But somebody else could describe the marvels your winters create: how the everflowing rivers come to a standstill as the freezing offers resistance to their current and their waves are turned into stone. And the neighbouring lake, which lacks any sign that reveals that it is in fact a marshy lake, has been turned by the frost into dry land, allowing, as is customary, those who want it to drive on horseback over its waves. And I know that the inhabitants of this region often contrive to get water from fire: by breaking off a lump of water and melting it in fire like a piece of bronze or iron, they turn this stone into water. Such was the situation at the time of their contest and from nature they received, to intensify their misery, chilly northerly winds, as one hears from those who narrate their marvels.

(153,3) After the martyrs had in a magnificent way publicly proclaimed the name of the Lord and by such a public proclamation had already showed themselves crowned, they advanced towards their perfection by death. And this was the sort of contest that was devised for them: an edict was issued by the tyrant that the athletes should be tortured by the cold. O the weakness of words and thoughts! How much does my sermon fall short in comparison to what they deserve! Their condemnation to death, the cold, their torture and their anticipation of such a punishment. The blessed youth arrived at the place of their punishment with laughter, childish amusement and intense joy. It was a race of athletes towards their suffering, a holy and intense race and the ambition to be the first to grasp the crown of their confession. Equal also was their zeal to attain victory: nobody was seen to lag behind in enthusiasm but all arrived one in heart at the place. As if this was reserved for public bathing and as if they were about to beautify their body by going to a public bath, they put off the cover of their tunics. Meanwhile they joined in Job's saying: '*Naked we came into the world, naked we will depart from it to Him who introduced us in it* (cf. Job 1:21). *We didn't bring anything with us into the world, nor ought we to take anything with us from it* (1 Tim 6:7). Rather, having arrived naked into the world, we depart from it full of the treasures of a good confession.' While saying these things and encouraging each other with similar words, they exposed their body to the frost. The nature of the elements was dominated by the frost but the martyr's nature was not the slave of it. Or better, their nature suffered what is proper and it was subject to pain, but the athletes' greatness of nature fought against nature itself. For the strength of their bodies was dissolved little by little, weakened and exhausted by the frost, whereas the fortitude of their spirit became only bigger. Their youthful bodies became black, their beauty withered away and the colour of their flesh faded. Their fingers fell off, mutilated by the frost little by little and all their limbs and sense-organs were pounded to pieces by the bitter cold. For after a time their flesh became livid and swollen, it became rent all around the limbs until it fell off the bones and they could experience in reality the decay of a corpse. In that way their near death was gradually protracted until it lasted for three days. During this time-span the martyrs' senses held out and they stayed on the very place where they had been posted from the start onwards: winners against the Adversary through all their sufferings.

(154,11) But who could narrate to me the events that followed in a way that does justice to them? What sermon will describe that divine procession, when the holy bodies were escorted on wagons to the fire? Or how, in exchange for the one stolen by the Devil, the jailer was by grace added to their number?[17] And who will tell me about that mother,[18] that worthy root for a martyr, who, when her son had been left behind by the executioner – because he was still alive he wasn't put together with the others on the wagon – and when she saw that act of humanity bestowed by the executioner on the hero, didn't bear the brutality and railed at him because he had separated the athlete from his fellow contestants. She herself was standing next to the martyr, who had already grown numb and motionless because of the frost. She saw that he was affected by the cold and weakness of breath, that he was alive only to the extent that he was able to suffer pain. With a fainting and weakened gaze he looked up to his mother, with a dying and slack hand he beckoned her and consoled her, he encouraged her to endure it in a noble way. When his mother had seen these things, did she experience any motherly feeling? Was she moved to the bottom of her heart, did she tear up her clothing or did she throw herself on her child to warm the withering body with the warmth of her arms? Not at all! Even to mention such a thing is absurd. *No, truly, by the fruit we recognise the tree: a diseased tree cannot produce good fruits* (cf. Matt 7:16–18; Luke 6:43–4). In consequence, since the fruit of martyrdom is good, praise the mother who gave birth to such excellent children because *she is saved through her child bearing*, as the Apostle says (cf. 1 Tim 2:15). For because she offered to God such a fruit, she made amends for the common nature of women. 'You are', she said, 'not my child, not the fruit of my labour during childbirth. Since you have received God, you were born in God. You received *the power to become a child of God* (John 1:12). Run to your Father, so that you are not left behind by your comrades, so that you do not arrive second at the crown, so that you do not render useless my maternal prayer. You will not hurt your mother when you become a crown-bearer, a winner and a trophy-carrier.' After she had said this, she braced herself beyond her strength, or rather, she was braced by the Spirit. She herself lifted her son on the chariot together with the others and with a shining face escorted the athlete.

What happened after that? The saints continued their contest in the air and they also sanctified the fire since, by adding themselves to it, they became fuel for the flame. They also carried over their blessing to the water. By all this the divine words were fulfilled: like the three young men (cf. Dan 3:66) they received both cold and heat together for common praise; the cold they received through the frost, the heat through their burning. Then *they went through fire and water* (cf. Ps 65:12).

(155,20)   But the sermon wishes to skip these well-known things and to have on this occasion a closer look at one of the issues which we were examining a few days ago.[19] When man was expelled from Paradise, a fiery revolving sword received the order to guard the entrance (cf. Gen 3:24). The reason for this forethought of God was to avoid man reaching the tree of life, taking from it and remaining immortal. Surely you remember what the examination was about and probably you also remember what we found out about the problem at hand. But if we were to go through everything from the beginning and to treat the entire homily, my sermon would extend beyond the time at my disposal. The problem was the following: is, because of the revolving sword, Paradise inaccessible, even to the saints? And, are the athletes also excluded from Paradise? What promise is left then for which they engage themselves in the contests for the faith? And will they then have less than the robber to whom the Lord said: *'Today you will be with me in Paradise'* (Luke 23:43)? And yet, the robber didn't approach the cross of his own free will. But, when he was close to his salvation, the quick and clever thief saw the treasure. Taking the opportunity that offered itself, he stole Life, using in a shrewd and clever way his skills as a thief by saying: *'Lord, remember me in Your Kingdom'* (cf. Luke 23:42). Thereupon he was deemed worthy of Paradise. But will the revolving sword then deny the entrance to the saints? The problem entails its solution! For this is the reason that the story showed the sword not always in an upright position facing those who enter, but made it also rotate: when it concerned unworthy people it appeared in front of their face whereas, in the case of worthy people, rotating, it passed behind their back, opening up to them the unhindered entrance to Life. Life, of which those became a part who, by the confidence they exhibited during their contests, passed the flame without being hurt. And may we, having made that passage with confidence, also enter Paradise, having received through their intercession the power for a good confession of our Lord Jesus Christ, to whom be the glory forever and ever. Amen.

Notes

1 Gregory here describes at length some of the devotional practices that took place in the martyrium (see also Introduction). It is striking that in general the tone of the passage is neutral and only at the end becomes a bit critical against the practices described. In general this is in agreement with Gregory's positive attitude towards the martyr cult (Skedros 2001).

2 In the above one sees how Gregory briefly touches upon the rhetorical topoi of the *patris* (fatherland), *ethnos* (a citizen from the whole world), *genos* (his family: he is of noble birth, *eugenos*), *epitèdeumata* (his occupation: he is a soldier). Much of what follows is a long exposition of his praxis, his major achievements: remaining steadfast during several interrogations and his burning of the temple of the Great Mother.

3 This chronological reference to Galerius interrupts the narrative and might therefore have been inserted in the text during the textual transmission. Given the fact that all manuscripts contain the sentence, this must have happened in a very early stage.

4 Gr. *daimôn*.

5 Gr. *andrikèn praxin*; the hero's *praxis* being one of the rhetorical topoi.

6 The cult of the Mother of the Gods was widespread in western Asia Minor in diverse local forms, of which Cybele is the best-known (Mitchell 1993: 19–22). In the province of Pontus the cult is attested in the cities of Amastris and Amisos. Hence it is not surprising that the goddess had a cult also in the metropolis of the province. Together with the Passion of Theodore, this passage is the only source for the cult of the Great Mother in Amasea.

7 Gr. *euparrèsiastos*, *parrèsia* being one of the 'standard qualities' of a martyr.

8 For a similar passage, see the *Life of Theodotus of Ancyra*, 23 (Franchi de' Cavalieri 1901: 75, l.22–3). There the governor Theotecnus offers the martyr the reward of becoming a high priest of Apollo and tries to convince him by stressing the influence and reputation he might acquire with this position. Mitchell 1982 connects this passage with the attempt of Maximinus Daia to install a pagan hierarchy; Nicholson 1994: 4 n. 17 is more careful.

9 Gr. *drosos*. Dew is an image for the blessing and the grace of (the knowledge of) God, used by Gregory in quite a few passages (cf. *Lexicon Gregorianum*, II, 494–5).

10 In this prayer Gregory requests of the martyr intercession with God as well as his effective help in the difficult situation in which the people of Euchaïta find themselves. The situation is dangerous because of the incursions of the Scyths, which are threatening the well-being, maybe even the life, of these people. Beyond the physical danger, however, there is also the religious danger of both paganism and heresies. One senses that Gregory is not only thinking here of the consequences of the barbarian attacks but also of the more general religious situation of the region, where besides a still vital paganism several divergent Christian groups were present (commonly labelled as 'orthodox' – the adherents of the Creed of Nicea, hence also Neo-Nicenes – and several forms of Arianism: homoeans, homoiousians and the Neo-Arians).

11 The words *anamnèsis* (remembrance) and *stèlografia* (inscription on a stone) refer to the Psalms in whose inscriptions these words occur. For *anamnèsis* these are the Psalms 37 and 69, for *stèlografia* the Psalms 15, 55 and 59. *Epilènios* (of a winepress) occurs nowhere *verbatim* in an inscription of a Psalm, but certainly refers to the *huper tôn lènôn* of Psalms 8, 80 and 83.

12 Both rivers mentioned by Gregory still exist. Today they are called the Mismil Irmak and the Kizil Irmak. The second is by far the largest of the two and was, as Gregory says, a famous river in antiquity. In fact the Halys, as it was called then, was the most important river of Asia Minor and is mentioned by many authors (e.g. Strabo, *Geography*, XII, 546–61 and Pliny, *Natural History* 6.6). Cf. Treidler 1967.

13 Presumably the very place were the martyrs had died in Sebaste was within eyesight of the sanctuary where Gregory was delivering this

panegyric. The homilist is stressing the unity of time and place: it was on that very spot on this day (9 March) that the Forty died.

14 Here Gregory signals for the first time to his audience that he is having trouble overcoming their noise. He then tries to resume his homily but does so in vain; barely a minute or so later the noise forces him to abandon his homily. This testimony about noise made by the public is not that exceptional: reactions from the audience in the form of cheering and applauding were rather common, though not every homilist welcomed it (Olivar 1991: 761–879; Kinzig 1997: 652–3). Here, however, we have a rather spectacular case in the sense that the homilist is forced to abandon his homily.

15 The homilist here stresses the unity of the Forty as a group. This theme is present in many texts about them: cf. Vinel 1997. Thereby he reassures his audience that they are partaking of the grace of the relics of the complete group, not of just one of them.

16 Gregory here narrates the well-known story of the rain-miracle that happened under Marcus Aurelius to the Legio XII Fulminata. This legion was stationed in Melitene, in the neighbourhood of Sebaste. Gregory thus weaves into his homily a tale belonging to regional history that might have been very dear to his audience. Yet, there is more to it than this. The story has been transmitted to us in several sources, both Christian and non-Christian, each ascribing the miracle to (resp. Christian and non-Christian) divine intervention. Among the sources: Tertullian, *Apology* 5; Eusebius, HE 5.4.3–5.7; Dio Cassius, *Roman History* LXX, 8.1–10.5; *Historia Augusta, Life of Marcus Aurelius* 24, 4. The scene is also depicted on the column of Marcus Aurelius. By narrating the story and connecting it to that of the Forty, Gregory is also joining in the battle to have this historical event attributed to an intervention of the God of the Christians. See Helgeland 1979: 766–73; Fowden 1987 and Sage 1987.

17 After one of the Forty had apostatised, he was replaced by the jailer who, impressed by the Forty's steadfastness and courage, joined them in their martyrdom. This story is a recurring element in the tradition surrounding the Forty. It is already present in the Passio, in Basil, and Gregory himself narrates it in full in his *Second Homily on the Forty*.

18 The story about the mother of one of the Forty is also a recurring element in texts about the Forty. Modelled after the mother of the Maccabees, she is already present in the Passio of the Forty as well as in Basil's panegyric.

19 An example of the homilist's freedom to choose or change his subject (cf. Introduction). At the same time one sees a connection with the subject of the panegyric: when, as a literal reading of Gen 3:24 seems to suggest, nobody can pass the angel guarding the gate to Paradise, how will the saints then be able to enter? After all, given the robber's fortune, the saints surely must have a way into Paradise. What was ultimately at stake here was not only the saints' fortune but that of all Christians, as the last lines of the homily make clear. Gregory comes up with a solution very similar

to the one brought forward by his brother Basil in his *Exhortation to Baptism* 2 (PG 31, 428C, 1–10). At the same time he touches in his exegesis upon several themes that occur often in the context of the late antique exegesis of Gen 3:24, most notably the robber from Luke 23 and the fiery revolving sword as an impediment to entering Paradise. Cf. Alexandre 1986.

III

JOHN CHRYSOSTOM

GENERAL INTRODUCTION

John's life and contribution

John's reputation as one of the greatest preachers of all time, in combination with the notoriety that his brief tenure as bishop of the eastern imperial capital in the early fifth century attracted, has ensured that we are relatively well informed about his life.[1] For similar reasons an unusually large number of his works survive (sixteen treatises; about 820 homilies; 245 letters; five commentaries and various fragments).[2] These works span some twenty-eight years (*c.* AD 378–406: the period from just prior to his ordination as deacon to the third year of his exile),[3] and were composed variously in Antioch, Constantinople and locations in Cappadocia and Armenia. The reason for the diversity of locations becomes clear when we review the circumstances of his life.

In *c.* AD 349, John was born at Antioch into a middle class Christian family of some means.[4] At eighteen he graduated from advanced rhetorical training, probably under Libanius, having been educated with the expectation that, like his father, he would take up a career in the civil service. In the following year he sought baptism by Meletius (bishop of one of the two pro-Nicene communities at Antioch), spending three years in his service, while also beginning attendance at the ascetic school of Carterius and Diodore (later bishop of Tarsus).[5] In *c.* 371 John first entered the ranks of the clergy as lector,[6] shortly afterwards leaving Antioch to further his ascetic education in the nearby mountains. He spent four years there under the tutelage of an elderly Syrian, spending a further two years in a cave alone, where he adopted extreme ascetic practices (Palladius, *Dial.* 5). At the end of six years, he returned to Antioch (this was around the same time that Meletius returned to the city from exile), where he resumed his duties as lector. Some two years later (c.381) he was ordained deacon by Meletius, who died shortly thereafter. It is during the five years he spent in this position that he appears to have written many of his treatises.[7] In 386 he was ordained presbyter by Meletius' successor, Flavian. For the next eleven to twelve years he preached a large number of sermons and seems to have worked on editing some into commentaries. During this time it appears that he was also groomed as Flavian's successor and took on some of that bishop's duties.[8]

In 397 Nectarius, the bishop of Constantinople, died. After some jockeying John was chosen as his replacement and formally took up office in that city early in 398. He served in that position for almost six years, during which relations with the imperial palace, the senatorial élite, the local clergy and the city's monks deteriorated, in contrast to his general popularity, which remained high. Here too he preached as often as possible and a range of homilies (and perhaps one or two treatises) can be located in this period.[9] In late 403 he was exiled by the emperor and almost immediately recalled. By February 404 he was banned from the churches of Constantinople and on 20 June 404 was again sent into exile. He was taken under military escort through Cappadocia to Armenia and during the next few years was shifted several times. He wrote two treatises and numerous letters during this period, hoping that his supporters and their allies would secure his return to the throne of Constantinople. On 14 September 407 he died while being escorted to a more remote destination across the Black Sea.

John's contribution is significant on a number of fronts. Although generally regarded as a theological lightweight in comparison to Gregory of Nyssa, Gregory of Nazianze and Basil of Caesarea, it has recently been argued that John is more than just a moral theologian and did indeed have a developed theological proposition that permeates and informs all of his work – the notion of divine accommodation or *sunkatabasis* (Rylaarsdam 1999). Equally recently the diversity and complexity of John's exegesis of the apostle Paul and the skilful accommodation to and exploitation of rhetorical norms in achieving this have been demonstrated (Mitchell 2000). A detailed description of his theology of martydom has also been put forward (Christo 1997). On the political front, John's well-developed philosophy of the relationship between secular and divine law and therefore the respective roles of emperor and bishop has just been brought to light (Stephens 2001). At the same time there is no doubt that his contribution as a preacher was outstanding and that he was also deeply devoted to the spiritual and physical well-being of those in his care (Mayer and Allen 2000). His treatises on education, the priesthood and on various aspects of the ascetic life have also been influential.

The martyr cult at Antioch and Constantinople

The divergent histories and topographies of the two cities in which John worked and lived ensured that the development of the martyr cult at the two locations differed markedly.[10] Antioch lay on a plain some miles inland from the east Mediterranean coast, bounded by mountains on one side and the river Orontes on the other; Constantinople was a coastal city, surrounded by water on three sides. The city life of Antioch was intimately connected with that of its elevated suburb, Daphne; the city of Constantinople proper formed a conurbation with the city of Chalcedon, on the opposite shore of the Bosphorus, and the suburbs of Galata and Sykae to the north of the waters of the Golden Horn. At Antioch the Christian community dated back to the time of the apostles; at Constantinople, although a small Christian community appears to have existed prior to the settlement of Constantine, Christianity only became prominent in the second quarter of the fourth century after Constantine developed the city as the eastern imperial capital. Consequently, at Antioch the martyrs who had died there over the third and fourth centuries lay buried locally in the countryside and in the cemeteries which lay to the south of the city next to the road to Daphne and to the west across the Orontes near the Romanesian gate. At Constantinople a much smaller number of martyrs were buried locally. Instead, Constantine's successors instigated a policy of importing the relics of martyrs from elsewhere in order to improve the city's status in this regard.[11] As bishop, John was himself active in acquiring relics and on at least two occasions presided over the solemn reception of such remains.[12] Another important distinction between the cult as experienced at these two cities is that at Antioch the traditional laws prohibiting the internment of human remains within the city walls continued to be observed throughout the fourth century, with the result that all of the martyria were situated in the suburbs or countryside and required those celebrating the festival to exit the city in order to hold a commemorative service at the martyr's tomb. The Church of the Maccabees, built in the Jewish quarter in the 380s, did not contravene this rule since, although it bore the name of the martyrs, it did not contain any actual remains.[13] In Constantinople Constantine's desire to locate his own tomb within the walls at the end of the major thoroughfare that led to the north-west saw the relics of imported apostles laid to rest in the church adjacent to his mausoleum, so that there some of the martyr festivals were also celebrated inside the city.[14]

The cult itself, on the other hand, followed the same basic pattern in both cities. The feast day was usually observed by the conducting of a stational service in the martyrium which contained the tomb of the martyr. In order to reach the martyrium in the first instance, the participants gathered at a predesignated point in the city and moved solemnly in procession through the streets to the martyrium. At the head of the procession was the bishop (or his delegate) and at times the most senior representative of secular authority available (e.g. the governor or emperor). Such processions were usually on foot and were often accompanied by the singing of the appropriate verses of a psalm. The crowds that attended these festivals tended to be drawn from all strata of society and there was a noticeable increase in atten-dance on such occasions (Mayer 1999, 2000b). At the martyrium itself the service included at least one, sometimes several homilies, in which the death and acts of the martyr were often detailed. In John's hands the martyr's story was rarely an end in itself, but rather an opportunity for moral instruction. In addition to the procession and homily, Scripture readings, a night-long vigil and celebration of the eucharist could all be incorporated (Mayer and Allen 2000: 20). On the days of the year other than that of the martyr's commemoration, private devotion was an important feature of the cult. Christians were urged to walk to the martyrium, to visit the tomb, to weep over the coffin, to annoint themselves with oil that had touched the holy remains, and to pray, using the martyr as their advocate.[15]

By virtue both of the greater length of John's tenure as presbyter and the greater variety of martyrs in the Antiochene festal calendar the majority of the martyr homilies of this preacher date from the period during which he was a presbyter at Antioch. In addition to the homilies on Julian, Babylas, Pelagia and on the martyrs in general, translated here, there survive from those years homilies on the Maccabees; Ignatius; Eustathius; the Antiochene virgins Domnina, Bernike and Prosdoke; Romanus; Lucian; Drosis; Barlaam; the sol-diers Juventinus and Maximinus; certain Egyptians; and the former

bishops of Antioch Philogonius and Meletius (in John's broad defin-
ition of the term, also martyrs; Christo 1997: 156–78). There also
exist two further homilies on martyrs in general.[16] From the period
of his episcopate there survive four homilies delivered on occasions
that cannot be identified,[17] in addition to one preached on the second
day of the celebration that occurred when relics of St Phocas were
introduced to Constantinople from Pontus.[18]

TEXTS

A homily on the Holy Martyrs

Introduction

Delivered at Antioch, since in the homily John makes it clear that
he is not the bishop of the city, *On the Holy Martyrs* is not strictly
speaking a martyr homily, in that it was not delivered as part of a
martyr's festival, although the topic of the value of the martyrs as
silent, yet eloquent preachers takes up a large part of the homily.
While it is delivered on the day of a martyrs' festival, the festival in
question is being celebrated in the rural area outside of Antioch,
rather than in the city itself. Thus the homily is likely to have been
preached at an ordinary service that took place in either the Old
Church (the Palaia) or the Great Church within the walls of Antioch,
rather than in one of the suburban martyria. It was delivered on the
day following the local festival of the Maccabees which, according
to the Syrian martyrology, was celebrated at Antioch on 1 August
(Wright 1866: 428).[19] There is no direct indication within the
homily as to the year to which it might belong, although the prob-
ability that it was delivered on a regular day of worship may allow
us to narrow the options. If we assume that the days of the week at
Antioch on which there regularly occurred a service in which a
homily was preached were Saturday and Sunday, and possibly also
Friday as well (van de Paverd 1970: 68), then the years 387–9 and
392–5, in which 2 August fell on other days of the week, can be
eliminated. As a result the homily can be dated to 2 August in either
386, 390–1 or 396–7.

The appropriation of the Maccabees as 'Christian' martyrs is of
particular relevance to the situation at Antioch, where there was a
prominent Jewish community with synagogues in the city quarter

known as the Kerateion and in the suburb of Daphne. Daphne was also the site of a Jewish shrine, the Cave of Matrona, which most probably contained relics of the mother of the Macabees, if not also her sons, and which was widely used for incubation by the inhabitants of Antioch, Christians and Jews alike, because of the relics' alleged healing properties (Vinson 1994: 183–4). Vinson's careful argument regarding the genesis of the Christian cult of the Maccabees at Antioch in the reign of Julian is of point here. Not only does she argue convincingly that the cult of the Maccabees was a powerful and 'highly visible symbol of the Jewish presence in Antioch' (Vinson 1994: 186–7), a presence aligned with Arian interests in the city, but she points out that the Christian Church of the Maccabees built in the Kerateion during the reign of Theodosius I must have been established in that region precisely as a means of forcing the distinction between the Christian and Jewish forms of the cult (Vinson 1994: 184–9). This church, while named for and associated with the Maccabees was not a martyrium in the same sense as other such buildings in the suburbs of Antioch, since it did not contain relics of the martyrs (which remained at Matrona, the Jewish locus of the cult). If, as John suggests in *On the Holy Martyrs*, the rural visitors on the previous day poured into the city to celebrate the Christian festival in the Church of the Maccabees in the Kerateion, then we have a rare example at Antioch of a martyr festival celebrated at a church located within the city walls. Extending the focus on martyrdom from that festival into the sermon preached at an ordinary worship service held in another intramural church on the next day would thus not have seemed unnatural to his audience.

Whereas on the previous day the audience was clearly swelled by the presence of visitors from the rural areas surrounding Antioch, it seems likely that the attendance had been reduced to more normal numbers by the next day. Certainly the size of the audience does not appear to have been diminished because of the martyr festival elsewhere, since John chides the audience for not reciprocating by flowing out of the city in crowds to attend it. This suggests that in general attendances at urban festivals were far greater than those at rural ones. Of significance in terms of the structure of the audience on each of the two days is John's comment regarding the speech of the rural visitors. It is different from that of the residents of Antioch, suggesting that he had a mixed audience of Syriac and Greek speakers on the preceding day, while on the present day the

audience is back to its Greek-speaking majority. Also of remark
is the bishop Flavian's absence on the present occasion. That he is
obliged to preside over rural as well as urban martyr festivals in
person indicates some of the extent of the jurisdiction of the bishop
of Antioch at this time, as well as the status of martyr festivals in
Syria in general. Conjointly if, as John states, at that time a greater
number of martyrs were buried at locations in the countryside than
in the suburbs of the city, and if the bishop was obliged to preside
over the feast day of each one, at certain times of year Flavian's
absences must have been frequent, while the interesting question
arises of what happened when there occurred a clash between an
urban and a rural festival. John's comments may also suggest that
there was a higher level of devotion to the martyrs in the countryside, given the absence of churches and of regular worship services
as an alternative focus.

This homily tells us little about the lives of particular individuals, since its focus is upon the role of the martyrs after death as an
encouragement to virtue and as witnesses to the ephemeral nature
of the sufferings in this life. The importance of their physical
presence as represented by their tombs is also highlighted, as is the
powerful effect of the tomb upon the visitor's conscience and behaviour – an effect more immediate and lasting, John suggests, than his
numerous sermons calling upon the listener to repent and moderate
their life.

Translated from the edition by B. de Montfaucon; PG 50, 645–54.

Text

1.   Yesterday was a martyrs' day, yet today too is a martyrs' day.
If only we were always celebrating a martyrs' day! For, if those
who are mad about the theatre and who have their eyes glued to
the clash of horses never get sick of those unnatural spectacles, so
much more should we be insatiable for the festivals of the saints.
There there is devilish pageantry; here, Christian festivity. There
demons leap around; here angels dance. There there is loss of souls;
here, salvation for all who are gathered. Yes, but do those spectacles contain some pleasure? Yet not as much as these. I mean,
what sort of pleasure is there in seeing horses simply running for
no good reason? Here you see not a pair of senseless animals but
countless martyrs' chariots, and God presiding over those chariots and driving along the road to heaven. For on the point that

the saints' souls are God's chariot, hear the prophet's words: *'God's chariot is ten thousandfold, thousands in abundance'* (Ps 67:18). For God has freely granted our nature too what he gifted to the powers above. He sits above the cherubim, just as the Psalm says: *'He ascended on the cherubim, and flew'* (Ps 17:11);[20] and again: *'{You} who sit above the cherubim, and view the abyss'* (Dan 3:55). On another occasion he gave this gift to us as well: above them he sits; in us he dwells. *For I shall dwell and walk among you* (cf. 2 Cor 6:16; Lev 26:12). They became a chariot; let us become a shrine. Did you see the relatedness of the honour? Did you see how he made peace between what is above and below (cf. Col 1:20)? That's why we are no different from the angels, if we are willing.

But, as I began by saying, yesterday was a martyrs' day, and today is a martyrs' day – not celebrating the ones in our vicinity, but those in the countryside. Rather, they too are in our vicinity. For, although city and countryside are distinct from one another in day-to-day matters, they share and are one in the reckoning of piety.[21] Please don't look at their alien speech but at their philosophical disposition. For what use is common speech when the cast of mind is poles apart? Conversely, what harm is there in different speech when the essentials of faith are in accord? According to this rationale, countryside is of no lesser value than city, for they bear equal honour in the chief of blessings. For that reason our Lord Jesus Christ didn't spend his time in the cities, while he left the country areas empty and deserted, but would journey through cities and villages, declaring the gospel and healing every illness and every infirmity. Our common shepherd and teacher has copied this, too, and left us and run off to them. Rather, in going off to them he hasn't left us, for he has gone off to our brothers and sisters. Indeed, just as the whole countryside poured into the city when the festival of the Maccabees was under celebration, so on this present occasion the whole city should have gone off to them while the festival of the martyrs there is under way. God planted martyrs not just in cities, but also in the countryside itself – indeed, more in the countryside than in the city – precisely so that on the basis of the festivals we might have a compelling motive for mixing with one another. I mean, God has given more abundant honour to the inferior, because that's the weaker part (cf. 1 Cor 12:23), which is why it has enjoyed greater attention. For while those who inhabit the cities enjoy constant preaching, those who live in rural society don't share in such great abundance.

Compensating for the poverty of preachers in the wealth of martyrs, God therefore organised a greater number of martyrs to be buried among them. Country people don't hear incessant preachers' tongues, but rather a martyrs' voice that speaks to them from the tomb and is louder in volume. To teach you that, even when silent, martyrs are louder in volume than we when we speak, when time after time many have preached to many others on the topic of virtue, they have achieved nothing; yet others, though silent, have achieved major successes through the splendour of their life. Consequently the martyrs have effected this to a greater degree, uttering voice not with their tongue, but with their deeds – a voice far superior to that which comes from the mouth. Through it they preach to humankind's whole nature, speaking the following words: 'Look at us, at what tortures we've suffered. For what did we suffer, when we were condemned to death and found eternal life? We were held worthy of shedding our bodies for Christ's sake. Yet if at this point we hadn't abandoned them for Christ's sake, a little later, even if we didn't want to, we would have divorced them from temporary life. Even if they (sc. our bodies) had continued on and not achieved martyrdom, death, shared as it is by nature, would have attacked and destroyed them. And so we don't cease giving thanks to God, in that for the salvation of our souls he held us worthy of being content with death, which is utterly obligatory, and received from us in the form of a gift and with the greatest honour that which is necessarily obligatory. Yes, the tortures are burdensome and unpleasant, but they last a brief flash of time, while the relief from them lasts throughout the aeons of eternity. Rather the tortures aren't burdensome for even a brief flash of time for those whose gaze is fixed on future things and whose eyes are glued to the President of the games.[22] After all, blessed Stephen too, when he saw Christ with the eyes of faith, for that reason didn't see the showers of stones, but counted up the prizes and crowns instead of them. Therefore you too transfer your eye from the present to the future and you'll catch not even a brief sensation of the tortures.'

2.   The martyrs say these things and much more and are far more persuasive than we are. If I say that torture is associated with nothing burdensome, I'm not convincing when I say it. After all, there's nothing irksome in offering philosophy like this in theory. But, when the martyrs give voice through their actions, no one can contradict them. Indeed it's the same as occurs inside the public

baths, when the pool of hot water is bubbling away, and no one is confident about getting in. For as long as the people sitting on the edge encourage each other with words, they rather convince no one. Yet when just one of them either sticks in a hand, or lowers a foot and then confidently dips in their entire body, in silence it is they who persuade those sitting up above to venture into the pool rather than the people who had a lot to say. It's the same way too with the martyrs. After all, in this case the fire lies in front of them instead of the pool of water. And so, even if the people standing around outside offer countless words of advice, they're not very convincing. Yet, when one of the martyrs lowers down not just a foot or a hand, but dips in their entire body, through their action they provide a proof more powerful than any counsel or advice, and banish the fear of those surrounding them.

Did you see how, even in their silence, the martyrs' voice is more powerful? That's why God left us their bodies. That's why even now they haven't as yet risen from the dead, though their victory was long ago. Rather, although they endured their trials such a long time ago, because of you and your need they haven't yet attained resurrection, so that, through thinking about that athlete, you, too, might be aroused to the same race. My point is that they receive no harm from the delay, whereas you derive considerable benefit from the stratagem. For they'll receive [their due] afterwards, even if they aren't receiving it now. But if God snatched them out of our midst now, we'd be deprived of much comfort and consolation. For truly substantial comfort and consolation comes to all human beings from these saints' tombs. You yourselves are witnesses to what I've said. At least, time after time, when we've threatened, flattered, terrified, or urged you on, you haven't taken on as much enthusiasm for prayer nor been stirred up. Yet when you've gone off to a martyrium without anyone prompting and have just looked at the tomb of the saints,[23] you've poured out copious fountains of tears and become enthusiastic in your prayers. And yet the martyr lies there voiceless in profound silence. What is it, then, that pricks your conscience and causes the torrents of tears to well up as from a spring? The image of the martyr itself and the memory of all their good deeds. For when the poor see others who are rich and in high office escorted by bodyguards, enjoying considerable honour in the emperor's circle, they lament bitterly as a result of learning their own poverty more accurately in the face of the prosperity of others. In

the same way we too weep and moan when we recall the bold
speech that the martyrs have with God, the King of all, and their
radiance and glory, and when we recall our own sins, recognising
our own poverty more accurately from their prosperity, and
understanding by how far we fall short of them. It's this that
causes our tears. It's for this reason that God left us their bodies
here, so that, whenever the crowd of affairs and multitude of day-
to-day worries spreads a thick darkness over our mind – whether
as a result of private or public concerns (the latter kind are
numerous), we might leave our house, exit the city, say a firm
farewell to these confusions and go off to a martyrium, enjoy that
spiritual breath of fresh air, forget our substantial preoccupation,
luxuriate in the peace and quiet, be in the company of the saints,
call on the President of the games for the benefit of our salvation,
pour out much supplication and, when we have shed the weight
from our conscience through all of these actions, go back home
with considerable refreshment.

Martyrs' coffins are nothing else but safe harbours and fountains
of spiritual streams and inexhaustible warehouses of abundance
that are never embarrassed. Indeed, just as harbours render safe
the ships they receive swamped by numerous waves, so too do the
martyrs' coffins render our souls quite calm and safe when they
receive them swamped by day-to-day affairs. And just as the fountains of cold streams revive bodies that are worn out and burning
up with fever, so too in fact do these coffins cool souls inflamed
by inappropriate passions. From sight alone they quench inappropriate desire and consuming envy and seething rage – in fact,
anything else of the sort that might be annoying – and are better
than warehouses of considerable abundance. For while monetary
treasures provide numerous dangers for those who discover them
and, when divided into many portions, decrease as a result of the
distribution, here it's nothing like that. Rather, the discovery is
risk-free, while the division causes no diminution – the complete
opposite of perceivable treasures. For when they've been frittered
away, as I said before, those get smaller, while these demonstrate their inherent abundance in particular when they've been
divided into numerous portions. For such is the nature of spiritual matters. They increase with distribution and multiply with
division. Meadows, that provide roses and violets for people to
look at, aren't as delightful as martyrs' tombs, that provide an
imperishable and indissoluble pleasure for the viewers' souls.

3.   So then, let's cling onto their coffins with faith! Let's set our minds on fire! Let's stir up laments! We've committed many wrongs and our sins are great. On that account we are in need of a great deal of treatment and of rigorous confession. The holy martyrs poured out their blood; let your eyes pour out tears. Indeed, tears have the power to quench sins' fire. The martyrs had their ribs crushed. They saw executioners standing around. Do this to your conscience too. Seat your reason as a judge on the throne of your impartial mind, lead all the sins you've committed into the public eye, position fearsome points of logic against your misdeeds, punish the inappropriate desires from which your sins arose, let them be crushed with considerable force.

If we practise judging ourselves in this way, we'll also escape that terrifying tribunal. For, regarding the point that, if a person judges themself now and demands of themself a precise account of their sins, they won't suffer punishment in the future, listen to Paul, who says: '*If we kept on judging ourselves, we wouldn't be judged by the Lord*' (1 Cor 11:31). For he said the following when he was criticising those who partake of the mysteries unworthily: '*The person who eats and drinks unworthily will be answerable for the body and blood of the Lord*' (1 Cor 11:27). What he means is like this. 'Just like those who crucified Jesus', he says, 'so too those who partake of the mysteries unworthily will suffer punishment.' Don't let anyone condemn the extreme nature of the statement. The Master's body is an imperial robe. The person who rips apart the imperial purple and the person who dirties it with unclean hands cause insult to the same degree. For that reason they receive much the same punishment too. It's the same in the case of Christ's body. While the Jews ripped it apart with nails on the cross, you, who live in sin, [dirty it] with your unclean tongue and mind. It's for that reason that Paul threatened you with the same punishment and added the comment: '*Because of this many among you are feeble and sick, and a fair number are asleep*' (1 Cor 11:30). Then, after demonstrating that those who demand of themselves an account of their sins here, who judge their misdeeds and no longer fall into the same [mistakes], will be able to snatch themselves away from that terrifying and inexorable vote to come, he added the following words: '*If we kept on judging ourselves, we wouldn't be judged. But now, when we are judged by the Lord we are trained, so that we might not be condemned along with the world*' (1 Cor 11: 31–2).

So then, let's crush our mind and harshly condemn those of our thoughts that are undisciplined. Let's wipe away our stains with our tears. The fruit of these laments is great, a great comfort and consolation. I say this because in the same way that the punishment for laughter and mirth is great, so too constant lamenting produces comfort. For scripture says: *Blessed are those who mourn, for they shall be comforted* (Matt 5:4); *Woe to those who laugh, for those same people shall weep* (Luke 6:25). It's for this reason that, even though he was conscious of no sin in himself, Paul spent the whole time in tears and wailing. Who says this? That blessed man himself. *'For three years, night and day'*, he says, *'I haven't stopped admonishing each and every one of you with tears'* (Acts 20:31). He [did it] for three years, we for scarcely a single month! He [did it] night and day, he [did it] for the sake of others' sins, we scarcely for the sake of our own misdeeds! He [did it] conscious of nothing in himself, we scarcely because of our own heavy conscience! For what reason does he weep? Why doesn't he just teach and advise, but adds tears as well? A loving father, who has an only-born child who has fallen ill and won't let the doctors' drugs near it but instead shoves them away, sits next to [the child] and offers flattery, kisses and embraces it, wanting by the extremity of the care to induce and persuade [the child] to receive the correction from the treatment. In a similar fashion Paul too, loving believers all over the world like an only-born son and seeing many falling into evil and an incurable illness of the soul and then not accepting the accusation readily nor the correction from the criticism, but leaping away, restrained them with tears so that, when they saw him weeping and lamenting and were moved at the sight itself, they might endure the medical help and, shedding their illness, return once again to good health. For that reason he constantly wept in admonishment.

If Paul expended so much thought on the sins of others, how much willingness should we direct toward the correction of our own? After all, in terms of being beneficial the power of grief directed towards God is considerable. When Isaiah was discoursing on this topic, or rather God through Isaiah, he expressed it in the following way: *'Because of {their} sin, I gave them a little grief'* (Isa 57:17). 'I didn't inflict a punishment', he says, 'commensurate with the misdeed.' In the case of good works, God exceeds due measure with his rewards, yet because of his love for human beings, in the case of sins often when he convicts he inflicts a brief punishment for the misdeeds. So, hinting at [this truth] in this instance, he said: *'Because of {their} sin, I gave them a little grief, and I saw that they were grieved and walking around in a gloomy state, and I healed their paths'* (Isa 57:17–18).

4.   Do you see how the benefit of repentence is extremely swift and substantial? 'After I punished the person a little on account of their sins', he says, 'when I saw them becoming downcast and gloomy I remitted even the small penalty itself.' Indeed, God is primed in this way for becoming reconciled with us and looks only for a scanty pretext. Let's therefore provide him with a stimulus for his love for us and both attempt to keep ourselves clean of sins and, if we're ever tripped up, quickly stand upright and with considerable severity mourn what we've done wrong, so that we might attain the favours associated with God. My point is that, if the person reversed God's attitude when they were grieved and walked around in a gloomy state, what won't the person achieve who applies tears as well and calls on him with considerable persistence? I know that your mind is now on fire. Even so, let's do this so that, when we leave and go outside, we don't let this ardour grow cold, but keep it retained within ourselves. The countryside of your mind is fertile. It receives the seeds and immediately gives forth ears of grain. It requires neither delay nor time. Yet I fear your enemy.

The Devil stands outside the church. For he doesn't dare enter this sacred sheepfold. I mean that where there's Christ's flock, no wolf shows itself. Rather it stands outside through fear of the shepherd. Whenever we go away from here let's not immediately surrender ourselves to inappropriate company or senseless conversations and fruitless pastimes. Rather, while we retain in our memory what was said, let's run home and each sit with our wife and children and accurately rehearse what was said. On the other hand, if you don't want to go home, gather around you the friends who shared in the instruction and sit together in private. Each offer from your own resources as much as you were able to preserve and reconstruct the sermon for a second time, so that you didn't gather here in vain. For the injunctions are God's lamp. *For the law's command is a lamp and a light and a life and an indictment and an education* (Prov 6:23). The person who lights the lamp doesn't stop at the marketplace but runs home, so that they might neither see the fire put out by a blast of wind nor waste the flame by hanging around for a long time. Let's do the same too. The Holy

Spirit has lit in us his own preaching. When we go out, then, and are full of the instruction, whether we see a friend, a relative, a household member, or any other sort of person coming towards us, let's slip past, so that the sermon's fire isn't put out in the meantime, while we're talking to them about silly and pointless things, but rather flourishes in our mind as if in a house, and lights up the whole interior, burning on the peak of our intellect as if on a lampstand. After all, it's quite absurd never to endure seeing the house in the evening without a lamp or light, but to put up with seeing the soul devoid of preaching. It's from this cause that the majority of our sins arise, namely that we don't swiftly light a lamp for our soul. It's from this cause that we stumble every day. It's from this cause that numerous thoughts lie randomly and as they occur in our mind, because when we receive the instruction from divine words, before we've even crossed the threshold of the church, we immediately throw it away, and walk accompanied by thick gloom as a result of putting out the light.

Well, if this is what was happening before this point, don't let it happen any longer. Instead, let's constantly have the lamp burning in our mind and beautify our soul rather than our house. For the one stays here [on earth], while we depart from here taking the other. For that reason we should expend even more care on it. But, as it is, there are some who are in such a pitiful state that they decorate their houses here from top to bottom with gold roofs and variegated tiles and coloured paintings and the splendour of columns and all the rest. But they overlook their mind, which in condition is more worthless than any empty inn, brimming with filth, smoke and appalling odour, an indescribable emptiness. The cause of all these deficiencies is the fact that the lamp of preaching doesn't burn for us continually. For this reason what is essential is neglected, while what is worthless enjoys considerable dedication. These words of mine are addressed not just to rich people, but also to the poor. I say this because they too often decorate their own house in so far as they can, but overlook their neglected mind. For this reason I address my sermon to both groups and admonish and advise them to take little account of things in the present life and bend all of their efforts towards the pursuit of spiritual and essential matters. Let the poor person see the widow who paid the two obols (cf. Luke 21:1–4), and not consider their poverty an impediment to doing works of charity and benefaction. Let the rich person reflect on Job and, just as that man acquired all of his possessions not for himself but for the poor, be like that too. I say this because the reason that he nobly endured their removal is because he practised their alienation even before the Devil's test.

You too, therefore, despise the money you have now, so that, if ever it goes away, you won't grieve. Spend it as needed whenever you can, so that, whenever it's taken away, you'll have double the benefit – both the profit stored up for you as a result of excellent spending and the philosophy inherent in despising it that will be beneficial for the time of its loss. My point is that 'money' is so named that we might use it as needed,[24] not so that we might bury it away. 'Possessions' are so called that we might possess them and not become their possessions. You are in control of a considerable amount of money. Don't, then, be a slave to that of which God made you master. You're not a slave to it when you spend it as needed, but don't bury it away. Nothing is as unstable as wealth. Nothing is so readily subject to change as abundance. So, since the possession of it is insecure and it often flies away from us more swiftly than any bird, and leaps away more thanklessly than any runaway slave, let's use it as needed for the time that we're its masters, so that we might render the benefits from the insecure money secure and inherit the treasure stored up in heaven. May we all achieve it by the grace and love for humankind of our Lord Jesus Christ, through whom and with whom be glory to the Father, together with the Holy Spirit, now and always, forever and ever. Amen.

A homily on Julian the Martyr

Introduction

Although it is clear that the homily was delivered at Antioch, since John explicitly mentions the city's famous suburb, Daphne, it is impossible to determine either the day of the year or the year itself in which it was preached. The suggestion that the audience forsake the attractions of Daphne for a picnic near the tomb of the martyr under the fig trees and grape vines narrows the time of year to mid to late spring or summer, since in autumn and winter the trees and vines would have been bare and the weather unsuitable for an outdoor meal. Early spring is unlikely also, since the leaves would not have sprouted sufficiently to provide the pleasant shade implied. The various calendars and martyrologies are of little help in narrowing the date, since they provide a variety of possibilities.[25] It is also pertinent to note that the Syrian martyrology, the closest in date and location, does not mention the festival.[26]

The one hope of narrowing the date of the homily to a month and year lies with identification of the pagan festival mentioned in the latter part of the homily. There it is said that the habit of attending the festival is long-standing, that it takes place at Daphne, that shared meals are involved and that a characteristic feature is troupes of male performers who sing earthy songs and utter suggestive words. While it is possible that a number of different festivals were staged at Daphne in view of its temples to Zeus and Apollo, its sacred grove of cypresses and other old and significant Graeco-Roman religious sites, there is one that the collective evidence associates in particular with male dancers who perform mimes and with dinner parties. That festival is the Maiuma, which fell at certain intervals in May. The nature of the evidence is such that the accurate cataloguing of the features of this festival is difficult, but we do know that it was celebrated in Antioch at Daphne (Libanius, *Or.* 41.16), that the rate of dinner parties increased dramatically at Antioch in May in the years of the festival (Julian, *Misopogon* 362D), and that it was associated with licentious theatrical spectacles (*Cod. Theod.* XV.6).[27] That the Maiuma was held in May neatly fits the indicators of the time of year contained within the homily. If we accept this identification, which is by no means certain, then the lifting of a ban on the Maiuma on 25 April 396 and reimposition of the ban on 2 October 399 in the legislation just mentioned might be thought to narrow down the year of the homily to 396/7. Unfortunately such legislation was clearly not always enforced or observed since the supposed final ban on a similar festival by the emperor Anastasius in 501 appears not to have been effective and it can be argued that a manifestation of that festival was observed at Antioch during the patriarchate of Severus (512–18) (Greatrex and Watt 1999: 15–21). In any case it may well be that the festival in question is not the Maiuma, but one with similar features that we have yet to identify.

Of equal interest is the information about the festival of St Julian that the homily contains. The relics of the martyr, who had been the bishop of a town in Cilicia, were evidently buried near Antioch, since John makes it clear that he is preaching in the vicinity of the coffin, talks of the benefit of seeing the relics, of their ability to bring about healing and perform other miracles, and suggests that he and the audience parade them in front of the city gate on the road leading to Daphne on the following day. How and when the remains of a Cilician bishop who was drowned at sea found their way to Antioch is unknown, but the festival seems to have settled comfortably into the Antiochene calendar by the time that this homily was preached. John himself suggests that the remains were acquired early not long after Julian was martyred. It is interesting that the annual celebration of the martyrdom of St Julian appears to have lasted for two days – that is, not just the day on which the present homily was delivered and its eve, but also on the day following. In no other of John's Antiochene martyr homilies do we observe such information. Rather, two-day celebrations are otherwise confined in his corpus to the festivities associated with remains newly translated to Constantinople.[28] The proposal to parade Julian's coffin on the second day may suggest that the coffin was also conveyed in a procession leading to the church where the remains normally resided and at which the service in which today's homily was preached was held, a practice hinted at in the homily preached on the festival of St Drosis.[29] A church complex dedicated to Julian, situated at a distance of three miles from Antioch, is documented by Procopius in the sixth century (*De bello Persico* 2.10.7–8), and also receives mention in the *Life of St Pelagia* as the site where a group of bishops gathered for a local synod were housed (*Vita s. Pelagiae* 3). Julian is also mentioned specifically, along with Babylas and the Maccabees, as one of the attractions that drew pilgrims to Antioch in the sixth century (*Antonini placentini itinerarium* 47). That Julian had already achieved some fame locally and that the martyrium was well established by the late fourth century is indicated by Theodoret, who records that the ascetics Theodosius, Aphrahat and Macedonius were all buried there alongside the martyr (*Hist. religiosa* 10.8, 13.19).

The desire of these holy men to be buried near a martyr of some reputation highlights the parallels between martyrdom and asceticism that are explicitly brought to the fore in the next homily (*On the Martyr Babylas*). In the present homily we see several classic features of hagiobiography: the martyr as imitator of Christ; focus on the trial, torture and eventual death of the martyr; the martyr's body as anathema to demons after death and as a visual prompt towards virtue.

Translated from the edition by B. de Montfaucon; PG 50, 665–76.

Text

1. If on earth the honours for the martyrs are like these, what sort of crowns are woven for their holy heads in heaven after they depart here? If the glory is so great before the resurrection [of the dead], how great will the splendour be after the resurrection? If they enjoy so much care and attention[30] from their fellow servants, how much approval will they meet with from their Master? If we, who are wicked, know so to honour and be amazed at those of our fellow servants who were successful when they competed for Christ's sake, how much more will our heavenly Father give countless blessings to those who have laboured on his own behalf? After all, he's a generous giver and loves humankind. Yet it's not for just this reason that great honours await them, but because he is also in their debt. The martyrs weren't butchered for our sake and yet we rush together to honour them. If we, for whose sake they weren't butchered, rush together, what won't Christ do, for whose sake they lost their heads? If Christ has given such great blessings to those to whom he owed nothing, with what valuable gifts won't he repay those to whom he's in debt? Before this point he owed the world nothing. *For they have all sinned*, says Paul, *and fall short of the glory of God* (Rom 3:23). Rather, he owed punishment and torture. But even though he owed us punishment and torture, he freely gave eternal life. If, then, he gave a kingdom to those to whom he owed punishment, what won't he give to those to whom he owes eternal life? And with what great honours won't he honour them? If he was crucified and shed his blood for those who hate him, what won't he do for those who shed their blood as a result of their confession for him? If he so loved those who turn their back and leap away that he even died for them, with what great approval and attentive care won't he receive those who loved him in the greatest possible measure? (For *no one has greater love than this, that a person lays down their life for their friends* [John 15:13].)

    So, while the athletes in the civic games wrestle and win and are proclaimed winner and crowned all in the same pit of sand, it isn't the same for these athletes of piety. Rather, while they did their wrestling in the present age, they are crowned in that age that is to come. They boxed here with the devil and proved superior, but are proclaimed winner there. In fact, so that you might learn that this is true and the crowns aren't given them here, but all the gifts await them there, listen to Paul who says: *'I've fought the good fight, I've finished the race, I've kept the faith. From now on the crown of righteousness is stored away for me'* (2 Tim 4:7–8). Where and when? *'Which the Lord, the just judge, will give me in return on that day'* (2 Tim 4:8). He ran here, he's crowned there. He won here, and is proclaimed there. You heard him just today crying out and saying: *'They all died in faith, not having received what was promised, but viewing and greeting them from a distance'* (Heb 11:13).[31] Why is it, then, that while the victories and the crowns are simultaneous for the secular athletes, for the athletes of piety the crowns aren't simultaneous with the victories, but [are awarded] after such a long interval of time? They sweated, they laboured here, they endured countless wounds, and [God] doesn't crown them at once? 'No', Paul says, 'for the nature of the present life doesn't receive the greatness of that honour. The present age is unstable and brief. That age is infinite and immortal and unending.'

It's for this reason that God assigned their labours to the brief and temporary age, but stored away their crowns for the undecaying and immortal age – so that both the burden of the labours might be cut short, halted by the brevity of the time, and the enjoyment of the crowns be lasting and unending, drawn out by the immortality of that infinite eternity. He thus delayed the gift out of a desire to honour them substantially. And it wasn't for just this reason, but so that from now on their pleasure might be unadulterated too. For the person who first lives in luxury and enjoys a life of ease, but afterwards suffers distress, has no perception of the present luxury out of anticipation of the torments to come. In the same way the person who first boxes and competes and endures countless evils, but afterwards receives a crown, has no perception of the present torments, renewed by hope for the blessings to come. [God] didn't just relieve them of the burden of their present labour through hope for the future, but also through organising that the distress occurred in sequence before the life of ease, so that, by setting their eyes on those rewards, they mightn't be too severely stressed by the present torments. In this way too, boxers receive their wounds enthusiastically when they set their eyes not on the blows, but on the crown. So too, when sailors are enduring countless dangers, storms, even a grim war, and are pitted against savage sea creatures and criminals on the seas, they take no account of these, but focus on the harbours and the wealth resulting from the trading venture. So too, when the martyrs were suffering countless torments and being stressed physically by diverse tortures, they focussed on none of these, but glued their eyes to heaven and the blessings that come from there. Indeed, so that you might learn that the things that are naturally burdensome and unbearable become light and easily borne with the hope of future blessings, listen to the first in rank for such blessings, who says: *'The light momentary distress is preparing us for an eternal weight of glory beyond all possible measure'* (2 Cor 4:17). Tell me, how? *'Since we look not at what's visible, but at what isn't visible'* (2 Cor 4:18).

2.   I haven't made these comments purposelessly, but for your sake, so that, whenever you see a person living in luxury and enjoying a life of ease in this life, but due for punishment there, you don't consider them blessed because of their present luxury, but call them wretched because of the punishment to come. And, again, [so that], whenever you see in distress and dire straits and beset by countless evils in this temporary life one of those due to enjoy considerable honour there, you don't weep because of the present torments, but call them blessed and consider them to be envied because of the crowns stored up for them in that infinite eternity.

The race of the Cilicians, which also bore Paul, bore this holy man. My point is that [Julian] was a fellow citizen of Paul and both men presented themselves to us from that region as servants of the church. When the stadium of piety opened up and the moment summoned him to the contests, he fell into the clutches of a savage beast, who was a judge at that time. Indeed, have a look at his stratagem. For when he saw that [Julian's] resolve was firm and how one couldn't undermine the strength of his zeal with the severity of the punishment, [the magistrate] threw him into the midst of hesitations and delays, continually having him brought in [to court] and taken out. He didn't hear the case and cut off [Julian's] head on a single day, lest the brevity of the punishment make the race easier for him. Instead, day after day he had him brought in, he had him taken out, he applied inter-rogations, he threatened countless tortures, he baited him with flattering words, he employed every possible stratagem in an effort to rattle the unshakeable foundation.

And for an entire year he humiliated [Julian] by having him taken all around Cilicia. Rather, contrary to what he thought, he rendered him more worthy of note. Indeed, the martyr cried out and sang with Paul: *'Thanks be to God who causes us to triumph in*

Christ Jesus, and reveals through us the scent of knowing him' (2 Cor 2:14). I mean that, in the same way that, for as long as it's lying in a single place, myrrh infuses only that air with its pleasing smell, but when it's drawn forth into numerous places it fills everything with its particular virtue, so too did it happen in the case of the martyr at that time. For although he was escorted around with the intention that he suffer humiliation, the opposite came about. The athlete became more famous as a result of that parading and he made all those who inhabit the region of Cilicia enthusiasts of his particular virtue. He was escorted around everywhere, so that the spectators mightn't just learn of his wrestling matches by hearsay, but also see the crowned victor himself. And the longer [the magistrate] made the courses for him, the more noteworthy all the races became. The larger he set the size of the pits of sand, the more remarkable he showed the wrestling matches to be. The longer he dragged out the affliction timewise, the more respected he rendered [Julian's] perseverance. Indeed, my point is that the more time that gold spends in intimacy with fire's nature, the purer it becomes. In the same manner too, as it was tortured then over time the holy man's soul shone more brightly, and [the magistrate] had the martyr escorted around as nothing else but a trophy against himself and the Devil, a condemnation of the cruelty of the Greeks, a demonstration of the piety of the Christians, a major proof of Christ's power, advice and counsel to the faithful to persist enthusiastically in the same contests, a herald of God's glory, a teacher of the science of such wrestling matches. I say this because he invited everyone to convert to his particular zeal, giving advice not just with his voice but also emitting a sound shriller than a trumpet with what he actually did. Indeed, just as the heavens proclaim the glory of God (cf. Ps 18:2) without uttering a sound – rather, they pass the viewer on to wonder of the creator through the splendour of the sight; so too did that martyr proclaim God's glory then, since he too was a heaven – one much more splendid than this one we can see. For the clusters of stars don't reveal a heaven as bright as the lymphatic fluid from his wounds revealed the martyr's body to be brighter.

Indeed, so that you might learn that the martyr's wounds were brighter than the stars fixed in heaven, consider. On the one hand, both humans and demons gaze at that heaven and its stars, yet on the other, while humans who are believers gaze at this man's wounds, demons don't dare to look straight at them. Rather, even if they should attempt to have a look, they're immediately blinded in the eyes, unable to bear the flash of light that leaps forth from there. What's more, I won't just guarantee this from what happened a long time ago, but also from what still happens even now. I mean that, if you grab someone who's demon-possessed and exhibiting manic behaviour and take them in to that holy tomb where the martyr's remains lie, without a doubt you'll see them jumping back and fleeing. For they instantly leap right out of the front doors as if about to set foot on hot coals, and they don't dare to look directly at the coffin itself. If now after so long a time they don't dare to look directly at the memorial nor at the bare bones of the saint, when he's become dust and ashes, it's obvious that then too, when they saw him reddened all over with blood, glistening with wounds more than the sun with its rays, they were panic stricken and left having taken a punch in the eyes.

3.   Did you see how the martyr's wounds are more radiant and wonderful and have greater power than the stars in heaven? What's more, the holy man was exposed to the public eye and cruel punishments surrounded him on all sides – [the] fear of what would happen, [the] effort of [enduring] the present, [the] pain of the attacks, [the] agony of what was expected. I say this because like savage animals the public executioners stood around and punctured his body in the ribs, crushed his fleshy bits, exposed his bones, strolled right into the innards of his intestines. Yet, even though they thoroughly searched every part, they couldn't rob him of the treasure of his faith. Certainly, in the case of the imperial warehouses, where gold is stored up and other indescribable wealth, if you just tear away the walls or open the doors, you immediately see the treasure lying in front of you. But here the opposite occurred in the case of this holy and Christ-bearing shrine.[32] The executioners tore down the walls and broke open his chest and neither caught sight of nor could seize the wealth stored up inside. But, as the men of Sodom experienced, when they stood right at the door of Lot's house, but couldn't find the entrance (cf. Gen 19:10–11), so these men too couldn't get their hands on the treasure nor empty faith's wealth, despite thoroughly searching every corner of the martyr's body. The good deeds of holy people's souls are like this – untakeable and unconquerable, stored up in the soul's courage as if in some divinely protected place. Neither tyrants' eyes see them, nor can public executioners' hands

grab hold. Rather, even if they tear down the heart itself, which guarantees the soul's courage above all, even if they cut it into tiny pieces, neither by this means do they empty the wealth, but make it even larger. God is responsible, who dwells in such souls. It's impossible for the person who does battle with God ever to win. Rather, they necessarily go away ridiculed and shamefully defeated.

For this reason the opposite to usual happened at that point. I say this because in every case actions beat words, but at that time words beat actions. How? They applied fire and sword and tortures. They applied punishments, penalties, whips. They punctured his ribs at every point and the victim remained invincible. All he did was speak and utter a single sound, and word conquered deeds. For the holy sound leapt out of the martyrial mouth and brought with it a light brighter than the sun's rays. The light from the latter is as long as the distance from the sky to the earth. No, rather, it can't even cross this entire span whenever a roof or a wall or a cloud or any other body intrudes in between. Instead, its forward momentum is blocked and walled off by such coverings. But the martyr's voice leapt forth from that holy tongue and leapt up into heaven. It passed the sky of heaven. Angels saw it and gave it room; archangels [saw it] and got out of the way. The cherubim and the other powers guided it on its way above and didn't step away until they'd escorted it to the royal throne itself.

After this sound, when the person who was judge at the time saw that all his machinations had been pointless and in vain and that he was kicking against the spur and beating on hard rock,[33] what did he do? From that moment on he walked towards the acknowledged defeat and withdrew the martyr from this present life. My point is that the death of martyrs who kill [themselves] is an obvious defeat, yet of those who are murdered, a splendid victory. Consider, if you will, how [the magistrate] contrived that the manner of his death was harsh and severe, sufficient to demonstrate that man's cruelty and the martyr's courage. What, then, was the manner of the punishment? He fetched a sack and filled it with sand and threw in scorpions and snakes and vipers and pythons, and threw the holy man in with them too, and hurled it into the sea. The martyr was certainly in the company of wild beasts and once again a righteous man was shut up with wild animals. I said 'again', so that you might please recall the old tale about Daniel. They shut him up in a pit; they threw this one into a sack. In that case the men put a stone on it; this person stitched the sack closed, making the prison more restricted for the righteous man. But in each case the wild beasts respected the bodies of the holy men, to the shame and condemnation of those who are honoured with reason and held worthy of being human, but reveal their savagery in the excess of their own particular beastiality – as was probably the case with this tyrant too. And one could see a strange miracle of no lesser magnitude than in the case of Daniel. For, just as in the past the Babylonians marvelled at seeing Daniel coming up out of the pit of lions after many days (cf. Dan 7), so too the angels marvelled at seeing Julian's soul ascending from the sack and the waves into heaven. Daniel fought and beat two lions, but they were visible ones. Julian fought and beat a single lion, but it was a conceptual one. For *our enemy, the devil*, it says, *circles like a roaring lion, looking for someone to devour* (1 Pet 5:8). But he was defeated by the martyr's courage. My point is that Julian shed sin's poison. For that reason it didn't swallow him up. That's why he was afraid of neither a lion nor the wild beasts' rage.

4.   Do you want me to recount another old tale, in which there are a righteous man and wild animals? Recall the flood that happened in the case of Noah and the ark (cf. Gen 6–8). For at that time too a righteous man and wild animals were together. Yet, while Noah entered as a human and exited as a human, Julian entered as a human but exited as an angel. The former entered from the earth and exited onto the earth again. The latter entered a sack from the earth, and went out of the sack into heaven. The sea took him – not so that it might kill him, but so that it might bestow a crown – and, after the crown, it gave us in return this holy chest, the martyr's body. This, which is a treasure of countless blessings, we retain right up to the present day. After all, God apportioned us the martyrs. Taking their souls himself, he gave us, I suppose, their bodies so that we might have their holy bones as a constant reminder of virtue. For even if a person is utterly lazy, they immediately leap up and become more enthused and bounce off to battle, when they see a fighter's armour (shield and spear and chestplate) bloodied, taking encouragement from the sight of the weapons to attempt the same deeds. Even if we're utterly timid, how then won't we have considerable enthusiasm when we see not weapons but the very body of the holy man that was honoured with being bloodied through its confessing Christ,

when this sight is falling into our mind like a fire and summoning us to the same contest? That's why God deposited in our hands the bodies of the saints until the time of the resurrection, so that we might have a rationale for a strict Christian way of life.[34] But, don't let the martyr's praises be diminished by the weakness of our tongue! Rather, let them await God, the president of the games. The person who crowns them will praise them too. For their praise is not from human beings, but from God. Moreover, what we've said, we've said not so that we might show that the martyr is more splendid, but so that we might render you more enthusiastic.

For our part, let's pass over the encomia and turn the full focus of the sermon onto you. Rather, it's not possible to pass over martyrs' encomia when one preaches in a church about what happened. Nonetheless, pay attention! Because today I want to excise a wicked and long-standing custom, so that we won't just be in the martyrs' presence, but might also imitate martyrs. I say this because it's an honour for martyrs not just for us to be in their company, but also for us to emulate their courage before-hand. That's why I have to mention the wicked custom first. For when the sickness is unrecognised it's not easy to apply medical help. For that reason I uncover the wound first and then administer the drug. So, what's the wicked custom? Under the influence of a certain laxity and naivety some of those gathered here today will leave us behind tomorrow and leap off to Daphne (heaven forbid that I accuse the whole church of such a charge!), squandering tomorrow what we've gathered today, and destroying what we've built. Therefore, so that their presence here won't be fruitless for them, we'll bring the sermon to a close by speaking a little about these things.

Why do you hasten off to the city's suburb, tell me? Behold the suburb of the Jerusalem above! Behold, a spiritual Daphne! There, there are springs of water, here springs of martyrs; there cypresses, trees that bear no fruit, here the remains of martyrs, their roots planted below and their branches stretching up into heaven. Do you want to see the fruit of these branches, too? Open up for us the eyes of faith and at once I'll show you the astonishing fruit's nature. For the fruit of these branches isn't from fruit or nut trees nor is it anything else from trees that decay and perish. Instead it's the healing of fevered bodies and forgiveness of sins, removal of evil, treatment of diseases of the soul, incessant prayer, bold speech with God – everything spiritual and brimming with heavenly blessings. When these fruit are continually harvested, they continually swell, and never desert their own farmers. Indeed, the trees that grow on earth produce once a year and, if you don't harvest them, when winter time is at hand lose their particular pleasing appearance as the fruit perishes and falls off. These trees know no winter or summer. They aren't subject to the strictures of seasons nor can one see them naked of their particular fruit. Rather, they're fixed all the time in the same pleasing appearance. Decay doesn't touch them, nor change of season. In truth, since this body was planted in the earth, how many people have harvested countless cures from this holy coffin and the fruit hasn't failed. They reaped the crops, and the ears of grain weren't spent. They drew water from the springs and the streams weren't emptied. Rather, the inflow is somewhat constant and doesn't fail, but perpetually provides a gushing miracle more than it is emptied.

It doesn't just work miracles but also persuades one to live a Christian life. For if you're rich and proud and have an inflated soul, when you come here and see the martyr, and work out the gap between your wealth and his riches, you'll at once suppress your conceit and shed your inflammation and so depart with considerable health in your soul. If you consider yourself poor and contemptible, when you come and see the martyr's wealth and scorn the money out in the world, you'll depart in such a way that you'll have filled yourself with much discipline,[35] even if insults or punishments or whips are applied. When you see that you haven't yet suffered as much as this holy martyr, you'll take back sufficient comfort from here. Did you see what kind of fruits come from these roots? How they're incorruptible? How they're spiritual? How they touch the very soul? I'm not forbidding you to go off to the suburb, but I am forbidding you [to do so] tomorrow. For what reason? So that the pleasure mightn't hold condemnation; so that the enjoyment might be pure and condemnation won't sneak its way in. After all, you can even indulge in the pleasure on another day and be free of sin. But, if you wish to enjoy pleasure right now, what's more delightful than this gathering? What's more gratifying than this spiritual theatre? Than your own limbs? Than being in the company of your brothers and sisters? But you wish to share an actual physical table? After the gathering is dissolved you can rest here near the martyrium under fig and vine and grant your body relaxation and free your conscience of condemnation. For the martyr, watching from nearby and being close at hand and standing next to the table itself, doesn't allow the enjoyment to give itself over to sin. Instead, like a tutor or an excellent father, he watches with the eyes of faith and checks the laughter, cuts out the inappropriate enjoyments, removes all the leaps of the flesh – things which one can't escape there. Why? Because choruses of men take over the suburb tomorrow. Often the sight of such choruses seduces even the person who wants to be sober into copying the same indecent behaviour against their will – especially when the Devil himself is present in their midst. For he certainly is present, summoned by the earthy songs, by the shameless words, by the demonic pageantry. You, on the other hand, rejected all this pageantry and ranked yourself in Christ's service[36] on that day on which you were held worthy of the holy mysteries. Therefore, remember those words and that contract and flee the transgression.

5.   I want to address both those who are present and those who aren't going up [to the suburb], and to entrust them with the others' salvation. After all, when a doctor visits the sick person, he says little to the person lying there. Instead, he summons their relatives and enjoins upon them all the instructions concerning drugs and diet and the rest of the treatment. Why, exactly? Because the person who's suffering doesn't accept the advice immediately, while the person who's healthy pays attention to what's said with considerable readiness. That's why, after [speaking to] these people, I want to address you too. Tomorrow let's occupy the gates ahead of time, let's keep a watch on the streets, let's pull them down from their vehicles, men [pulling] men, women [pulling] women. Let's bring them back here; let's not be ashamed. Where there's a brother's or sister's salvation at stake, there's no shame. If they aren't ashamed of going up to the illicit pageantry, all the more shouldn't we be ashamed when we're about to bring them back to this sacred festival. When a brother's or sister's salvation lies ahead, let's refuse nothing. For, if Christ died for us, we ought to endure anything for them. Even if they lay on blows, even if they get abusive, hold back and don't stand aside until you bring them back to the holy martyr. Even if it requires you to set up a law court made up of passers-by, let those who wish, hear. Say: 'I want to save my brother/sister. I see a soul being destroyed and I can't bear to overlook the relationship. Let who wants to, criticise. Let who wants to, condemn.' Rather, no one

will criticise. Instead everyone will actually speak in praise, everyone will be welcoming. My point is that it's not for the sake of money, nor out of vengeance because of a private hatred, nor for the sake of any other worldly concern that I struggle and fight, but for the sake of a brother's or sister's salvation. Who won't approve of these actions? Who won't be amazed? Even though we have no relationship to one another in terms of a relatedness of the flesh, our spiritual relatedness makes us more loving than fathers. If you like, let's take the martyr with us too. For he isn't ashamed of coming and saving our brothers and sisters. Let's set him in front of their very eyes, make them fear his presence, be ashamed at him when he urges and entreats. My point is that, if his Master urges our nature (Paul says: '*We are ambassadors for Christ, seeing that God urges through us: "Be reconciled to God"*' [2 Cor 5:20]), how much more will the servant do this. Just one thing grieves him – our destruction. One thing delights him – our salvation – and for this reason he won't deny doing anything for its sake.

So, then, let's neither be ashamed nor consider it to be pointless. My point is that, if human hunters traverse cliffs and mountains and crevasses and every inaccessible place out of a desire to hunt either a hare or a deer or anything else of this type, or even, as is often the case, those wild birds, would you simply hold back and blush when you're about to bring back from destruction not a worthless irrational creature but a spiritual brother or sister for whom Christ died, and exit not mountains and valleys but the [city] gate? Tell me, what pardon will you have? Don't you hear a certain sage, who advises and says: '*There is shame that introduces sin*' (Sir 4:21)? Well, are you afraid that someone will criticise? Transfer the responsibility onto me who said it. Say: 'The teacher ordered thus'. I'm prepared to be judged by those who criticise and to provide accounts. Rather, not a soul – not even if they're completely shameless – will criticise either you or us. Instead, they'll all approve and will marvel at our solicitude (not just the people in our territory, but also those who live in the neighbouring cities) because love is so great a tyrant among us, our enthusiasm for caring is so great. But why do I mention human beings? The Master of the angels himself will approve us. Knowing the reward, then, let's not despise the hunt, nor simply come back tomorrow, but let each person attend worship with their catch on them. If you're on the spot for just that hour during which the person leaves their house and takes to the road and you divert them into arriving here, there'll be no irritability from that point on. Instead, when the time has passed, that person will be very thankful to you and everyone else will praise you and marvel. And, what is more significant than anything, the Master of heaven will provide you with many rewards for their sake and will multiply this investment and the praise.

Therefore, considering the reward that attaches to us from the action, let's all pour out in front of the city and grab hold of our brothers and sisters and bring them back here so that tomorrow too our theatre may be filled and the festival in this way concluded. As a result the holy martyr will receive us into the eternal tents with great confidence on account of our zeal here. May we all attain these blessings through the grace and love for humankind of our Lord Jesus Christ, through whom and with whom be glory to the Father, together with the holy and lifegiving Spirit, now and always, forever and ever. Amen.

A homily on the Martyr Babylas

Introduction

Delivered at Antioch, since once again the suburb Daphne is explicitly mentioned, this homily was delivered on 24 January,[37] the feast day of Babylas. Babylas was a bishop of Antioch who was martyred during the time of the Decian persecution. The fortunes of this martyr after his death are of particular significance to the Nicene Christian community at Antioch, for whom he became something of a patron. Initially buried in the common cemetery that lay to the south outside the city walls, during the reign of the caesar Gallus (351–4) Babylas' remains were disinterred and translated to a martyrium built next to the temple of Apollo at Daphne, ostensibly as a curb on the licentiousness for which that suburb was famous. When Gallus' brother Julian became emperor (361–3) and initiated a campaign to restore the old Graeco-Roman religions, the war on the Persian front took him to Antioch, where he visited the temple of Apollo with a desire to consult its famous oracle (Socr., HE 3.18; Soz., HE 5.19). Frustrated that the oracle was no longer functioning properly, he diagnosed the cause as the presence of Babylas' remains next door and demanded that the Christian community disinter the body and remove it from the oracle's vicinity. This was done with deliberate ceremony in which those who accompanied the remains back to their original resting place registered their protest by singing the verse of a psalm with obvious anti-Julian overtones (Theod., HE 3.10). Under the bishop Meletius (360–81), plans were made to build a church dedicated to the martyr across the river Orontes. This was begun in either 379 or 380 (Downey 1938: 47) and seems to have been completed in time for Meletius (d. 381) to be buried in it, after his body had been returned from Constantinople to Antioch. At around this time the remains of Babylas must once again have been disinterred from the common cemetery, and translated to their final resting place in the purpose-built sarcophagus at the centre of the church constructed in his honour (Downey 1938: 46).

Regarding the actual year in which the homily was preached, it has traditionally been assigned to 388 on the basis of its location within a series of homilies on the rich man and Lazarus (Mayer 2003: ch. 1), but this date relies on the secure location of another series of homilies in 387 which, given the recent challenge to the dating of some of the homilies in that series (Brändle et al. 2001), may now no longer be certain. Another factor against this date is the statement by John at the beginning of the homily that he was set to continue preaching on a particular topic, but that the festival of Babylas, with its demand that the subject of the feast day be addressed, has intervened. This suggests that 24 February fell in this particular year on a regular day of worship. If we again consider that at Antioch those days were Friday, Saturday and Sunday, then only the years 386–7, 391–2 and 396–7 fulfil that demand. The traditional date of 388 should therefore be discarded until the relationship of this homily to the series *De Lazaro* (CPG 4329) and to those thought to have been preached in 387 has carefully been reassessed.

Of interest liturgically is the indication that not only John but a number of other preachers, including the bishop, are expected to preach at this festival. It is also noteworthy that relating the martyr's life in a chronological fashion is not considered necessary, since John has taken as his subject events more than a century after Babylas' death and expects that the other preachers and Flavian will cover the details of Babylas' life and martyrdom in the homilies that follow. That the homily was delivered in the Church of St Babylas itself is made clear towards the close of the homily when John refers to the martyr's final translation from the cemetery to the church and says that even 'here' the martyr was not alone.

In this homily several themes are brought into prominence: that the martyr teaches that death is trivial in comparison to the blessings that await the virtuous in heaven; that the remains of the martyr are imbued with the animating force of the Holy Spirit and can thus perform miracles; that demons are no match for the spirit-filled relics; and that the ascetic life (here exemplified by Meletius) is another form of martyrdom.

Translated from the edition by J.-N. Guinot; SC 362, 294–312.

Text

1.   Today I was wanting to repay the debt that I promised you when I was here recently. But what can I do? In the meantime blessed Babylas has appeared and called us to him without uttering a sound, but rather grabbing our attention with the brightness of the vision. Don't be upset, therefore, at my deferral of the repayment. Truly, the longer the time period becomes, the more your interest will increase. For we'll pay back this silver with interest, since the Master who entrusted it has ordered it so.[38] Confident, then, on the grounds that both the capital and the earnings await you in respect of the loan, let's not pass over the profit that's crept in today. Rather, let's luxuriate in the achievements of the blessed Babylas.

2.   How he led the church in our community, then, and saved this holy ship in storm and choppy sea and waves; and how bold the speech was that he exhibited towards an emperor; and how he laid down his life for his sheep (cf. John 10:11) and submitted to that blessed slaughter – these and similar acts we'll leave to the more senior preachers and our common father to speak about.[39] For our old men are able to relate beautifully the more remote events. Young as I am, I shall relate to you all that has happened recently and in our generation. I mean the events after his death, those after the martyr's burial, those [that occurred] when he was spending time in the suburb.[40] Yes, I know that Greeks[41] will laugh at our promise, if we promise to speak of the courageous acts after his death and burial of a person who's buried and disintegrated into dust. Regardless of that fact, we won't be silent. Rather, we'll speak especially because of that particular fact, so that, by truly proving this incredible matter, we'll turn the laughter back in their face.[42] For an ordinary person couldn't accomplish achievements after death. But a martyr could accomplish numerous achievements of substance, not so that they might become more famous (for they have no need of glory among the

masses), but so that you, the unbeliever, might learn that for martyrs death is not death, but the beginning of a better life and an introduction to a more spiritual society, and a change from a worse to a better situation. Indeed, don't look at the fact that the martyr's body lies before you naked and bereft of animating energy. Rather consider this, that a second power, greater than the soul itself, infuses it – the grace of the Holy Spirit, which, through the miracles it performs, confesses to all about the resurrection. My point is that, if God has granted bodies that are dead and disintegrated into dust a power greater than any living thing, to a far greater degree at the time of the crowns will he grant them a life better and more blessed than their first. So, then, what are his achievements? Wait, don't get rowdy if we take the story back a little. After all, those who want to show off their paintings to advantage, position the viewers back a little from the tablet.[43] In this fashion they uncover the paintings, making the view clearer for them by means of the distance. For this reason, then, be indulgent too as the storyline draws you back.

3.   When Julian, who surpassed everyone in impiety, ascended the imperial throne and took possession of the tyrant's sceptre, immediately he both raised his hands against God who created him and ignored his benefactor, and, looking from earth below towards heaven, barked in the manner of rabid dogs that snarl indiscriminately at both those who don't and do feed them. Rather, he displayed a madness more savage than even they. I mean that the latter shun and hate both their own kind and strangers indiscriminately. But this man, on the one hand, would fawn upon the demons hostile to his salvation and flatter them with every kind of service; on the other, he continually shunned and hated the benefactor and saviour who for his sake didn't even spare his only-begotten [Son]. He also vilified the cross – an artifact which righted the world that was lying on its face, and chased away the darkness from every corner, and introduced a light brighter to us than the rays of the sun. And he didn't even halt his madness there, but proclaimed that the race of Galileans (this is the way he used to label us) would be snatched violently from the midst of the world.[44] And yet, if he thought that the name 'Christians' was an abomination and that the matter was full of a great deal of shame, why didn't he call us by that name, if he was keen to disgrace us? It was because he clearly knew that it's a great distinction for not just humans but also angels and the powers

above to be named by their relationship to Christ. That's why he did everything in his power to rob us of this distinction and destroy the message. But that was impossible, miserable wretch, just as it was impossible to annihilate heaven and put out the sun and shake apart the foundations of the earth and throw them down. And Christ prophesied these very things, when he said the following: *'Heaven and earth will pass away. But my words will not pass away'* (Matt 24:35). But you can't stand what Christ says. Therefore accept the voice of what happened. I say this because I, who am entrusted with knowing how strong and incontestable a matter God's declaration is, whatever it is, am convinced that this is more reliable than both natural consequence and the experience of everything that happened. But you, who still crawl along on the ground and are inclined towards a scrutiny of human reasons, accept the witness offered by what took place. I contest nothing, nor do I argue.

4.   So what do the events say? Christ said that it is easier for heaven and earth to be destroyed than for any of his words to fall away. The emperor contradicted those words and threatened to abolish [Christ's] teachings. Where, then, is the emperor who made those threats? Dead and perished, and he's now in Hades awaiting his inexorable punishment. And where is Christ, who made those declarations? In heaven, occupying the highest throne of glory on his Father's right hand. Where are the emperor's blasphemous utterances and unbridled tongue? They've become ashes and dust and the food of worms. Where is Christ's declaration? It shines out of the very truth of what happened, flashing out of the outcome of the deeds as if from a golden column. And yet at the time the emperor neglected nothing in anticipation of taking up the war against us. On the contrary, he would summon seers and assemble sorcerors and bring together all his father's (sc. the Devil's) machinations. Staining the air with smoke, the earth with blood, he would summon all the demons from every quarter and invite them to take part with him in the fight against us. And everything was full of demons and evil spirits. So what were the consequences of this cult? The destruction of cities and a famine more severe than any other.[45] Of course, you know and remember how the marketplace was empty of goods, while the workshops were full of turmoil with each person jostling to be the first to snatch what appeared, and leave. And why do I mention famine when the springs themselves – springs which eclipse rivers in the

abundance of their flow – ran dry of water? But since I've recalled springs, come, for the rest let's go up to Daphne and draw the argument toward the martyr's achievements. Yet you're keen to continue parading forth the Greek indecencies. Well, even though I too am inclined to do so, let's back away. For, truly, where there is recollection of martyrs, the shaming of Greeks occurs there too.

5.   So this emperor went up to Daphne, then, and constantly annoyed Apollo, praying, beseeching, entreating him and butchering countless herds of cattle so that he'd reveal something about the future to him in an oracle. So what did the seer, the great god of the Greeks [do]? 'Dead bodies are preventing me from speaking', he said. 'Break open the coffins, dig up the bones, transfer the bodies!' What could be more impious than these instructions? The demon was introducing alien laws of grave-robbing and conceiving of novel methods of expelling foreigners. Who ever heard of dead bodies being deported? Who saw lifeless bodies being ordered to change locations, just as [Apollo] commanded, overturning nature's common laws from their foundations? My point is that these are natural laws, common among all peoples – to bury the departed in the ground and put them in a tomb and wrap them in the folds of the earth, mother of all things. And no Greek, no barbarian, no Scythian, no person more savage than they has ever disturbed these laws. Instead they all respect and preserve them, so holy and venerable are they to everyone. But the demon, after lifting his mask, stood bareheaded against nature's common teachings. 'The dead bodies are pollution', he said. It's not the dead bodies that are pollution, utterly wicked demon, but the evil will that is a defilement. If one must say something astonishing, the bodies of the living are more full of wickedness than those of the dead are impure. My point is that the former serve the soul's commands, while the latter lie motionless. What is motionless and bereft of all sensation would also be free of any charge. Except that I personally wouldn't say that the bodies of the living are by nature impure, but rather that in every case the wicked and distorted will is accountable for the charges brought by all.

6.   A dead body isn't polluted, Apollo. But to pursue a young woman who wants to be modest and to ruin a virgin's dignity and lament when you fail at the shameless act[46] – that deserves both criticism and punishment. At any rate, there have been many marvellous and great prophets among us who foretold many things about the future, and in no instance did they order the persons

posing questions of them to dig up the bones of the dead. On the contrary, in one instance Ezekiel stood near the bones themselves and not only was he in no way impeded by them, but he also clothed them in flesh and nerves and skin and brought them back to life (cf. Ezek 37:1–10). In another instance the great Moses didn't stand near bones of the dead, but foretold the future after taking charge of Joseph's complete corpse (cf. Exod 13:19). And rightly so! For their words were a gift of the Holy Spirit. The words of these demons, on the other hand, are misleading and the falsehood cannot be disguised in any way.

7.   That these words were a pretext and excuse and that he was afraid of blessed Babylas is clear from what the emperor did. For he left all the other bodies and moved just that martyr. And yet, if the emperor did this not out of fear but out of a disgust for him, he should have ordered the coffin smashed, drowned, taken off into a wilderness, [or] liquidated by some other method of destruction. For that is the mark of a person in a state of disgust. That is what God did when he spoke to the Hebrews about the disgusting practices of the nations. He ordered [the Hebrews] to smash their columns, to not bring the polluted objects from the suburbs into the cities.

8.   And so the martyr was moved, but the demon didn't in this fashion enjoy indemnity. Instead he immediately learnt that while it's possible to move a martyr's bones around, it's impossible to escape a martyr's hands. For at the same moment that the coffin was being dragged toward the city a bolt of lightning flew from heaven onto the head of the wooden cult statue and incinerated the lot.[47] And yet, if not in fact before then, it would at that moment at least have been reasonable for the impious emperor to become enraged and unleash his anger on the martyr's martyrium. But he didn't dare it even then. So great a fear held him back. Instead, even though he saw that the conflagration was intolerable and he knew the precise cause, he kept silent. And it isn't just this that's amazing – that he didn't raze the martyrium to the ground – but that he didn't even dare to replace the roof on the temple. For he knew, he knew that the strike was the work of God and he was afraid that if he planned anything further he might call that fire down on his own head. It's for that reason that he endured seeing the temple reduced to such great desolation. For there was no other reason why he didn't right what happened, other than fear alone. Because of it he kept silent against his inclination, even

when he knew how much shame devolved upon the demon and how much honour upon the martyr.

9.   Indeed the walls now stand in place of a trophy, uttering a sound clearer than a trumpet, relating through the sight to those in Daphne, those in the city, those arriving from afar, those who live here, those people who will exist hereafter, everything – the contest, the struggle, the martyr's victory. For it's likely that the person arriving at the suburb from afar and seeing, on the one hand, the martyrium empty of the coffin, on the other, the temple with its roof missing, will seek out the cause of each of these events. Next, they'll depart from there in possession of the whole story. Such are the martyr's achievements, the ones after his death.

10.   I consider your city blessed too, because you demonstrated a great deal of enthusiasm for this holy man. After all, at the time that he came back from Daphne our whole city poured out onto the road and while the marketplaces were empty of men, the houses were empty of married women and their chambers were deserted by young single women.[48] So every age group of each sex bounded out of the city as if about to receive a father who was returning after a long time from a lengthy journey. And although you gave him back to the band of like enthusiasts,[49] God's grace didn't allow him to remain there forever. Instead he transferred him once more beyond the river[50] so that many regions might be filled with the martyr's sweet smell.[51] And not even when he came here was he destined to be alone. Rather, he quickly received as neighbour and co-inhabitant a man of like temperament.[52] For he shared the same office as Babylas and displayed the same boldness of speech for the sake of piety. For that reason (not by accident, as it might seem) this admirable enthusiast of the martyr received the same dwelling as him. My point is that he laboured there for a long time, constantly writing letters to the emperor, harassing government officials and offering the martyr the service of his body. Of course, you know and remember that he used to walk there every day in summer with his circle of administrators when the sun's middle rays occupy the sky, not just as an observer, but also as a person intending to take part in what was going on. Indeed, he often helped grab hold of a stone and dragged on a rope, and when he was doing construction work submitted to anyone who asked before the labourers [could do so]. For he knew, he knew how valuable were the rewards that would be in store for him because of these actions. It's for this

reason that he spent time cultivating the martyrs, not just with magnificent buildings nor constant festivals, but in the way that's better than those. What is this way? He copied their life, he was an enthusiast of their courage, through every action, in so far as he could, he preserved in himself the martyrs' image. Consider! They gave up their bodies to slaughter. He mortified the components of his flesh that are on earth. They stood firm against fire's flame, he quenched the flame of his will. They fought against the teeth of wild animals, but he quelled even the most savage of the passions in us – rage.

11.   Let us give thanks to God for all these gifts: that he favoured us with such noble martyrs, and shepherds that are worthy of martyrs, *for the perfecting of the saints, for the building up of the body of Christ* (Eph 4:12). With [Christ] may glory, honour, power be to the Father, together with the holy and lifecreating Spirit, now and always, forever and ever. Amen.

A homily on Pelagia, Virgin and Martyr

Introduction

There is nothing to locate this homily at Antioch except the description of Pelagia as an Antiochene martyr in the title to the homily.[53] On the other hand, there is no reason to suspect that the homily did not belong to the period of John's priesthood, since the hagiographies associate no less than two separate Pelagias with that city (Petitmengin *et al.* 1981: 13–18) and the Syrian martyrology locates her festival there on 8 October (Wright 1866: 430). It is perhaps also significant that towards the close of the homily the festival is said to have been celebrated locally for quite some years without any abatement in the enthusiasm for it. There has been some attempt to assign the homily to 386, the first year of John's presbyterate, but no secure grounds for doing so have yet been given (Mayer 2003: ch. 1).

What is curious is that the Pelagia whose martyrdom is detailed here is not the Pelagia featured in the widely disseminated *Lives*. The Pelagia of those documents was a beautiful actress/prostitute who resided at Antioch and was converted by the sermon of a visiting bishop, Nonnos, which she heard in passing. She received baptism, gave her wealth to the poor and departed for Jerusalem, where she took up the monastic life. She died there after performing numerous miracles.[54] The Pelagia of this homily is the Pelagia mentioned by Ambrose (*De virginibus* 3.7.33–7). She was a virgin, also of Antioch, ✓ arrested for being a Christian during a time of persecution. Her house surrounded by the soldiers sent to arrest her, she asked permission to change her clothes, utilised the opportunity to escape to the roof of the house and leapt from there to her death, astonishing with her determination to preserve her virginity the soldiers and the magistrate who had ordered her arrest. Ambrose adds the detail that she dressed herself in bridal finery before going to meet her spiritual bridegroom. He also claims that her mother and sisters, likewise devoted to the ascetic life, embraced voluntary martyrdom by drowning. The detail he provides matches the acts of the Antiochene martyrs Domnina, Bernike and Prosdoke (Wilmart 1920; Nardi 1980) and, if accurate, would place Pelagia's death during the time of Diocletian. This is in contrast to the eleventh-century menologion of the emperor Basil II, which claims that she was martyred under the reign of Diocletian's predecessor, Numerian (Petitmengin *et al*. 1981, 1984: 13–14). In the menologion her commemoration is located on the same day as that of the other Pelagia (8 October). ←

In regard to the festival itself John tells us that it was both old and popular. The crowd was evidently substantial and largely consisted of Christians, including 'heretics'. John gives no clue within the homily as to what kind of heretics they were. The area where Pelagia's remains are buried (also the site at which the homily is being delivered) contains other tombs, some of which belong to the wealthy. The site is some distance from the city and people tend to make their way home in a disorderly and irreverent fashion. Indeed, John hints that more is going on at the festival (including drinking and dancing) than just the liturgy and that the behaviour of some on the homeward journey – perhaps those not paying attention to the homily – is simply an extension of their immoderate behaviour during the festivities.

A key theme in this homily is the promotion of suicide as a valid means of martyrdom for ascetic women, in contrast to his claim in *On Julian the Martyr* that for (male) martyrs suicide is a defeat.

Translated from the edition by B. de Montfaucon; PG 50, 579–84.

Text

1.   God be blessed! Even women now poke fun at death and girls mock passing away and quite young, unmarried virgins skip into

the very stings of Hades and suffer no ill effects. All of these blessings we experience because of Christ, born of a virgin. For after those blessed contraction pains and the utterly awe-inspiring birth the sinews of death were unstrung, the devil's power was disabled and from then on became contemptible to not just men, but also women, and not just women, but also girls. Just as, when a particularly good shepherd catches a lion putting terror into his lambs and doing injury to the whole flock, he cuts out its teeth and excises its claws and shears off its hair and makes it contemptible and ridiculous and then hands it over to the little shepherd boys and girls to poke fun at, so too did Christ take death which is feared by our nature and terrifies our entire race and put an end to its fear and handed it all over, so that even virgins might poke fun at it.

It's for this reason that blessed Pelagia too ran to meet death with such great delight that she didn't wait for the executioners' hands nor did she go to court, but escaped their cruelty through the excess of her own enthusiasm. For while she was prepared for tortures and punishments and every kind of penalty, even so she was afraid that she would destroy the crown of her virginity. Indeed, that you might learn that she was afraid of the sexual predation of the unholy men, she got in first and snatched herself away in advance from the shameful violence. None of the men [in her situation] ever attempted any such act at all. Instead they all filed into court and displayed their courage there. Yet women, by nature vulnerable to harm, conceived for themselves this manner of death. My point is that, were it possible both to preserve one's virginity and attain martyrdom's crowns, she wouldn't have refused to go to court. But since it was utterly inevitable that one of the two would be lost, she thought it a sign of extreme stupidity, when it was possible for her to attain each victory, to depart half crowned. For this reason she wasn't willing to go to court or to become a spectacle for lecherous eyes, or to give opportunity for predatory eyes to revel in the sight of her own appearance and crudely insult that holy body. Instead she went from her chamber and the women's quarters to a second chamber – heaven.

I say this because, while it's a serious thing to see executioners standing around and puncturing ribs, the one is no less serious than the other. I mean that for those whose sensibility has already been consumed by the diversity of the tortures death no longer seems frightening, but rather a release and respite from the pressing torments. The woman who hasn't yet experienced anything of the sort, on the other hand, but still has a body that's untouched and who hasn't yet felt any pain requires a great and noble resolve, if she's going to take herself out of this present life through a violent death. In consequence, whenever you revere those men for their endurance, revere this virgin for her courage. Whenever you admire those men for their patience, admire this virgin too for her noble resolve, in that she boldly entered into such a death.

Don't simply pass over what happened, but consider how it's likely that she was raised as a gentle girl, knowing nothing beyond her chamber, while soldiers were posted against her en masse, standing in front of the door, summoning her to court, dragging her into the marketplace on serious and weighty sorts of grounds. There was no father inside, no mother present, no nurse, no female attendant, no neighbour, no female friend. Instead, she was left alone in the midst of those executioners. I mean, how isn't it right that we be astonished and amazed that she had the strength to come out and answer those executioner soldiers, to open her mouth and utter a sound, just to look, stand, and breathe? Those actions weren't attributable to human nature. For God's influence introduced the majority. Most assuredly, at the time she didn't just idly stand around, but displayed all her personal qualities – her enthusiasm, her resolve, her nobility, her willingness, her purpose, her eagerness, her bustling energy. But it was as a result of God's help and heavenly goodwill that all these qualities reached maturity. In consequence, it's appropriate both to marvel at her and to consider her blessed – to consider her blessed because God was her ally, to marvel because of her own enthusiasm. I mean, who wouldn't rightly be astonished when they heard that in the space of a moment she planned and executed and put into effect so great an intention? For of course you all know that when the time comes that demands that we try out what we've often been practising over a long time, and a little fear takes hold of our mind, we tend to throw away all our plans, suddenly scared by the effort. Yet she had the fortitude to entertain and resolve and in practice to implement so frightful and terrifying a plan – all in the space of a moment. Neither fear of those present, nor the swiftness of the moment, nor the desolation that comes from being the subject of others' plots, nor being shut up alone inside, nor anything else of the kind disturbed that blessed virgin. Instead she

did everything with confidence, as if some friends and acquaint-
ances were at her side. And rightly so! For she wasn't alone inside,
but had Jesus as an adviser. He was by her side, he touched her
heart, he cheered her soul, he alone cast out her fear. He didn't do
these things at random, but because the martyr had made herself
worthy of his help.

2.   And so she went out and asked a favour of the soldiers, that
she might go inside and change her clothes. And she went inside
and changed decay for incorruption, death for immortality, being
clothed in momentary life for eternal life. In addition to what's
been said, I marvel as well at how the soldiers granted her the
favour, how the woman deceived the men, how they didn't suspect
any of what was about to happen, how they didn't work out the
deception. After all, one can't say that no one [ever] effected
anything of the sort. For many women, it seems, gave themselves
up to a cliff or hurled themselves into the sea or drove a sword
through their breast or fastened a noose. That time was full of
numerous dramas of that kind.[55] But God blinded the soldiers'
hearts so that they wouldn't openly see the deception. That's why
she flew up out of the middle of their nets. When a deer falls
right into the hands of the hunters and then escapes from there
to a mountain peak that's difficult for hunters' feet to tread and
is unreachable by weapons' discharge, it halts its flight at that
point and looks down with confidence at those who were plan-
ning to do it harm before. In this same way when she fell right
into the hands of the hunters and was left behind inside the
walls as if in nets, she ran up not onto a mountain peak, but onto
the very pinnacle of heaven, where it wasn't possible for them to
pursue her any longer. Next, as she watched them go away from
that spot empty-handed, she rejoiced on seeing that considerable
disgrace was being prepared for the unbelievers. I mean, consider
how it was. The law court's sitting, the executioners are standing
ready, the tortures have been readied, the entire crowd is assembled, the soldiers are expected, everyone's drunk with pleasure,
expecting to have the catch, and those who went off for the
purpose return with their heads hanging and relate the drama that
took place. How much shame, how much pain and disgrace is
likely to have been poured on all those unbelievers? How [isn't
it likely] that they returned with their heads hanging and hiding
their faces after learning as a result of what took place that their
battle was not against humans but against God? At the time when

Joseph was being plotted against by his mistress, he left with the foreign woman the cloak that her foul hands were holding onto and went away naked (cf. Gen 39:7–12). This virgin didn't even allow her body to be held onto by their lecherous hands, but ascended with her soul bare and left her holy flesh among her enemies and thus threw them into considerable helplessness. For they couldn't work out what they should do with the remains after that.

God's achievements are like that. He leads his servants from difficult circumstances into a state of considerable ease; he throws his opponents and enemies from what might even seem to be resourceful circumstances into the utmost helplessness. For what was more difficult than that helplessness into which the girl had fallen at that time? And what was more abundant than that ease in which the soldiers were at that time? They had her inside, left behind alone, locked up in the house as if in a prison, and yet they left, having lost their game. Again, the girl was bereft of allies and helpers and could see no way out of her troubles on any front. Although she was near those wild animals' mouths, she snatched herself, so to speak, from their very throat and fled their plots and got the advantage of soldiers, judges and magistrates. Indeed, while she was alive, they all expected to get the better of her. But when she was dead, at that point they fell into greater helplessness, so that they might learn that a martyr's death is a martyr's victory.[56] The same happened as if a ten-thousand-talent tonnage merchant ship brimming with valuable pearls escapes the thrust of a wave that is about to swamp it and smash it to pieces at the very mouth of the harbour and is then thrust forward by the very force of the water and conveyed at full speed towards the harbour. It was like this too for blessed Pelagia. My point is that the approach of the soldiers and the fear of the expected tortures and the threat of the judge, which attacked her more severely than any wave, drove her to fly up toward heaven at full speed; the wave that was about to sink the ship conveyed her to the calm harbour; and her body, brighter than any flash of lightning, tumbled down and struck the Devil's vision. A thunderbolt released from the heavens isn't as frightening to us as the martyr's body (more severe than any thunderbolt) put terror into the ranks of demons.

3.   Indeed, that you might learn that these events didn't take place without God's aid, it's especially clear from the inspired nature

of her enthusiasm and from the fact that the soldiers didn't recognise her deception and that they granted the favour and that the action achieved its end. On the other hand, one can recognise this from the manner of the death itself no less than from what I've said. At least, lots of people who've tumbled from a high roof haven't suffered any ill effect. Others, in turn, despite suffering permanent disability to some part of their body, have lived for a long time after the fall. But in the case of that blessed virgin God didn't allow any of these options to happen. Instead, he ordered the body to release the soul immediately and received it on the grounds that it had struggled sufficiently and completed everything. For death wasn't caused by the nature of the fall, but by God's command. From that point the body wasn't lying on a bed, but on the pavement. Yet it wasn't without honour as it lay on the pavement. Rather the pavement itself was held in honour, because it received a body clothed in such great glory. And so for that very reason, in particular, that body was held in greater honour in that it lay on the pavement. For the insults that we receive for Christ's sake provide us with an abundance of honour. For this reason, then, that virginal body purer than any gold lay on the pavement, on the street. And angels dressed the corpse, while all archangels honoured it and Christ was present. My point is that if, when the more faithful among their household-servants die, masters give them a funeral and are unashamed of it, even more so would Christ be unashamed to honour with his presence the virgin who had released her soul for his sake and undertaken so great a risk. It's for this reason, then, that she lay, with martyrdom as a substantial shroud, decorated with the jewellery of confession, clothed in a dress more honoured than any imperial purple robe, than any precious purple cloth – a dress that was double, being that of virginity and that of martyrdom. With these burial clothes she will stand next to the tribunal of Christ.

Let us too strive to be clothed in such a dress, both living and dead, knowing that if a person adorns their body with clothes of gold, it's of no benefit. Instead they in fact attract much criticism, on the grounds that even in death they can't step away from vainglory. But if a person is dressed in virtue, even after death they will have much praise. Indeed, wherever there lies a body that lived life with virtue and piety, that tomb will be more notorious among everyone than the imperial palace itself. You are all witnesses to this fact, seeing that you rushed past the coffins of the rich as though they were caverns, even though they have clothes of gold, and ran with considerable enthusiasm towards this holy virgin, because the martyr died after dressing herself in martyrdom and confession and virginity instead of golden clothes. For that reason, then, let's copy her in so far as we can. She despised life; let us despise luxury, let us ridicule lavish expenditure, let us step away from drunkenness, let us flee gluttony. I'm not saying these things now without point, but because I see many running off to drinking and pub-crawling and the tables in inns and other shameless behaviour after this spiritual spectacle is let out.[57] For that reason, I ask and request that you have this holy virgin in your memory and mind all the time, and neither disgrace the festival nor strip ourselves of the frankness that we inherit from this feast. I say this because we pride ourselves on the long standing of the feast in no usual way when we converse with Greeks and put them to shame and say that in death and after so many years a single girl year after year attracts to herself an entire city and such a large population, and no passage of time has interrupted the sequence of this honour. But if they were to catch sight of what happens in the festival, we would be stripped of the majority of the praise. My point is that, if this crowd that's here now were present in an orderly fashion, it would be a very great distinction for us. But if [it's present] with indifference and considerable contempt, [we attract] shame and criticism.

4.   So that we may take pride, then, in the magnitude of your affection, let's go home in the same orderly fashion in which those who've been in the presence of such a martyr ought to depart. For if someone doesn't go off home in this fashion, not only is it of no benefit, but they also attract very great danger to themselves. I know that you are free of these diseases, but this isn't a sufficient excuse for you. Rather, you should also lead your disorderly brothers and sisters into the utmost good order and get them settled in the appropriate deportment.[58] Did you honour the martyr with your presence? Honour her with the straightening of your own limbs too. If you see immoderate laughter, and shameless running, and uncivilised walking and inappropriate deportment, approach and give a piercing and fearsome glare at those who are doing them. Well, do they pay no attention and ridicule [you] severely? Take two or three or even more brothers or sisters with you so that they become more respectful because of

the numbers. On the other hand, if one can't even touch their idiocy in this way, make these offenders known to the priests (cf. Matt 18:15–17). Rather, it's inconceivable that they'd sink to such great shamelessness that, when they're reproved and asked politely, they wouldn't give in and pay attention and resile from their disorderly and childish revelry. If you win over just ten, or three, or two, or even one, you'll have come in with a sizeable load of merchandise.[59]

The length of the road is considerable. Let's avail ourselves of that length, then, for the purpose of summarising what's been said. Let us fill the highway with incense. For the road wouldn't seem as venerable, if someone waved a censer along its entire length and perfumed the air with the sweet smell, as it would now, if everyone passing along it today were to relate to themselves the martyr's struggles and so walk home, each making their tongue a censer. Don't you see with what precision the soldiers in their armour walk in ranks on each side when an emperor enters a city, quietly encouraging one another, and that they proceed with great anxiety so that they appear well worth viewing to the spectators? Let's copy them. For we too are leading the way for an emperor – not one we can see, nor one on earth, but the Master of angels. For this reason, then, let's also enter in an orderly fashion, encouraging one another to walk in front with even pace and formation, so that we may astound those watching not just with our numbers but also with our decorum. Above all, even if no one else were present and instead we were walking along the road by ourselves, even so we shouldn't disgrace ourselves in this way, because of the unsleeping eye that is present everywhere and sees everything.[60] But as it is, consider that there are many heretics mingled with us.[61] If they see us dancing, laughing, shouting, drunk like this, they'll go away condemning us completely. If a person who causes offence to a single person awaits inexorable punishment,[62] what sort of penalty shall they pay who cause offence to so many? But heaven forbid that after these arguments and this advice anyone is found guilty of what I've said! I say this because, if you dared these things and they were unpardonable before this point, after this advice and reproof they bring a much more inexorable punishment upon both those who do them and those who cast a blind eye at them being done. So that you might both free them from punishment, therefore, and supply for yourselves a greater reward, take on the care of our

JOHN CHRYSOSTOM

brothers and sisters, include them in the summarising and the discussion of what I've said, so that, by spending time on these arguments for the length of the entire road you might bring the remains of this table back to those who stayed at home and kept away, and make the feasting there magnificent too. In this way we'll catch the maximum sensory experience of this feast, as well as inducing the holy martyr to greater kindness, by honouring her with an honour that's genuine. For to go away having profited and received some spiritual benefit will bring her much greater pleasure than to be present here and be noisy. May it be that, through the prayers of this holy virgin and of those who've endured the same contests as hers, you retain a precise memory of both these comments and the rest of what I've said and that you demonstrate them all through what you do, and so continue to please God in all things, to whom be the glory and the power forever and ever. Amen.

DEMONSTRATE

Notes

1 For a survey of the sources see Kelly 1995: Appendix A. Two biographies of John have appeared in the last decade (Kelly 1995 and Brändle 1999), the latter directed more toward the introductory level than the first. Both are well presented and sound studies of his life. A useful overview of the social and historical context as well as his life is provided in Mayer and Allen 2000: 3–16. See also Allen and Mayer 2000, for a different perspective.

2 These are set out in detail in Geerard 1974: 491–540; CPG 4305–495. More than a thousand works passed down under his name or compiled from extracts of his genuine writings also survive (Geerard 1974: 540–672; CPG 4496–5197), attesting to his popularity.

3 The letters cease in 406. For an outline of the results of the recent redating of his correspondence see Delmaire 1997.

4 Regarding the date see Kelly 1995: 296–8.

5 In this he may have been influenced by the example of his mother. Widowed at a young age and when John was barely more than an infant, she refused to marry for a second time, instead adopting an ascetic life (John Chrysostom, *On the Priesthood* 1.2; Kelly 1995: 5).

6 The *anagnôstès* read the Old Testament and epistle lections during the liturgy (van de Paverd 1970: 100–1).

7 See e.g. Adkin 1994, who dates *On Virginity* to 382. But see Lochbrunner 1993: 110–17, who locates the important work *On the Priesthood* most probably in the years between John's return from the mountains and his ordination to the diaconate (378–81), and Stephens 2001: 26 n. 43, who convincingly argues that *On Babylas against Julian and the Pagans* was composed *c.*378.

157

8 For the first substantial support for this hypothesis see Mayer 2001a.
9 There has been some argument that because of administrative duties he preached much less often once he became bishop. For a counter to that argument see Mayer 2001b. It is also possible that a treatise on the *subintroductae* (virgins who live in a 'spiritual' marriage with ascetic men), if not the ones that survive, was produced during this time. See Adkin 1992.
10 For a useful summary of the similarities and differences between the two cities see Mayer and Allen 2000: 11–16.
11 See Woods 1991 regarding the acquisition of the relics of Andrew, Luke and Timothy in 360 by Constantius.
12 A translation of the homily preached on one of those occasions is provided in Mayer and Allen 2000: 85–92. For the homily preached on the reception of the relics of St Phocas see John Chrysostom, *On Phocas* (PG 50, 699–706). John also received a letter from Vigilius bishop of Tridentum promising him relics of three Italian martyrs (PL 13, 552–8).
13 See the introduction to *On the Holy Martyrs* below.
14 Regarding the development and function of the Church of the Apostles see Mayer 2000a: 62–5. Once the precedent had been set other remains were also buried within churches inside the city. See Liebeschuetz 1990: 164 regarding the burial in *c.*381 of the remains of the former Constantinopolitan bishop Paul, who had died in exile in Armenia, in an urban church. For a survey of the churches and martyria at both Antioch and Constantinople see Mayer and Allen 2000: 17–23.
15 See *On the Martyrs* (Mayer and Allen 2000: 96).
16 All of these are found in PG 50, 515ff. For translations of the homily on Philogonius and one of the homilies on the martyrs see Mayer and Allen 2000: 93–7 and 184–95.
17 *Nov. hom.* 1–3 and 15. The first two were delivered on successive days when some new relics were taken from the Great Church to their final resting place beyond the walls of Constantinople.
18 PG 50, 699–706. On the popularity of Phocas at this time, and the significance of locating relics of a patron saint of sailors at Constantinople with its many harbours, see the introduction and notes to Asterius of Amasea: *Homily on Phocas*, below.
19 Aigrain 1953: 23–5 dates the martyrology to between 362 and 411, arguing that it belongs closer to 362. If this is the case, the martyrology is an important witness to the status of the calendar of martyr festivals at Antioch in the second half of the fourth century.
20 John cites the psalm verse with cherubim in the plural (Gr. *epi tôn cheroubim*), where the Septuagint reads *epi cheroubin* (sing.).
21 Gr. *eusebeia*. On the importance of this term in the preaching on martyrs see Asterius of Amasea: *Homily on Stephen* n. 80.
22 Gr. *agônothetès*. On Christ as the president of the games as an important motif in martyrial homilies see Leemans (forthcoming).
23 The punctuation in the text provided by Montfaucon (PG 50, 648, 38) requires the translation: '. . . looked at the tomb, you've poured out

copious fountains of holy tears . . .'. In terms of sense it seems preferable, however, to place the comma after *tôn hagiôn*, which would attach it to 'tomb', than before it, as in Montfaucon, thereby requiring it to qualify the observer's tears.

24 John exploits a wordplay here: *chrèmata* (money), *chraomai* (to use).

25 Delehaye 1933: 200 lists 22 Jan., 14 Feb., 16 March, 21/22 June, 12/25 Aug. and 26 Dec., but argues that the last of these dates, accepted by Baur 1959–60: 200 n. 71, is an error in the Hieronymian martyrology for the festival of Marinus, buried in the church of St Julian, not Julian himself.

26 Regarding the date and provenance of this document see Aigrain 1953: 23–5.

27 For a careful analysis of all of the extant evidence in regard to the festival see Greatrex and Watt 1999.

28 See *On Phocas* (PG 50, 699–706) and *New hom. 1–2* (PG 63, 467–78).

29 *On Drosis* (PG 50, 685, 12–16).

30 Gr. *therapeia*.

31 Evidently Heb 11:13 formed part of the lections read on the day of the festival.

32 For a similar use of the motif of the martyr as Christ-bearer see Asterius of Amasea: *A Homily on Stephen* 9.1.

33 Lit. 'adamant', a term used to describe an extremely hard substance of metal or rock. An equivalent phrase in English would be 'beating his head against a brick wall'.

34 Gr. *filosofias megistès*. On the use of the term 'philosophy' to refer to the Christian life in general see Asterius of Amasea: *Homily on Stephen* n. 90. In John's writings it is also used to refer more specifically to the ascetic life and in the context of a discussion about virtue it is likely that the term has these overtones here. For John's description of asceticism as a form of martyrdom see Christo 1997: 155–84.

35 *Pollès filosofias*. Difficult to translate exactly in this instance. The idea being promoted is that the virtue taught by the martyr's example will lead to a more disciplined frame of mind and restrained, perhaps even ascetical, lifestyle.

36 John deliberately echoes the words of the baptismal formula at this point, which at Antioch involved renouncing Satan, his pageantry, his service and his works (Wenger 1970: 80–1).

37 There is no dispute regarding the date of the festival, which is clearly listed in the Syrian martyrology on this day (Wright 1866: 424). The three boys mentioned in the martyrology are the three youths in the furnace of the Old Testament, who came to be associated with the Babylas story in the time of the emperor Julian (Vinson 1994: 174 n. 26). They are still found listed together with Babylas as a hagiotourist attraction in the sixth century, as witnessed by the Piacenza pilgrim, *Itin.* (*rec. alt.*) 47.

38 An allusion to the parable of the talents (cf. Matt 25:27, Luke 19:23).

39 A reference to presbyters more senior than John and to the current bishop of Antioch, Flavian.

40 I.e. Daphne. A reference to the years during which Babylas' remains resided in the martyrium next to the temple of Apollo in that suburb.

41 The term is used by John to refer to those who observe the Graeco-Roman religions in the first instance, but more generally to those who don't fall within the categories 'Jew' or 'Christian'. This was common terminology for the time. Cf. the emperor Julian, *Against the Galileans* 43A.

42 Lit. 'on their head'.

43 *Pinakiskos* here refers to the wooden panel on which a picture was painted.

44 Julian's disagreement with Christian teaching is exemplified in his philosophical treatise *Against the Galileans*, in which he challenged the Christian claim to Jewish roots.

45 Lit. 'all other famines'. Chrysostom here refers to the drought that set in during the winter of 361/2. The destruction of cities may refer to the activity on the Persian front, which led to the build-up of troops at Antioch from 360 onwards, contributing to a local increase in inflation and exacerbating the economic and human effects of the drought.

46 The allusion here is to the legend of Daphne, daughter of a river god, who, in order to escape Apollo's advances, was transformed into a laurel tree. See Ovid, *Metamorphoses*, 1.452–567. In the discourse *On Babylas against Julian and the Pagans* (SC 362, 180–2) John claims that the metamorphosis took place on the site of Antioch's now famous suburb.

47 The fire is mentioned by Ammianus Marcellinus (*Hist.* 22.13.1) and Sozomen (HE 5.20). Julian suspected the Christian community of arson (Amm. Marc., *Hist.* 22.13.2). The possibility also arose at the time that the fire may have been started accidentally by a candle left burning by an itinerant philosopher named Asclepiades (Amm. Marc., *Hist.* 22.13.3).

48 *Parthenoi* (virgins). In other homilies this is a technical term for women who practise asceticism, but in this instance it most likely refers simply to young women who have not yet been married.

49 I.e. the fellow martyrs and saints buried in the common cemetery outside the city gate next to the road leading to Daphne. He may here be referring to a specific martyrium containing the remains of a number of martyrs.

50 I.e. to the church of St Babylas.

51 The sweet smell of the martyr's relics is an important theme in martyr homilies. Putrid smells signified mortality and sin, sweet odours incoruptibility, participation in the divine order and eternal life. As Susan Ashbrook Harvey points out in her recent analysis of the significance of olfactory experiences in late antiquity, 'the promise of salvation was heralded in the rich fragrances exuded by relics' (Harvey and Ashbrook 2001: 92).

52 John alludes here to Meletius, the bishop of Antioch who preceded Flavian. Meletius died at Constantinople while presiding over the second ecumenical synod of 381. It appears that his remains were temporarily located in the Church of the Apostles in that city before being brought

back to Antioch for reburial in the double sarcophagus in which Babylas' remains had been placed (Mayer 2000a: 63 n. 56).

53 'On the holy martyr Pelagia in Antioch' (PG 50, 579). On the unreliability of homily titles, some of which were penned by later editors, see Mayer (2003: ch. 3.1).

54 See Petitmengin *et al.* (1981, 1984) and the summary provided in the introduction to vol. 1 (1981: 14).

55 John appears here to be referring to the time of the Diocletian persecution. For an example of women resorting to suicide at the time, see the Antiochene martyrs Domnina, Bernike and Prosdoke, a mother and daughters who drowned themselves in a river. Their festival was celebrated at Antioch on 14 or 20 April (John Chrysostom, *On Bernike and Prosdoke*: PG 50, 629–40; Wilmart 1920; Nardi 1980).

56 The Greek, which has 'martyrs' in the plural and 'death' and 'victory' in the singular, translates better if both nominative and genitive are made the same number.

57 Cf. John's similar comments in *A Homily on Martyrs* (PG 50, 663–4; ET Mayer and Allen 2000: 95–6).

58 Gr. *schèma*. This term refers to how one presents oneself to others, in physical appearance, dress and deportment. In another homily delivered on a similar occasion he argues that the outward appearance, including one's comportment, gaze and gait, should reflect the inner effects of visiting the martyr (*On the Martyrs*, PG 50, 665–6).

59 Chrysostom exploits here both the literal re-entering the city after returning from the martyrium, and the idea of a merchant ship entering the harbour with cargo on board.

60 The concept of the everwatchful eye of God occurs a number of times in John's homilies and treatises. For a list of examples, none of them in martyr homilies, see Leyerle 2001: 54.

61 John uses the term to refer to a wide variety of heterodox groups. If he is referring to members of the dominant heterodox communities at Antioch he may be referring either to Anomoeans (a form of Arianism) or to Apollinarians (Mayer and Allen 2000: 3, 13).

62 John may be alluding here to Matt 18:6, Mark 9:42, Luke 17:2; or to a similar saying attributed to Jesus which does not appear in the Scriptural canon.

IV

ASTERIUS OF AMASEA

GENERAL INTRODUCTION

Amasea

Already in pre-Christian times Amasea was a city of some import-ance. It was a metropolis of Asia Minor in the province called Helenopontus (from Constantine onwards), now in the north-east of Turkey. The famous geographer Strabo was born there (69 BC) and left us in his *Geography* a description of his native city.[1]

Christianity may have been introduced to Amasea very early. A hagiographical tradition related to Basileus of Amasea refers to the apostle Peter as the one introducing Christianity.[2] Another tradition connects this with the missionary activities of the apostle Andrew.[3] There is no firm evidence, however, that predates the beginning of the fourth century (Vailhé 1912: 964–70). At that time the Great Persecution produced victims in Asterius' city. A famous example is the soldier Theodore, who presumably died in Amasea the martyr's death after having set fire to a pagan temple.[4] According to a story of a heavily hagiographical character, Basileus, one of Asterius' prede-cessors, suffered martyrdom under Licinius.[5] Eusebius, finally, testi-fies that Licinius was extremely severe to Amasea: several churches were closed or destroyed.[6] By the end of the fourth century, however, Christianity was firmly established in Amasea. Yet Asterius, its bishop in this period, still had to warn against the continuous influence of paganism in the Christians' daily life.[7]

Asterius of Amasea

'Our information on the life of Asterius ... is far from perfect' (Datema 1970: XVII). There are no contemporary sources about him[8] and this silence lasts until the eighth century, when some of his works are quoted during the second council of Nicaea (787) devoted to the problem of iconoclasm. Asterius then appears as an authority in support of the veneration of the holy images.[9] Afterwards, several iconophile authors quote the bishop of Amasea.[10] He receives his hour of glory in the *Bibliotheca* of the famous Byzantine partiarch Photius, in which no less than ten of his homilies are quoted (cod. 271).[11]

What little that can be known of Asterius' life is easily summarised:

– Asterius' education by a Scythian slave of an Antiochene citizen is mentioned in a homily quoted by Photius.[12]
– An allusion to the reign of Julian the Apostate (*hom.* 3,10) may imply that Asterius was an adult in 360/1.
– Many authors assume that Asterius actually saw in a church in Chalcedon the image of Euphemia he describes in his *Ecphrasis* (*hom.* 11). This would then imply that he spent some time of his life in that city (before his episcopate?).[13]
– Asterius' episcopal ordination must be dated after 378: in that year Eulalius (his immediate predecessor?) is known to have returned from exile. On the other hand, Palladius, one of Asterius' successors in the Amasene episcopal see, was present at the Council of Ephesus (431).[14]
– The best assured date is that of the year 400: in his fourth homily against the Calends (the pagan New Year) Asterius refers to the fall and death of some high dignitaries (among them Eutropius), an event that can be safely dated in the year before.[15]

As a result we are left with only one assured fact: his fourth homily must be dated in AD 400. Consequently his birth should be placed between 330 and 335 and his death between 420 and 425.[16]

Asterius' writings

Asterius is only known by his homilies. Moreover, modern criticism had to separate his works from those of other authors with the same name, as well as to restore to Asterius homilies attributed to other orators.[17] In particular, Asterius' homilies had to be separated from the *œuvre* of his namesake, the so-called Sophist, an Arian theologian of the first generation, now more aptly referred to as 'the Cappadocian'.[18] In addition, it has been established that the Homilies on the Psalms, in the Migne edition still printed with the other homilies of Asterius, must not be ascribed to the Amasene bishop.[19]

As a result, sixteen homilies can now be ascribed to Asterius. To this corpus four more are to be added that are known by the quotations of Photius. The catenae on Luke seem to contain more material, which is not impossible given Asterius' interest in this Gospel (Speyer 1986: 628). Altogether we have seven homilies on biblical subjects (plus four in Photius).[20] The other homilies are paraenetical (nos 3, 4, 13 and 14) or are devoted to the martyrs (nos 8–12).[21] The complete list is as follows:

Homily 1:   On Lazarus and the Rich Man (Luke 16:19–31)[22]
Homily 2:   On the Unjust Steward (Luke 16:1–15)
Homily 3:   Against Avarice[23]
Homily 4:   Against the New Year's Feast
Homily 5:   On Matthew 19:3–12[24]
Homily 6:   On Daniel and Susannah
Homily 7:   On the Man Born Blind (John 9)
Homily 8:   Encomium on Peter and Paul
Homily 9:   Encomium on Phocas
Homily 10: Encomium on the Martyrs
Homily 11: Ecphrasis on Euphemia
Homily 12: Encomium on Stephen the Protomartyr
Homily 13: On Repentance
Homily 14: On the Beginning of the Holy Fast
Homily 15: On the Two Sons (Luke 15:11–32)
Homily 16: On: 'Two Men Went Up to the Temple to Pray' (Luke 18:9–14)

Asterius the homilist

The bishop of Amasea knows his 'classics'. In the introduction to the *Ecphrasis on Euphemia*, he tells us that he was studying Demosthenes. Elsewhere in his homilies there are also traces of acquaintance with pagan education.[25] Asterius does not neglect the usual rhetorical topoi, though this might also be partly due to his dependence on the already existing Christian rhetoric. No doubt the Cappadocians influenced him in this regard (Datema 1970: XXVIII–XXXII). But if we may believe that Asterius' oration against the Calends (the New

Year's feast) is a direct attack on Libanius' much more favourable treatment of the matter, it must be agreed that the bishop of Amasea possesses also some individuality and thus is more than an imitator of the Cappadocians. This impression is only confirmed by his personal adaptation of popular currents in philosophy and literature: many passages betray the influence of the Stoic diatribe and the aretalogy of the philosophers (Bretz 1914). Nevertheless the impression remains that in comparison to many of his famous Christian predecessors (such as the Cappadocians) Asterius displays some ambiguity. However deeply indebted to the classical tradition he may be, he is also its critic. After all, Christianity is in his view the true philosophy, the true religion. Rhetoric is merely at the service of the Christian truth. Consequently, Asterius does not hesitate to criticise Plato (*hom.* 5.12,5), to question the importance of Demosthenes or Socrates (*hom.* 8.5,4) or to disdain Greek mythology (*hom.* 10,9).[26] Neither does he fail to criticise the use of rhetorical techniques (*hom.* 8.2,1–2 and 5.4), even though the influence of classical models of panegyric and funeral oration is clearly visible in his homilies.[27]

Above all, Asterius is a Christian orator who is convinced of the preponderance of the Bible and the Christian tradition. It may be said that his theological profile is rather low,[28] but this certainly cannot be taken to mean that important theological questions escaped his attention. The homily on Peter and Paul (*hom.* 8.14) directly criticises Arius and Eunomius. In his *Homily on Stephen the First Martyr* Asterius shows an awareness of the meaning of the Protomartyr's vision for orthodoxy: it rebukes Sabellianism as well as the wrong doctrines on the Holy Spirit (*hom.* 12.12–13). One could argue that in the latter case Asterius is dependent in the first place on his 'model', Gregory of Nyssa (Bretz 1914: 71–5). But it could be true as well that at the end of the fourth century not all traces of Eunomianism had disappeared and that the discussion about the person of the Spirit was still alive. Finally, Asterius' remarks about the Incarnation reveal his consciousness of the necessity of a precise formulation of the two natures in Christ (*Homily on Stephen* 1 and *hom.* 8.12,4).

As a Christian orator at the end of the fourth century, Asterius also takes a specific anti-Judaic position. This is obvious in the *Homily on Stephen*, but other homilies, such as the one on the man born blind (*hom.* 7) or the one delivered on the occasion of the beginning of Lent (*hom.* 14), also develop into heavy anti-Judaic diatribes. Yet, Asterius still hopes that the 'son of the murderers, descendant of the slaughterers of the Lamb' will convert and leave the synagogue of the evil-doers to hurry to the church of the pious (*hom.* 14.15,2).

The homilies on the martyrs

As shown above, Asterius' homilies can be divided into three categories: biblical, paraenetical and martyrial or encomiastic texts.[29] Yet, these divisions shouldn't be taken too strictly. So the paraenetical 'tone' prevails in almost every homily, meaning that the 'biblical homilies' are less exegetical than 'moral'. The same holds for many passages in the encomiastic texts, in which the saints function as the models for Christian life *par excellence*. Again, an encomium such as that on Stephen could be considered a biblical homily too, as it follows inevitably the story of Acts. Thus, each division has its limitations. As the following pages will be devoted to the introduction to and translation of three martyrial homilies, it may be useful to have a short look at the two other texts that belong to this group.

First of all there is the *Encomium on Peter and Paul* (*hom.* 8). Though the concrete liturgical context is not clear, one can safely assume a connection with the liturgical celebration of the two apostles. Asterius himself indicates that the calendar in Amasea, as well as in Cappadocia, had as a continuation to the Christmas feast (25 December) the feast of the Protomartyr and, the day after that, of the apostles Peter, James and John.[30] Chrysostom, in his turn, testifies that Paul was celebrated on 28 December (Piédagnel 1982: 13–20). Yet, the combination Peter and Paul is not unattested, be it on another date.[31] It is evident that in his homily Asterius considers both apostles from the point of view of martyrdom: 'Customary usages such as these, celebrating the martyrs according to the tradition, are sacred memorials and remaining monuments about those who were brave for God's sake' (*hom.* 8.1,1). The homilist then dwells on each of the apostles, referring to their rich missionary career, but stressing especially their martyr's death. He also knows the tradition of Peter in Rome and his crucifixion under Nero with his head downwards.[32] Since the same Nero was also the murderer of Paul, both the apostles received the crown of martyrdom by his hand and he (Nero) 'left to us and to the whole world the passion of these saints as a festival and the occasion for this celebration' (*hom* 8.33,4).

Asterius' *homily* 10 is devoted to all the martyrs, though the precise occasion for the celebration is not clear. Interestingly enough,

Asterius takes in this homily the opportunity to answer a criticism which was in his day levelled against the martyr cult: that the Christians worship ordinary men and women. This criticism was voiced by pagans and some heretics alike, especially by the Euno-mians.[33] Asterius explains that the Christians do not adore the martyrs but only honour those who were excellent in the contest about religion. The latter part of the homily also defends the martyr cult on the basis of its Old Testament background: the care for the remains of the deceased and the importance attached to his or her intercession is already present there, Asterius argues.[34]

TEXTS

A homily on Phocas

Introduction

By the end of the fourth century, the fame of St Phocas, a martyr of humble descent,[35] had reached Rome, as Asterius testifies in his homily, and also Constantinople. John Chrysostom refers to a two-day celebration on the occasion of the translation of relics from Pontus to the capital (*On Phocas* [CPG 4364] PG 50: 699–706).[36]

Asterius' homily doesn't mention any precise circumstance for Phocas' martyrdom. There is no description of trial or tortures; the decapitation is scarcely mentioned (8.3). Instead, the text focuses on the noble attitude of the saint who is a model for Christian life. Later on, the homily expands on the traditions about Phocas and the martyr's continuing influence and intercession. The context must have been a panèguris (7.1), an occasion fully exploited by Amasea's bishop to present the cult of the martyr as the successor to pagan religious practices. The celebration was held in Amasea, in a sanctuary devoted to Phocas (cf. 9), probably after 400. This date depends on the assumption that Asterius, in the same passage, refers to the introduction of the martyr's relics in Constantinople, an event that on the basis of the testimony of John Chrysostom can best be situated around AD 400 (cf. Datema 1970: XXIII–XXIV, XXX). This encomium of Asterius has been revised by Symeon Metaphrastes for his *Menologion* (the text of this revision is printed in parallel with Asterius' text in the edition of Datema 1970).

The text can easily be divided into the following three parts:

1   1–4: introduction on the prevalence of practical teaching
2   5–8: the story of Phocas
3   9–13: Phocas' continuing importance as helper and mediator.

Translated from the edition by C. Datema; Datema 1970: 114–27.

Text

1.1   The commemoration of the saints is good and useful, especially for those who strive for what is noble. Those who long for virtue and true religion are not only taught by words but also have in front of them, as visible lessons, the deeds of people who lived in a just way.[37] Therefore, Our Lord also, giving rules for the best of behaviour, says: '*Anyone who does so and teaches in the same way will be called great*' (Matt 5:19) and elsewhere: '*Let your lamp shine before people so that they see your good works and praise your Father who is in heaven*' (Matt 5:16). 1.2 Theoretical education is a lesser and weaker teacher than real action; in the measure that sight is said to be more accurate than hearing, action can prevail over the word. In this manner we learn various bodies of knowledge. In art we are trained first by words, how to acquire, and then to master by the hand and by experience what remained dark. 1.3 A land-measurer not otherwise studies first on the books and is full of his master's voice, but only catches the meaning of varying forms when he understands the points and lines and circles on his tablet. Or the one who wants to study astronomy is not only informed by word, but his teacher will show him also before his eyes the movement of the firmament by turning the axis of the globe. The doctor, even labouring on Hippocrates and the other authorities, remains inexperienced until he has visited many sick and has learned from those who are ill how to heal them.[38] 1.4 So we also as disciples of the martyrs take the deeds of these valiant people as teaching our confession and learn to preserve the true religion even in extreme danger; and therefore we keep our eyes on their holy shrines as inscribed monuments showing us precisely their struggle of martyrdom.[39]

2.1–2   People who approach the oak of Mamre or the cave bought for the burial of Sarah from Ephrem the Chattean, where the patriarch himself rests with his children, renew after their observation of the places the representation with their mind and see the faithful patriarch with their spirit, the firstling of faith, his circumcision. And they consider also the offshoots of the same root, Isaac, Jacob and so with the recollection of these men they become spectators of the complete history of the patriarchs. In the same way[40] do I approach today the venerable sepulchre of the thrice-blessed Phocas, and by the spot itself am I filled with the memory of all the stories about him. I see the gardener by occupation, the uneducated soul, the hospitable fellow, the jewel of this coastal region, the benefactor of the inner country, that most holy man, famous more than all those who are famous because of Christ.

3.1   The long list of noble martyrs is holy and venerable, those who gave thanks by their sufferings for the One who suffered, their blood serving as a recompense for the Blood of the Saviour of us all. But among them, honour is not equal, they do not obtain their prizes according to the same measure. Even the enumeration of the Saints can't escape from a 'first' or a 'second'.[41] The reason, I think, is the strict impartiality of their Judge. 3.2 Indeed, He considers the measures of the punishments and the steadfastness of their endurance, he makes the proof of the contest and gives recompense to the athletes according to their value. It is not strange that righteousness is evaluated like that by God, if we ourselves don't consider military leaders and presidents of games equally with the bravest fighters or the combatants, but they receive a reward according to the extent of their successes.

4.1   I made this digression to show that the one who is the occasion of our assembly today is excellent among his companions and fellow combatants. Those others are not all known by everybody nor is their courage generally spoken of, but nobody ignores Phocas. As the beams of the sun spread over everybody's eyes, so this martyr's fame reaches the ears of everyone. In one word, who knows Christ our Lord, knows his faithful servant. Therefore I refrain from praising what he has in common with all others, in order to develop special stories about him for you, lovers of the martyr.

5.1   Our holy man, that helper of Christians, was born in Sinope, not far from here, an ancient city of fame, abounding in valiant people and philosophers.[42] There is no need to point to differences of religion, the question is whether this city was as a mother nursing excellent men. Phocas was a cultivator and gardener. On a piece of land he owned before the city-gate, on the isthmus, he exercised his job diligently, producing means of life for himself and for those who needed it. 5.2 He liked to open his small and humble house for guests, and as he lived near the main road, he could offer what he had to travellers, another Lot, not among the Sodomites but among the Sinopeans. In due times he did not fail to receive his reward, because his hospitality[43] was the reason for his lifegiving death. You will hear about that as I go back a little bit in time.

6.1   When the message of our true religion was announced and the divine preaching was heard by everybody, making known Christ and His mysteries, according to the Psalm *the nations were in turmoil and the kings and rulers came together*, the erring people raged against Jesus' reign (cf. Ps 2:1–2),[44] every Christian was sought as an evil-doer, those at hand were executed, those far away traced back. Phocas could not hide, though as gardener, his occupation was humble; but he was manifest as an initiate of Christ.[45] And so there came up to him the people who should lead him away without trial or defence from this wretched, unstable life. The only charge made against this excellent man was that he confessed with a clear voice: even if not questioned, his deeds were manifest, but interrogated, he confessed with joy.

7.1   Those entrusted with the execution went out – at the same time being the reason for our celebration – and halted exactly at the dwelling of the one they sought, not knowing him, nor recognised by him. Meanwhile they held the reason for their presence secret, wanting first to be informed by those outside the city, who Phocas was, and where he lived, so they could appear at once and catch him as the Jews did with the Lord in the garden, with the help of Judas.[46] 7.2 It escaped their notice[47] that they already had the hunted in their nets, as the dogs the lamb, the wolves the sheep, the crooked robbers the dove, according to the prophet Isaiah, who says: '*The kid lies together with panthers, the lamb grazes together with the wolves, the lions share their food with the calf*' (Isa 11:6).[48] When, as usual, the talk at the table had brought them to confidence, the martyr questioned who they were and why they came to his city. 7.3 As they appreciated the fine hospitality of the man, they begged him urgently not to tell anybody what they were going to say, and they made known to him their secret goal by revealing their plan: to seek out Phocas for execution. And they urged him for the sake of hospitality to do them the favour of helping with the hunt for their victim.

8.1   The servant of the Lord heard it and received the message with an unshaken mind. He had no low or unworthy feelings nor did he want to escape the danger because of cowardice.[49] He had every opportunity to run away but instead he approved their demand. 'I shall lend you my help for your task', he said. 'I know the fellow, and am well able to discover him and make him known. It won't take long, just one day. Meanwhile, take your rest in my humble dwelling.' 8.2 After confirming his engagement in that way, he confined himself to a double task: to entertain his murderers and to prepare his own grave. When he had finished the trench and prepared his burial, he approached them the next day and said: 'I sought Phocas eagerly; now, the prey is ready, you can take it if you want'. They answered with considerable joy: 'Where is he?'. And he said: 'Not far away, just near, it is me. So fulfil your command and accomplish the aim of your journey and the object of your trouble.' 8.3 The men were deeply struck on hearing these words,[50] they stood as frozen, remembering the salt and the table, the generosity of their host in all his poverty. He however admonished them to undertake the execution, not to postpone even a little as the crime was not due to their hands, but the work of those who sent them. With his words he convinced them, and suffered; decapitated he was a holy offering to God.

9.1 A pillar and a support of the churches of God, so do we have him from that moment until now, gentlemen. Among the martyrs, he is most famous, he keeps the first place among the bravest and the best. One star is different from another in splendour according to common opinion and the word about the elect vessel.[51] All over the world he is considered the most prominent among the saints. 9.2 He draws and brings everybody together to his dwelling. The thoroughfares from every country are full of people coming to this place of prayer. This splendid shrine is a place of relaxation for the afflicted, a resource for the needy, a surgery for the sick, an Egypt for the hungry.[52] 9.3 Phocas after his death nourishes more lavishly than Joseph did when alive; the latter indeed exchanged money for food, our man freely gratifies the poor. As when in wintertime the doves through need of food fly to the recently sown land and gather there, so the host of wandering poor assembles on the Isthmus of Sinope as at a common storehouse. 9.4 But elsewhere also our martyr has established through small relics some colonies of the metropolis, remarkable places to be sought by Christians; and this is also true for this holy place of assembly for those who celebrate. *Precious for the Lord is the death of His saints* (Ps 115:6),[53] and even when the relics are scattered all over, the fame of the thrice-blessed saint everywhere remains complete.

10.1   Even in the imperial city, the head of Italy, the empress of the world, he has a bodyguard and a renown and a magnificent house, beautifully decorated. The Romans serve Phocas no less than Peter and Paul.[54] Therefore, as the story goes, they eagerly tried to obtain the head of our martyr, driven by a purpose contrary to that of Herodias. She, through thirst for blood, was claiming the head of the Just to injure it, but they wanted it to preserve it with honour, to their benefit.[55]

11.1   The seamen and sailors everywhere, not only those who sail through the Euxine (Black Sea) but also those cutting through the Adriatic and the Aegean, or the Western ocean or the bays of the Eastern lands, have adapted the usual songs for the relief of their labour into a new eulogy of our noble man. The thrice-blessed saint is on their tongue as he shows evidence of his help in need. 11.2 Often he has been seen at night, when a storm was expected, awaking the helmsman who was dropping asleep over his rudder, at another moment stretching the ropes and taking care of the sail, looking forward from the prow to the shallow waters. It has become customary for sailors to have Phocas as a guest at table. And as it is impossible for someone incorporeal to share our life, hear how they contrived the impossible by pious consideration. Everyday they reserve at table an equal part of their food for the martyr. 11.3 One of them buys it for money, the next day another, and so on. So the buying is allotted daily to someone for acquiring a part. When a harbour receives them and they go on land, the money is divided among the needy: that is the part of Phocas, to look after the poor.

12.1   The emperors are amazed about this most valiant and God-beloved man: they decorate God's temple with honouring treasures. Those who come after contend eagerly to exceed their elders. And there is no wonder that, if those who piously govern the Roman empire, people brought up in law and order, have such a devotion for the servant of Christ, his marvel is told also among the barbarians. 12.2 The most uncultivated Scyths who inhabit the other side of the Euxine and dwell on the banks of the Maiotis and the Tanais river, also those who occupy the Bosphorus, stretching out until the Phasis river, all of them accompany as guards our gardener. Most different as they are from us as to customs and behaviour, they agree with us on this single point, civilised by the Truth from their uncultivated ways. 12.3 One of their leaders, a king, put down from his head his golden crown glittering with gems, together with his cuirass made of precious matter – the full armour of the barbarians is as a rule sumptuous and delicate – and sent them both as votive offerings, so that they, sanctified because of our martyr, became signs of his power and status. It is evident that the crown was a thank-offering for his kingdom, the cuirass for his power over his enemies.

13.1[56] How could one enumerate the unceasing effects of the dream-visions and healings enjoyed by those who are ill, as it remains impossible to touch only with words all his achievements? At least we can say this much to those who adhere to the error of polytheism, that we have *one* servant of Christ, our co-servant who fulfils the operations of many so-called gods. 13.2 Let the oracles be silent, as they were silenced by foretellings done among us by the Just. Let the places of healing be idle, Asclepius be no more venerated. Let people no more think about the Dioscuroi as saviours; sailors know too well who is their helper. Where is the Pythia, the pseudo-prophetess, who gives slanting and obscure answers to people so that she prepares an apology for her failures and lies in advance by using ambiguous words. Where is the source of the so-called prophetising water? Isn't this all nonsense and idle talk that, in the way of popular leaders, brings wretched people to error? 13.3 Adore God, Whose true servants receive such grace, who do nothing of their own power, but look after their co-servants in so far as they have been granted. This is what happened after their departure and their separation from the body. Recognise from the servants of the house the magnanimity of their Lord, glorify God who is truly above all, to whom adoration is due, now and always forever and ever. Amen.

Ecphrasis on the Holy Martyr Euphemia

Introduction

This text is not a homily but for the greater part the description of a painting. The notion 'ecphrasis' refers to a digression of a descriptive character and was much appreciated in ancient rhetoric. Also Christian authors such as the Cappadocians use it and in Asterius' *œuvre* we find another example in his homily on the man born blind (*hom*. 7.4; Downey 1959; Hohlweg 1967, esp. 43–7).

Taking into account that the ecphrasis is a literary technique, it is far from certain that Asterius' description corresponds exactly to what he might actually have seen (see Grabar 1972: II, 72–4). Moreover, the writing can be considered as a text written with the explicit purpose of being published, not for oral delivery. Then it could have been directed primarily to a readership that still had to be won for the Christian religion. That the text displays knowledge of ancient art as well as the use of a religious terminology that certainly was familiar to pagans certainly points in that direction (Speyer 1971).

But all this does not exclude that Asterius indeed has seen a representation of Euphemia's death; in any case he follows one particular branch of the very diverse hagiographical tradition.[57] Yet Asterius' 'account' is rather sober and despite all literary art, it finds a balance between realism and engaged description, to the effect that while reading one gets the impression of 'historicity', much more than is the case with the later Passiones.

The fame of Euphemia was already widespread in Asterius' lifetime and it is well accepted that there existed a martyrium near Chalcedon before the end of the fourth century.[58] A full description of this building has been given two centuries later by the church historian Evagrius Scholasticus (HE 2.3). Moreover the sanctuary had by then become much more famous than in the fourth century due to the great council of 451 that had taken place within its walls (see Schneider 1951). Consequently, one cannot be sure whether the building described by Evagrius had not undergone modifications compared to when Asterius might possibly have seen it.

The ecphrasis of Euphemia has been translated before into English; see Mango 1972: 37–9; Castelli 2000: 464–8. Our translation is based on the edition of Halkin 1965: 4–8.

Text

1.   The other day, gentlemen, I had the great Demosthenes in my hands – that [oration] of Demosthenes in which he assails Aeschines with bitter words.[59] I spent a long time with the text, and as my spirit was burdened, I needed the distraction of some walk, so that my soul could recover a bit from her labour. Having left my room, I walked with some friends in the marketplace, and

from there I went to the temple of God[60] for some quiet prayer. It happened that I passed through one of the roofed passages; and there I saw a painting, the view of which overtook me completely. A masterpiece of Euphranor, you might say, or of some of those artists of old who raised the art of painting to great height, so that their paintings seem almost alive. If you want – and if there is time for an explanation – I shall describe the painting. For we – children of the Muses – have in no way less satisfying colours than painters.[61]

2. A holy woman, named Euphemia, a virgin who consecrated her chastity to God, at the time of the persecution of the pious by a tyrant,[62] chose willingly the danger of death for herself.[63] The citizens who shared the belief for which she died, in full admiration for the virgin's courage and holiness, built in honour of her a tomb near the church with the coffin therein, and honour her with a yearly festival and a public celebration. And the ministers of God's mysteries always honour her memory, teaching carefully the assembled people by a public speech how she completed her contest of endurance.[64] But the pious painter by his art placed the whole story with vigour on a canvas and placed the painting near to the holy tomb.

This is the masterpiece.

3. High upon his throne sits the judge who looks in a severe and hostile way at the virgin; indeed, even with inanimate matter, art can rage whenever it wants. Then the guards of the office and many soldiers, the secretaries with their tablets and styluses; one of them has lifted up his hand from the wax and observes intensely the condemned, his face turned towards her as if he was ordering her to speak louder so that he, struggling to hear, should not write down any manifest mistake. The virgin stands, dressed in a grey frock and a mantle signifying philosophy,[65] as it was the artist's conviction, and with a courteous look, [a beauty] representing, however, for me the adornment of her soul with virtue.[66] She is led to the ruler by two soldiers, the one drags her forward, the other presses her from behind. The virgin's face shows a mixture of shame and firmness[67] – she inclines her head as if she blushes before the eyes of men and yet she stands without panic, fearless before the struggle to come.

I always praised other painters, I saw the drama of that woman of Colchis,[68] how she is going to kill her children with the sword, her face divided between pity and anger – one of her eyes looking with wrath, the other revealing the mother in fear and sorrow. But now I have turned away my admiration from the concept of that painting to this one, and highly I praise the artist who, more than the brightness of colours, mixed shame and courage, virtues that struggle by nature.

4.   The representation continues: some executioners, under their short tunics almost naked, begin their work: one has already grasped the head and bowed it down so that the face of the virgin is ready for the punishment by the other. This one stands ready and cuts out her teeth which are like pearls. A hammer and a borer seem to be the instrument of torture.[69] I weep from now on – I am too shocked to speak; the painter has indeed depicted the drops of blood with such realism that you would say they really stream from her lips – lamenting I turn away.

The prison follows. Anew the holy virgin sits down, alone, in grey clothes, stretching her hands to heaven, calling on God, the helper in distress.[70] And while she is praying, the sign that Christians worship and depict appears over her head, a symbol, I believe, of the suffering that awaits her.[71] Immediately, a little further, the painter lit a tremendous fire, with red colour giving life to the flame from all sides.[72] He put her in the middle with her hands stretched towards heaven. No burden is manifested by her face; on the contrary, she looks rejoicing because she moves towards the bodiless, blessed life.[73]

Here the painter stayed his hand and I my speech. It is time for you, if you want to complete the description,[74] so that you can see with precision whether our explanation was not failing.

A homily on Stephen the First Martyr

Introduction

Apart from Asterius' homily, other examples of encomia on Stephen are known. Under the name of John Chrysostom several homilies on Stephen are transmitted but it is difficult to be sure about their attribution. Other famous homilists, such as Proclus of Constantinople and Hesychius of Jerusalem, also have devoted encomiastic orations to the Protomartyr (see Aubineau 1989 and 1978). Most near to Asterius' work, however, we must situate the two homilies by Gregory of Nyssa, the first of which may have been a direct source of inspiration to Asterius.[75] Certainly nothing speaks against the idea that Asterius may have had a small collection of Gregory's homilies at his disposal (as he may also have been acquainted with some of Basil's homilies) (Datema 1970: XXVIII–XXXII). Yet, Asterius was more than a late imitator (Bretz 1914: 71–5). Moreover, his homily on Stephen as the Protomartyr has some particularities: in one way or another, the biblical text must play a role in the homily and the same is true for the fact that he was killed by the Jews (and not by one or another Roman authority). These elements give a certain direction as well as limitation to the possibilities of the homilist.

The date of the homily can only be roughly established. It probably postdates Gregory of Nyssa's *First Homily on Stephen the Protomartyr*, which highly likely served to some extent as a source of inspiration for the bishop of Amasea (Datema 1970: XXIII, XXXII). As *terminus ante quem* one can safely take the year AD 415. In December of that year the remains of Stephen were discovered near Jerusalem and solemnly transferred to the city on the 26th. It is unlikely that Asterius would have left this fact without mention if he had pronounced the homily after AD 415.

The homily can be structured as follows:

1   1–4: the celebration of the Protomartyr preceding that of the apostles
2   5–10: the martyrdom of Stephen
3   11: transition – the role of Paul as persecutor
4   12–13: conclusion – the theological importance of the vision of Stephen.

Translated from the edition by C. Datema; Datema 1970: 165–73

Text

1.1 How truly holy and beautiful is the cycle of events delightful to us. Feast follows upon feast, the one celebration comes closely after the other.[76] We are invited from prayer to prayer: the birth of the Lord[77] is followed immediately by the honour given to His servant. And even if someone looks back to the begetting of the One who yesterday was born according to the flesh, existing eternally according to the godhead, or [considers] the testimony[78] about Him given by His noble servant today, they will find many various events but one purpose: that we are instructed about true religion.[79] 1.2 Yesterday indeed we learned by the periodically

177

returning celebration that the Saviour[80] of the world was born,[81] that the One without flesh put on the flesh, the one without body put on the body, and so then also accepted the suffering for our sake, and was elevated on the wood[82] for nothing else than for his concern about us. Today we look upon the brave fighter[83] stoned for Him, so that he gave thanks with his blood for His blood.

2.1   Stephen who assembled us for this celebration, calling us to the present festivities by leading the city to this place[84] – he was the first of the martyrs, the teacher of suffering for Christ, the foundation of the good confession (cf. 1 Tim 6:13). Indeed before Stephen nobody shed his blood on behalf of the Gospel. 2.2 But as Cain,[85] the murderer of his brother – as the story in the book of Moses teaches me (Gen 4:8) – accomplished this murder instead of natural love, preferring contentious jealousy, and as the first introduced murder on earth – so was Stephen the thrice-blessed[86] first to sanctify the earth with his own blood, by a pious contest, second in time after the apostles but first by his brave deeds.[87] 2.3[88] Don't be displeased, Peter, don't be irritated, James, nor discontented, John, if I not only compare the man with your love of wisdom, but even want to assign him something more. Rather rejoice, as fathers without jealousy, able to glory in the successes of their sons, gladly overcome by their children with regard to virtue. If indeed there is something noble and great about Stephen, it is completely yours, as you are his educators and leaders into the mysteries.[89] 2.4 The good fame[90] of the athletes is an honour for the trainer. Now that I have begged briefly your permission, I shall freely say what the subject inspires in me as a plea for the hero of Christ.

3.1   Yes, you are the elder of the disciples, holy Peter, proclaiming Jesus Christ before all the others.[91] But when you were announcing the word of the Gospel, passing from city to city, crossing from place to place in labour for the message, this one entered the stadium, carrying off the crown[92] of the contest. He went to heaven and was glorified, even when you were still on earth. And the climax was that the Father Himself and the Son summoned him by a wonderful vision.[93] As far as Peter is concerned, may my words suffice: it would be bold to contest more with the fathers about the places of honour. 3.2 Let us also consider you, James, brother of John. You were the preacher of Christ, His second prey, after Peter.[94] Who wouldn't admire your faith? You were simply called and without hesitation you followed. You left

your boat, and your father Zebedee. You followed Christ as a true
disciple. You suffered for faith eagerly, I recognise: Herod, the
tyrant, slew you with the sword, though much later than Stephen.
3.3 But why should I name them one by one? Our man took away
before all other saints the prize of martyrdom, being the first to
meet the devil[95] in battle and to vanquish him, in imitation of
David,[96] but by an opposite deed: with stones David vanquished
Goliath (1 Sam 17:49), with stones Stephen the devil too, but the
former with stones he threw, the latter with those by which he
was hit. Let us, people of Christ, cry out like once the army of
Israel and shout in triumph for the victory, as if we saw him
present, admiring him as he keeps upright.

4.1   Everyone who fights for the true religion is eminent, even if
he follows as a second or a third the fighters before him. But he
deserves not the same admiration as the first. A second is led by
his zeal to imitate the preceding and is drawn in that way to his
goal. But he who has no predecessor needs invent his bravery on
his own and rightly receives the vote of precedence. 4.2 Mighty
was the zeal of our man, mighty therefore also the honour;
immortal his remembrance, no forgetfulness covered it, no time
darkened it. As the tale has been passed down from generation to
generation,[97] without interruption we celebrate his feast: priests,
people, children, men, women. But we must consider again the
story, so that we, as it were touching the facts, may admire all
the more the man.

5.1   Stephen was the first of Christ's deacons, sanctified by grace,
a vessel filled by the Spirit.[98] He daily fortified the household [of
the Lord] and made the erring return to the right way. But
because his teaching was more straightforward, he hindered more
than the other apostles their enemies, and prominently their chief
enemy, the Devil. For the Devil fixes his eyes more fiercely and
wildly upon those who manifest their adherence to the true
religion. 5.2 He roused an assembly of Alexandrians[99] to direct
opposition. Certainly you know about the people of that city, how
quick to anger they are, how heated once they have something
in mind. When he caught sight of a crowd of them rushing to
confront him, he did not understand the event. But he found,
however, an ingenious way of addressing them with harmonious
and gentle words. There is indeed no better remedy to cure anger
and excitement than by mild and well formulated advice. 5.3 'Tell
me please', he says, 'the reason for your hatred, why you stretch

out your hands against me in such a way, ready to tear me in pieces.' When they answered: 'Because you destroy the decrees of our Fathers and you introduce foreign teachings', the blessed man stood up in their midst, though he was uneducated and unprepared as a rhetor[100] – he did not speak by means of training but according to the inspiration of the Spirit – and said: 'Gentlemen, brothers and fathers, listen'.

6.1   How wise the introduction, how excellent the beginning of the speech to those heated people. The gentleness and mildness of the words were like some honey or soft oil diminishing the fiery heat of the wild beasts.[101] Then he went back in memory until Abraham, beginning with ancient times and stretching forth widely his account, and so caused them by the long interval to forget their anger so that it disappeared. And developing his long oration, he demonstrated that also Moses prophesied about Christ,[102] by the thrustworthiness of the Lawgiver quite naturally as well as stealthily introducing the word of faith. Prudently he brought forward what could serve to benefit the audience. But when he saw that their wickedness did not disappear and their mind remained incurable, he became filled with freedom of speech, and neglecting this life below, he abandoned his flattering eloquence, addressing them openly: 'Stiffnecked, uncircumcised, strugglers against the Law, waging war against the Spirit ...' (cf. Acts 7:51). And what happened thereafter? *Many dogs and fat bulls they surrounded him* as they did the Lord, according to the Psalm, *they overcame* the Just (cf. Ps 21:13, 17).[103] He stood alone, encircled on all sides by the mob of murderers. Noone was near him at that hour, no friend nor intimate, no kinsfolk, though it brings some encouragement for those in danger to see someone of acquaintance nearby.

7.1   The high President of this mighty contest[104] knew that this man needed a supporter – however noble he was, he was also afflicted by human feelings. He appeared immediately as [Stephen] gazed to heaven, and showed him the Son standing at the right hand in the form of the incarnation. What philanthropy, what goodness! The athlete saw those for whom he contended in a vision. And the God of All more or less spoke to him this message. 7.2[105] 'Do not suffer unworthy feelings, Stephen. You have no human companions, no friend supports you in this hour of fear, but I, together with my Beloved, am watching your holy action. Your rest is prepared, the gates of paradise are open.[106] Be steadfast just a little longer, and than leave this transitory existence and strive for the everlasting life[107] without end. While in the body, you see God, an event of greater value than anything in the innercosmic nature. 7.3 You have been introduced by the elder apostles to [the knowledge that] the Father has a real beloved Son. Look, now I manifest myself to you, as far as you can bear it. My Son stands at My right side, so that you know by His position the honor He holds.[108] At the time it scandalised many that God embraced a body on earth. But now consider Him on high together with Me as celestial and even supracelestial, to confirm in His human shape the economy of salvation. Therefore, while you are being killed by the stones, don't cower now, don't give up. 7.4 Look at the president of the games, and you will not fear the contest. Abandon your body, despise it as an earthly bond, a house of decay, a perishable vessel of the potter.[109] Run up hither as a liberated man, the crown of virtue[110] is ready for you. Leave that earth for heaven. Abandon your body for this murderous people, as food for dogs. Leave that raging mob and join the chorus of angels.'

8.1   For this reason God appeared[111] Himself to the valiant man: that he should not manifest some cowardice nor should diminish his zeal by the greatness of danger. Therefore He did not send an angel as support, as He did later for the apostles in prison, nor any ministering power or co-servant, but He showed Himself to him. 8.2 He became the first fruit of martyrdom, and this deserved perfection, so that the martyrs to come could build upon him, having the strength of his zeal as a basis, not becoming imitators of cowardice. So it happens as well in normal warfare.[112] One of the soldiers leads the attack and gives the sign of battle. If he behaves victoriously and courageously, his own people will be fortified and the adversaries are overthrown. But if he manifests some weakness, fear overcomes his people and they get filled by fear, and he turns into a signal for flight. For that reason God appeared from heaven.

9.1   Stephen who was worthy of this magnificent vision[113] as no other, did not keep silent about what he saw, but immediately cried out: '*Behold, I see the heavens opened and the Son of Man standing at the right hand of God*' (Acts 7:56). In his opinion, to mention openly the vision to the unbelievers could possibly make them change their mind. But to them his words became a reason for even greater anger and mania; they closed their ears to his word as if it were a blasphemy and conspired immediately about murder. They dragged the Christ-bearing man out of the city (Acts 7:58): he carried his endurance as the Lord the cross. They cured evil by evil, by a murder they defended themselves because of the murder, to the cross they added the stones. 9.2 They put the thrice-blessed on a flat spot, his tall body, the high trophy[114] of martyrdom. That people of blood and anger surrounded him, imitating the formation of a dragnet as they call it in war: they threw stones at the servant of the cornerstone (cf. 1 Pet 2:6–7; Isa 28:16). Every Hebrew hand took part in the murder. The martyr was the mark of their throwing, he stood between them as the target of the archer. 9.3 His body, wounded at all sides and washed with blood was bending from the right position, shaking and almost ready to fall down, tall like a plane-tree surrounded by many carpenters. But he didn't fall down unseemingly as many others do, nor did he bend forward or lean to his side or on his back. He knelt down with the worthy attitude of someone in prayer,[115] and ended his life urging the separation of his soul from the body, by his prayer crying to the appearing Lord: '*Lord Jesus Christ, receive my spirit*' (Acts 7:59–60). 9.4 He pressed on as for a migration, a change of abode from a foreign land to his own country, to a radiant city out of a desert and dry place. And he added to his prayer an imprecation about those throwing stones – involuntarily they were his benefactors: by the stones they saved him, by their murder they made him alive, separating him from the mud they sent him to the kingdom.

10.1   But let us also consider the words of his prayer, to what aim he says '*Lord, do not hold their sin against them*' (Acts 7:60). He prays not, as some incorrectly presume,[116] that the sin of his enemies should remain unavenged and guiltless. That would make him opposing the Divine intention: he would seem to rectify the righteous judgement and the legislation which would give the murderers what they deserved. 10.2 But what does he say? '*Lord, do not hold their sin against them*', that is, 'Give them fear because of compunction; bring them to regret what they dared, let them not die away in circumcision, draw them through repentance to knowledge[117] about you, kindle in their hearts the flame of the Spirit. If they repent[118] in that way, it will be manifest that you hold not that sin against them, but by the bath of grace[119] they will wash away your and my blood and be free of any charge.' 10.3 So it happened and the drama came to its end. The host of angels were rejoicing, amazed about the contest, and led Stephen with a numerous escort to his own inheritance.[120] The devil on the contrary turned away empty, in complete distress, or to say it more concretely about this spirit which walks in the air, imitating a prophetic saying, *with a face like a burned pot* (cf. Joel 2:6; Nah 2:11). He achieved the contrary to what he intended, and by his attempt to diminish the Christians, he made the list of the martyrs increase.

11.1 And what now about St Paul?[121] He indeed was one of the murderers, a real Benjamin, a snatching wolf. He did not personally throw stones but he guarded the clothes of those who were throwing and so he was serving the rapacious pack. But after a little I'll see you, who are now so swelling with pride and breathing like a fierce beast, as an old feeble woman led by the hand, when you are brought to Ananias (cf. Acts 9:8ff.), after having made the acquaintance of Truth. 11.2 I shall laugh in a while pleasantly when I hear you speaking about your troubles because of the Gospel, and mentioning among other dangers: 'On one occasion I was stoned'.[122] It was appropriate that you had to defend yourself by stones because of the stones and that you have solved the charge of sins by the same suffering.

12.1 Neither are we allowed to leave the vision[123] of Stephen unexplored. As the God of all who foresees the future knows what in the life of men will happen as sins and prepares their treatment, He has done also the same in this case. When the theophany on its own was useful for the contestant, a voice from heaven sufficed, as it happened at the baptism or later at the metamorphosis, or as happened to Paul on the way to Damascus (cf. Matt 3:17, 17:5 and Acts 9:4). 12.2 But since in our days that evil Sabellius[124] from Lybia appeared in the churches of God and introduced the evil doctrine of the mixture of the persons [of the Trinity], therefore, as an anticipation of the future and a confirmation of the souls beforehand, God shows Himself to Stephen in His very own glory; and moreover He shows the Son as a person on His own, standing at His right side, so that by a clear distinction of the Persons the hypostases are manifest.

13.1 But probably someone would say: 'The question about the Father and the Son has been treated sufficiently by you, but what about the Holy Spirit?'.[125] If for the safety of faith the Father and the Son appeared from heaven, then it was fitting that the Holy Spirit too was present, so that by the vision a direct introduction to the mystery was achieved for men. The one who puts forward this reasoning against us, must be answered as follows. O very wise man, you who question what is read must have a right insight and trained memory in order to have every piece of Scripture present. 13.2 If you look for the presence of the Spirit, return a little before the stones and the murder, and you will find the Spirit mentioned before the vision, present with Stephen and preparing him as an athlete. At the very beginning of the narration we find the following text: *Stephen, filled with grace and truth and power, worked miracles and great signs among the people. But some stood up from the synagogue that is called from the Freedmen, and from the Cyreneans and the Alexandrians and those from Cilicia and Asia, and started to debate with Stephen and they could not stand against him because of his wisdom and the Spirit through whom he spoke* (Acts 6:8–10).[126] 13.3 You see that Scripture clearly presents us the person of the Spirit. Even if this is written a little earlier, and the Father and the Son are coming later, this change of order does not harm faith in any way. To do this is customary for Scripture: one time it mentions the Son alone, another the Spirit with the Son. Sometimes it starts with the Father, to finish with the Spirit or on the contrary takes a beginning at the Spirit and leads by the text through the Son to the Father. 13.4 And this customary mode of expression can be seen happening almost negligently in the case of the great Paul.

But now our duty to Stephen is fulfilled. If not properly because of the size of the subject, it might be sufficient because of the ability of the speaker. Glory to our God, forever and ever. Amen.

Notes

1 Strabo, *Geography* 12.3.39: on Amasea, see EEC I, 27 and Ireland *et al.* 2000: 1–6.
2 On Basileus, see now LTK[3] II (1994) 66; for the text on Basileus' martyrdom, see BHG 239 and Honigmann 1953.
3 See the acts of Andrew (Prieur 1989): Andrew's connection with Amasea goes back to the *Life of Andrew* by Gregory of Tours, which is based on a Latin version of the Acts.
4 See Gregory of Nyssa, *On Theodore*, with Leemans 2001b.
5 See n. 2.
6 Eusebius of Caesarea, HE 10.8.14; *Life of Constantine* 2.12.
7 See the homily against the feast of the Calends, the pagan New Year. It has been argued in recent research that Asterius' audience may have been composed also of rather superficially christianised people, or even half-pagans.

8 Even Jerome has nothing to say about Asterius in his *On Illustrious Men*.
9 During the fourth session, the *Ecphrasis on Euphemia* (*hom.* 11) was read, as well as a passage from *hom.* 1. Chs 2–4 from the Ecphrasis were read anew during the sixth session. On Asterius' position, see Thümmel 1992.
10 E.g. Theodore the Studite, pope Hadrian I, patriarch Nicephoros. About the latter's use of Asterius, see Alexander 1958 and Featherstone 1997. On the whole it may be that Asterius himself had no objections against images of saints in church buildings (contrary to Epiphanius of Salamis, to name just one) but he was not in favour of an uncontrolled use of religious images on clothing etc. (*hom.* 1). Cf. Maguire 1996: 134.
11 Photius, *Bibliotheca*, ed. Henry 1977: 79–100.
12 Photius, *Bibliotheca*, ed. Henry 1977: 91–2.
13 The argument is only valid if Asterius has actually seen the painting and in Chalcedon: in Asterius' time Euphemia's fame was already widespread!
14 Vailhé 1912: 968 restricts his episcopal career to the years 380–410.
15 The case was also treated, and most directly, by John Chrysostom in his homily *On Eutropius*. For an ET, see Mayer and Allen 2000: 132–9.
16 So the most recent editor (Datema 1970: XXIV); cf. Speyer 1986: 626–7. Other authors, however, prefer an earlier date for his death: Vailhé 1912 (410) and Schneider 1951 (around 410).
17 So the homily on Stephen, translated below, has been attributed in the textual transmission to Proclus of Constantinople as well as to Gregory of Nyssa; see now CPG 3260.
18 See Vinzent 1993; this Asterius should be dated between 260–80 (birth) and 341 or later (death).
19 Kinzig 1990; the homilist must have been an adherent of the Nicene Creed, living in Syria (or in Palestine), *fl.* 385–410. Cf. PG 40, 389–477; *hom.* 1–14 on col. 163–389.
20 Photius (CPG 3261) quotes from the following homilies: (1) The good Samaritan (Luke 10:30–7); (2) Zachaeus (Luke 19:1–10); (3) the Centurion (Luke 7:1–10); the daughter of Jairus and the hemoroissa (Luke 8:40–55 par.). The latter quote demonstrates Asterius' knowledge of the tradition on a statue of the women, also present in Eusebius, HE 7.18. Of this, there is also a trace in the catenae; cf. E. von Dobschutz, *Christusbilder*, Leipzig 1899: 255*.
21 Moreover, an encomium on Asterius' predecessor Basileios has been attributed to him (cf. BHG 240), though the text is known only through Symeon Metaphrastes. See against the authenticity Bretz 1914: 26–9.
22 Possibly this homily is incomplete. Cf. Speyer 1986: 628.
23 The homily begins as an encomium on the martyrs but soon (*hom.* 3.2,3) turns to the topic of avarice as a continuation of his homily the day before.
24 Possibly this homily is not complete. Cf. Speyer 1986: 628.
25 For a detailed discussion, see Speyer 1986: 628–33.
26 To Asterius, all kinds of pagan beliefs are an occasion for mockery. See again *hom.* 16, where he derides the importance of the Zodiac:

'... that's what I hear from you, Greeks ...'. Cf. other examples in the Cappadocians, e.g. Gregory of Nazianzen, *Oration on the Theophany*, 5–6; *Oration on the Holy Lights*, 4–6.

27 See the Introduction and e.g. Basil of Caesarea, *On Gordius*.

28 Speyer 1986: 634; Id., LTK³ I (1993) 1101: Asterius evades the theological problems because of his pagan or half-Christian public.

29 See on this esp. Bretz 1914: 46–71; the *parainèsis*, at the service of which the diatribe is used, gives also more insight into Asterius as a socially engaged author (Vasey 1986).

30 On the phenomenon of the 'accompanying feasts', see Baumstark 1954 (esp. 82–3). Also from Gregory of Nyssa's encomiastic orations on Stephen it appears that Christmas was followed by the feast of Stephen and then by that of the apostles.

31 As in the case of Hesychius of Jerusalem. Cf. Aubineau 1978: 463–509, esp. 492–4; for John Chrysostom see Mayer and Allen 2000: 23 and Kelly 1995: 138–9.

32 Cf. the martyrdom of Peter, in the *Apocryphal Acts of Peter*. The tradition of the Roman martyrdom of both Peter and Paul goes back to Tertullian, cf. *De praescriptione haereticorum* 36.3; under Nero: Tertullian, *Scorpiace* 15.3; *Apologeticum*, 5. See Eusebius, HE 2.25 for the common presentation of their martyrdom.

33 Also the radical ascetics of the fourth century rebuked the celebration of the martyrs near their tombs, as is shown by canon 20 from the synod of Gangra.

34 For examples of the continuing criticisms against the martyr cult, see Dihle 1998.

35 Another Phocas, bishop and martyr, also of Amasea, is known in the hagiographical tradition. He might be a 'derivation' of the gardener. A third Phocas, a martyr of Antioch, is known as well. See for our Phocas the material in BHG 1535g–1540b (hortulanus).

36 See about this event Kelly 1995: 139–40; Mayer and Allen 2000: 22–3. Phocas' fame can also be glimpsed from a poem by Gregory of Nazianze (*Carmina* 2.3, 77–80).

37 The theme of the homily is given in the very first lines. Phocas will be the model of *askèsis*, i.e. of virtuous life and the defence of the true religion (cf. Datema 1970: XXVIII).

38 Such comparisons are not uncommon in Christian homiletics (cf. Gregory of Nyssa, *On Basil* 27). Here they function to point the audience's attention more to the model-function of the martyr: his life should be imitated in practice; cf. Leemans 2000.

39 Here as well as in 2.2 Asterius stresses the importance of the pictorial representations in the cultic context; cf. the *Ecphrasis on Euphemia* and Leemans 2000.

40 The comparison with Abraham puts Phocas on the same level as the 'saint' from the Old Testament. This element of *sunkrisis* is usual in

rhetoric; its application gives Asterius the occasion to prepare already the theme of hospitality.

41 See also 9.1; cf. the development in the *Homily on Stephen* 2–3 or on Peter in *hom.* 8.8,4.

42 The Cynic philosopher Diogenes was born in Sinope. Asterius adopts the topos of the origin by contrasting it with the humble descent of the martyr; cf. his treatment of Peter in *hom.* 8.5,5 and 6.2 as well as his general remark, ibid., 2.1–2: '. . . therefore, I shall keep silent about their provenance, the fame of their ancestors should not hinder our presentation . . . these citizens of heaven, we want not to honour them because of earthly and wordly reasons . . .'. Cf. Basil, *On the Forty Martyrs of Sebaste* 2; *On Mamas* (this martyr was a simple shepherd). A close parallel to Phocas' humble position as gardener is that of Conon in the *Martyrdom of Conon* (ed. Krüger 1965: 64–7).

43 The theme of Phocas' hospitality will be fully developed in the context of the account of the events leading to his martyrdom. It is again a standard element in the laudatio of a person but in this homily it also functions as a continuation to the comparison with the traditional theme of the *filoxenia* of Abraham.

44 Cf. the use of this Psalm text in Acts 4:24–6.

45 This passages echoes the terminology of the mystery cults: Christ and his mysteries (6.1); *mustès*, initiate (6.2).

46 The parallel with the Passion Narrative underlines the comparison of the martyr with his model, Christ.

47 The story that now follows can be compared with the *Passion of Athenogenes* (BHG 197b) 17–18.

48 The quotation is far from precise.

49 The topos of the martyr's steadfastness is also present in Asterius' *Homily on Stephen* 7.2–8.1. Cf. also *Martyrdom of Polycarp* 9.1.

50 See for this as well as the preceding paragraph again the *Passion of Athenogenes* and the *Martyrdom of Polycarp* 7.2.

51 In Acts 9:15 Paul is called 'the elect vessel' (tool of Christ's mission). Asterius is using the notion to speak about the martyr's body (cf. 10.4,1). See also *On Stephen* 5.1 where Stephen is designated as the vessel filled with the Spirit.

52 For 9.2 and 9.3 cf. *hom.* 10.4,4; for the comparison with nature see also *hom.* 14.3,2.

53 This quotation from Ps 115:6 is not uncommon in martyrial homilies: see also *hom.* 10.18,5 and Gregory of Nyssa, *On Theodore* (GNO X, 1/2, 64). Cf. Leemans 2001b.

54 Asterius knows about the Roman veneration of the two apostles and puts his hero on the same level as those 'pillars'.

55 Again a comparison based on a biblical narrative (Mark 6:19–28), here turned into a contrast.

56 Also in other homilies Asterius confirms the importance of the intercession of the martyr in many ways, cf. in detail *hom.* 10.4,1–4; cf. Leemans 2001b.

57 Euphemia's death is traditionnally situated under Diocletian (AD 303). According to Asterius, she died by fire. The Passiones make her die in the arena, killed by beasts. A third tradition wants her to be decapitated (Schrier 1984).

58 In 399 the emperor Arcadius and the Gothic leader Gainas met in Chalcedon, in the 'martyrium, there where the body of the martyr Euphemia lies' (Socrates, HE 6.6.12). But even earlier, in 384, the famous Egeria made during her pilgrimage to the Holy Land a stop in Chalcedon to visit the very illustrious martyrium of Euphemia, known to her of old (*Peregrinatio Egeriae* 23.7; Maraval 1997).

59 Asterius refers here to Demosthenes' oration *On the Crown*. For a less favourable reference to the Attic orator, see *hom.* 8.5,4.

60 Asterius uses a number of circumscriptions that seem to avoid naming Christianity explicitly: par. 1: the temple of God (the Church); par. 2: the belief for which she died (Christianity); ministers of God's mysteries (priests); par. 4: the sign that the Christians worship (the Cross). See Speyer 1971. He also prefers some terms belonging to the pagan religious language as if they were more familiar to his readership: mysteries, hierophant and many other cases in his other homilies, also in his orations in praise of Phocas and Stephen.

61 'Children of the muses': the comparison, not to mention the competition, between literature and visual art was often used as a rhetorical topos (cf. Basil, *On the Forty Martyrs of Sebaste* 2). Elsewhere, Asterius writes about a man praying to God exemplified by Ps 38:5: 'you can see *as if upon an icon* how the state of mind of the one praying becomes visible; how, helpless, he looks forward to the future . . .' (*hom.* 2.8,2).

62 The description of the persecution is vague on purpose. Also for non-Christians it might make sense that a 'tyrant' persecutes 'the pious'; cf. *hom.* 8.4,4.

63 The virginal state of the woman martyr is stressed more than once. Cf. Eusebius, *On the Martyrs of Palestine* 7.1–2; 8.5–8; 9.9.

64 Asterius evidently knows about a martyrium and a yearly panèguris, but whether he has Chalcedon in mind or not, is difficult to establish. See also his description of the Christian practice in *hom.* 10.8,1.

65 As Christianity is the true philosophy, those who embody it excellently like the martyrs can be called philosophers; so also the apostles (*hom.* 1.10,4; *hom.* 2.1 and *hom.* 14.1). During the fourth century philosophy is connected with a life in perfection, in particular an ascetic life (that can include or lead to the path of suffering). The virgin's sober dress accentuates her firm disposition with regard to suffering and martyrdom. (On the meaning of the mantle, see N. Hyldahl, *Philosophie und Christentum*, Kopenhagen 1966, 102–12). In the *Acts of Philip*, the apostle is recognised as a philosopher by his (ascetic) dress; cf. ed. Amsler 1999: 40–3.

66 Asterius transposes the classic motif of the beauty of the woman martyr to Euphemia's inner qualities, as outer beauty has to correspond with the (inner) moral disposition (cf. his treatment of Susannah in *hom.* 6.5,5).

67 Cf. again *hom.* 6 on Susannah, indicating how the young woman became a model for Christian martyrs.

68 Medea, of whom there existed an illustrious image by Timomachus.

69 This torture was also the fate of the martyr Apollonia; cf. Eusebius, HE 6.41.7.

70 One thinks again of the story about Susannah; cf. Dan 13:35, 42–3. The gestures are almost liturgical, parallel with many presentations in the Acts of the martyrs.

71 For the sign of the Cross, cf. *Martyrdom of Lyon and Vienne* 41, about the woman martyr Blandina. For the connection of the Cross with prayer, see Asterius, *hom.* 16.

72 Death by fire for women: cf. Agathonikè in the *Acts of Carpus* 46; Julitta: Basil, *On Julitta* 2; Apollonia: Eusebius, HE 6.41.7.

73 The joy of the martyr is a topos. See e.g. Agathonikè in *Acts of Carpus* 44.

74 In Greek the meaning of *telein* can be 'to complete the way', that is: to go (and see the picture for yourself). Cf. Halkin 1965: 8 n. 3 and Datema 1970: 237–8. Thus, the last lines of the text are an invitation to the reader to follow the martyr's example in her virtuous life.

75 GNO X, 1/2, 73–94 and 95–105.

76 The introduction seems to be inspired by Gregory of Nyssa's *First Homily on Stephen*. There also it is manifest that the celebration of Christmas as a separate feast was introduced about that time in Cappadocia (Mossay 1965). Gregory's homily also points to the existence of a series of celebrations after Christmas: the day after Stephen, the following day the apostles (cf. Gregory of Nyssa, *On Basil* 1). The sequence of celebrations is indicated by Asterius in his homily *On the Martyrs* (*hom.* 10.10,1–2). Here, as elsewhere (e.g. *hom.* 4.3) Asterius insists on the spiritual character of the celebration.

77 Gr. *theofaneia*. As such it means 'appearance of the divine' (cf. 12.1) but as in the writings of the other Cappadocians the word can also take on the more precise meaning 'birth of Christ' (cf. Gregory of Nazianze, *On the Theophany* 3).

78 Gr. *marturion*, allows a shift of meanings and *double entendre* between testimony and martyrdom (cf. *hom.* 10.3,2).

79 *Eusebeia*; Christianity is the true religion; cf. 4.1 and 5.1. The homiletics on the martyrs will stress that their martyrdom is a proof of that truth. See further *hom.* 3.1,2; *hom.* 8.1,4; 7.1; 27.5 and *hom.* 10.1,2.

80 *Sôtèr* (saviour), *theofaneia* (in 1.1), *mustagôgos* (2.3) are examples of a religious terminology that might have been familiar to Asterius' audience. Cf. also 'Saviour of the world' in John 4:42.

81 As in the preceding passage, Asterius focuses on the orthodox presentation of the divine and the human in Christ and the correct understanding of the Incarnation. In 1.1 the 'existing always' of the Son certainly is a hint against the Neo-Arians (cf. Basil, *Against Eunomius* II.12). The 'One without flesh' (*asarkos*) is said about the Logos before the

189

Incarnation; cf. Gregory of Nazianze, *Oratio* 38.2. The 'right' doctrine about the Incarnation is of course also often present in Christmas homilies (e.g. Gregory of Nyssa's *On the Nativity*).

82 'The wood' is of course the Cross (cf. Acts 5:30 and *hom.* 8.6,1; 29.1). Asterius accentuates the soteriological dimension of the Incarnation.

83 *Gennaios agonistès* (brave fighter) belongs to the language of the stadium, so often exploited in language related to martyrdom. At the same time, however, it is not to be excluded that for Asterius this terminology also covers a moral meaning as developed by the Stoic ethics: the exercise in virtue. Also in that respect the martyr's life is a model. For Stephen as a model, see e.g. Gregory of Nazianze, *On his Father* 24.

84 The panèguris (cf. Introduction) is the occasion for the homily: elsewhere Asterius also describes how 'the whole city' assembles for the celebration of the martyrs (cf. *hom.* 3.1,1 and *hom.* 9.1,1). The paragraph introduces at the same time the main issue of the homilist's introduction: to explain why Stephen is the first and precedes the apostles.

85 A play of words impossible to translate: *Cain-ekainizen*, 'introduced as sth. new', murder. For another example of the often applied rhetorical strategy of comparison (*sunkrisis*) with biblical figures, see David in 3.3.

86 A common epithet for the martyrs; cf. 9.2.

87 Stephen precedes: this whole chapter can be read as a christianisation of the 'Erfindertopos' (Speyer 1986). In *hom.* 8 Asterius applies the topos to Peter, 'who ran before the other apostles' (11.1–2).

88 Asterius cannot refrain from anticipating the celebration of the next day; cf. 3.1–2. But the apostles shouldn't follow the example set by Cain.

89 Gr. *mustagôgoi*: here and elsewhere (e.g. 7.2–3; *hom.* 3.10,3; *hom.* 11.2,2) Asterius uses the language of the mystery religions (Speyer 1986: 632–3). Origen already considered the apostles as *mustagôgoi* (*Expos. in Psalmos* 36.21). Before, Asterius has referred to the apostles' *filosofia*, again a way of introducing Christianity in a popular tone; in *hom.* 1.10,4 he introduces the apostles as 'philosophers'; cf. *hom.* 14.2,1 with Malingrey 1961.

90 Asterius will use time and again the language of the stadium.

91 Peter was the first of the disciples, called together with his brother Andrew (Mark 1:16).

92 Note the pun: 'crown' is in Greek *stefanos*. Besides this topos of the etymological explanation of the martyr's name, there is also the further application of the athletic imagery; neither have the ethic implications disappeared. Cf. 7.4 and *hom.* 10.10,2.

93 The homilist announces already here the importance of Stephen's vision which enhances the martyr's priority position.

94 The call of James, cf. Mark 1:19; his death: Acts 12:1–2 (but there Herod is the 'king'). The designation of 'tyrant' is not uncommon in a martyrological context: Christians were persecuted by 'tyrants', not by regular leaders. Cf. *Ecphrasis on Euphemia* 2; *hom.* 8.4,4; *hom.* 10.5,1).

95 Martyrdom as a struggle with the Devil is so frequent an application of the athletic terminology that it became a commonplace in early Christian

literature (see below 5.1; 10.3); but Asterius will not fail to continue to combine the idea of that struggle with the idea of the struggle for the true religion.

96 Again a comparison with a biblical character, concentrating on the element of the stones.

97 Asterius stresses also elsewhere the long tradition of the celebration of the martyrs; cf. *hom.* 8.1,1.

98 A paraphrase of Acts 6:5–8. Asterius' insistence on the presence of the Spirit in Stephen is of importance for the theological argumentation at the end of the homily, but functions here as well as an explanation for his eloquence. These contexts often refer (implicitly) to the promise that the disciples will be inspired by the Holy Spirit at the moment of trial (cf. Luke 12:11–12 etc.; cf Acts 6:10).

99 Asterius drops here the exact quotation (cf. 13.2) and focuses on the confrontation with the Alexandrians; in this way the context of the Sanhedrin session and the direct parallel with the Passion Narrative remain unmentioned.

100 The presentation of the 'uneducated' speaker is often present in early Christian literature as an adaptation of the 'Unfähigkeits'-topos (Speyer 1986). In his homily on Peter and Paul Asterius also presents Peter as the uneducated (*hom.* 8.5,5 and 6.2) in full contrast to Demosthenes and Socrates. But at the same time Stephen's address sounds very diatribic!

101 Asterius' presentation is that of the Cynic philosopher who tries to convince with sweet words but does not hesitate to use freedom of speech (*parrèsia*) when the audience does not pay attention (cf. *hom.* 3.2,1). The theme of *parrèsia* became a topos, applied to the martyr standing before his/her judge (cf. already Acts 4:27–8). The term is also used with regard to the martyrs' freedom as mediators in heaven (cf. with regard to Phocas *hom.* 10.11).

102 The history of salvation culminating in the coming of Christ is also a theme in *hom.* 8.6,3 about Peter's oration of Acts 3.

103 Psalm 21 has a long tradition of christological interpretation in the early Church, from 1 Clement and Justin Martyr onwards. Asterius quotes the same text in *hom.* 8.5,2 on Peter. In the text on Stephen it accentuates the parallellism between the Lord and his martyr.

104 Christ or the Lord as the president of the games (*agônothetès*) is an important element in martyrial homilies (Leemans (forthcoming)). For Asterius this is also the real context of Stephen's martyr story; at the same time it underlines the importance of the vision as a revelation about the meaning of the Incarnation. In that sense the celebration of Stephen is again presented as a continuation on the celebration of the birth of the Lord.

105 The direct speech betrays the influence of the diatribe, whereas the terminology is almost close to the language of the mystery religions (*epopteuô ta dromena*).

106 The martyr has the privilege of passing immediately into the 'other world'; cf. Luke 23:43.

107 A classical theme in the Acts of the Martyrs, as the result of their brave behaviour.

108 The vision stresses the equality of being between the Father and the Son, against the Arian position (cf. Asterius' position in *hom.* 8.14,2). This could also have been the reason why the homilist puts Stephen in direct confrontation with 'the Alexandrians' (Arius was an Alexandrian).

109 Asterius doesn't avoid the Platonic presentation of the body as a hinderance, even as something dirty (Speyer 1986: 631). To join the chorus of angels refers again to the belief in the direct transition of the martyr into the heavenly life.

110 The 'crown of virtue' is an allusion to Stephen's name (*stefanos* = crown). Cf. *hom.* 10.10,2: 'Stephen who was duly named in that way . . .', in which an agonistic terminology is used which is ethical as well.

111 The theme of the vision is as such not uncommon in martyrological literature, but here it is enlightening the idea of the 'protomartyr': Stephen is to be portrayed here as a model of courage as well as a champion of orthodoxy.

112 The image of warfare is popular in the Stoic diatribe.

113 The description of the vision and the reaction to it confirms the parallel with the Passion Narrative. Stephen, like other martyrs, is called 'Christbearer'; cf. Gregory of Nyssa, *Second Homily on Stephen*. For the meaning of the vision see also *hom.* 8.22,1 and 23,2.

114 The trophy is the sign of victory. In the middle of military language, Asterius uses a word that had for the Christians a deep meaning; also for him the Cross is 'the trophy' (*hom.* 8.6,1); here, however, it is not the Cross but the martyr's body (Datema 1970: 238).

115 The story of Acts permits the homilist to give now full attention to the prayer of the martyr, the content of which constitutes again a similarity to Christ's passion (Luke 23:46, cf. Ps 31:6 and Acts 7:59). A similar tendency can be discovered in the description of the martyrdom of James by Hegesippus, in Eusebius, HE 3.23.13–16.

116 The prayer is interpreted seemingly in correction to others, who read in it the theme of the forgiving of the enemies (even a direct correction of Gregory of Nyssa's homily; Datema 1970: 238).

117 Gr. *epignôsis*. Knowledge of divine truth is the martyr's achievement *par excellence*. In the *Martyrdom of Polycarp*, Polycarp in his prayer for this knowledge brings thanks to God (*Mart. Pol.* 14.1).

118 Apparently, Asterius' interpretation develops into the possibility of the conversion of the Jews. It is formulated again in a very diatribic fashion, so that it seems as if the martyr himself furnishes the explanation.

119 An allusion to baptism.

120 The image of the escort of angels is not uncommon in martyrological literature (cf. e.g. *Passion of Perpetua* 11).

121 *Hom.* 8 presents Paul evidently in a more favourable way; cf. esp. par. 18–20.

122 An allusion to 2 Cor 11:25 connected by Asterius with the story of the stoning. The style of par. 11 is again that of the diatribe.

123 After the digression on Paul, Asterius returns to the context of the vision (see another explanation in *hom.* 8.22). Probably following Gregory of Nyssa's lead, he insists on the 'dogmatic' meaning of the revelation.

124 Asterius attacks modalism, labelled as usual in the fourth century as Sabellianism. It is a common conviction that Sabellius came from Lybia, though no early source confirms this. However, his doctrine is identified with each form of monarchianism that leads to a confusion of the persons in the Trinity.

125 Following (probably) Gregory, Asterius continues his explanation of the vision in contrast to the Pneumatomachian reading of it. But Gregory amply develops this question with a biblical argumentation. Asterius reduces his reaction to the argument that the Spirit is present in the larger context of the vision and that this is the way in which Scripture proceeds. It might be wrong, however, to think that Asterius is writing here only in the guise of an imitator of Gregory and that his concern about orthodoxy is inspired by tradition. Discussions about the Holy Spirit may have continued after the Council of Constantinople (381) had 'settled' the issue. In that context Asterius may have seen in this part of the story of Stephen a convenient opportunity to present the vision as a personal revelation to the martyr about the true concept of the Trinity.

126 The full quotation of Acts 6:8–10 is given here (cf. 5.2), with the addition of (full of . . .) *truth*. The martyr is the witness to truth *par excellence*.

V

HESYCHIUS OF JERUSALEM

GENERAL INTRODUCTION

Hesychius of Jerusalem is the only homilist represented in this volume who never achieved episcopal status. A fifth-century presbyter who had formerly been a monk, he remains a shadowy figure to us, although he was held in high regard by his contemporaries.[1] He was a supporter of Cyril of Alexandria in the Nestorian controversy, and attacked the exegesis and the christology of the Antiochene theologian, Theodore of Mopsuestia. A prodigious scholar, he composed biblical commentaries and homilies on biblical books, a church history of which only a fragment survives, and homilies for liturgical and festal occasions. The anonymous sixth-century pilgrim from Piacenza informs us that the tomb of Hesychius at the main gate of Jerusalem was the site of the distribution of bread to the poor and to pilgrims.[2]

Three of Hesychius' martyrial homilies have come down to us.[3] Apart from the homilies on Stephen and Procopius, translated here, we have also a homily on the martyr James,[4] all three saints having intimate connections with the city of Jerusalem.

Hesychius preached his homilies in at least five different locations: in a church 'at the third mile' along the road from Jerusalem to Bethlehem, at the martyrium of Constantine where the relic of the cross was kept, at the large church of St Sion, and in the church of the Resurrection (Anastasis).[5] His audiences must have been fond of his rhetorical style, full of repetition, anaphora, antithesis and unusual words, and of his intensive use of scripture, a dramatic feature of the liturgy of Jerusalem, in which the biblical pericopes and the visual impact of the holy sites they described went hand in hand (see Hunt 1984: 114). The city was also notable for the early development of a rich stational liturgy, although there is no evidence of this in either of Hesychius' martyrial homilies (see Baldovin 1987: 35–104).

TEXTS

A homily in praise of Stephen the First Martyr

Introduction

Hesychius delivered his homily on the protomartyr Stephen in the church of St Sion, probably in the *diaconicon*, the chapel to the left of the central nave.[6] Unlike the church of Amasea, which honoured Stephen on 26 December, the church of Jerusalem celebrated his feast on 27 December. According to the homilist (par. 2), there were several feasts of the martyr celebrated in Jerusalem. Stephen's relics were solemnly enshrined in St Sion on 26 December 415, and in 438/9 Eudocia began building the imperial basilica dedicated to the saint. Consequently, Hesychius must have delivered his homily between these two dates.

There is nothing in the homily to indicate the nature of Hesychius' audience on this occasion. They were presumably in the main residents of Jerusalem, because the homilist takes great pains to glorify the city, while at the same time exaggerating the feats of its first martyr, the protomartyr of all Christians. While staying close to the text of Acts, the homilist manages to embellish Stephen's importance by means of rhetorical flourishes.

Translated from the edition by M. Aubineau; Aubineau 1978: 328–50.

Text

1. In Stephen's honour let all the earth celebrate his feast: indeed he cultivated all of it constantly by his words, and filled the inhabited world, with all its people, with holy laws. He sowed everywhere doctrines of piety, the churches in their entirety he allowed to strive for the light of his teaching. And just like the sun, when it rises somewhere from one corner of heaven, has been allotted the task of illuminating visible creation in its entirety,

so the Crown[7] of graces, beaming rays out of Jerusalem, filled entire cities and regions, nations and peoples, tribes and languages with a knowledge of God that is inextinguishable.

2.   But it is we who rightly owe him more numerous feasts, because he is a citizen of the cross, a relative of Bethlehem, a descendant of the Resurrection, a table-attendant of Sion (cf. Acts 6:2), a herald of the Ascension.[8] It is in our midst that he fixed his abode and his tents (cf. Gen 26:25 etc.); it is in our midst that he obtained the election to his ministry and the part of his martyrdom (cf. Acts 8:21). In this spot he had his sacrificial altar and the bema[9] of his blessing, the field of his teaching, the theatre of his eloquence. From this spot he was taken up into heaven, and left us to go to Christ.

3.   This explains the frequency of the festal spectacles we hold in his honour, and we often put crowns on his nuptial canopy, frequently we go up leaping for joy to his wine-press, and we sing a marriage hymn as we say the words of the harvest song: '*Lord, you have crowned us with the shield of your favour*' (Ps 5:13). In fact, Stephen's zeal is a shield for believers, and his tongue is a sword for the pious, and his frank speech is a preparation for confession, his courage is an exhortation to bravery, his eloquence is material for theology, his teaching is the catechesis of the law, the knowledge of prophets, the realisation of gospels, his contemplation of heavenly mysteries – I should say more than heavenly – is an exegesis.

4.   But who is equal to the task of reciting the praises of Stephen in detail? Indeed, what should I call him? Witness to the light, minister of life, soldier of Christ, lampstand of the Word, pearl of the Spirit, flower of patience, foundation of philosophy, example of impassibility, first fruits of teachers, pillar of the church, pedagogue of grace, ladder of virtues, monument of progress, precursor of the apostles, first-born of the martyrs, guide to knowledge?

5.   He was in service to widows (cf. Acts 6:1), but by his own initiative he became appointed to the service of the churches: ordered to deliver food, he delivered doctrines instead. He changed tables (cf. Acts 6:2) into altars; he used bread from heaven, not from earth. He transformed the mixing bowl of drunkenness into cups of grace: instead of wine he mingled the Spirit; instead of material water he poured mystical and spiritual water.

6.   He was forceful in both speech and action, in teaching and miracle working, in refuting the Jews, in driving out demons, in

196

healing at the same time the sicknesses of the body and those of the soul. He opened his mouth and captured everyone's attention; he moved his tongue and death took to flight, falsehood was chained, charity progressed. Although a lamb, he fought on the shepherd's behalf against the wolves (cf. John 10:11); although a dove (cf. Matt 10:16), he subjected snakes to the eagle. He presented the character of an angel (cf. Acts 6:15), while being silent before judges. He laughed on seeing his accusers circling around him (cf. Acts 6:13), and, observing the false testimonies which were brought forward (cf. Acts 6:13), he said to himself these words from David's song to the cithara: 'Their blows have become children's darts' (Ps 63:8). I mean that however numerous the arrows of the false accuser, the artisan of truth is not wounded. However numerous the darts thrown by the evil one, they fly and are impelled in vain – they do not pierce the upright person, they do not hit the guileless person, they do not bite the pure person.

7.   So what was the nature of the false accusation? *This man does not stop discoursing against this holy place and against the Law* (Acts 6:13). *This man.* Which one? 'The one who works superhuman signs and prodigies (cf. Acts 6:8), the one who draws on the source of wisdom in its entirety (cf. Acts 6:10), the one who empties into himself the treasures of grace, the one who performs miracles which we cannot bear. We are consumed with rivalry and envy towards him. The deaf person obeys his call, and the blind person looks at him with eyes he has received from him, the lame person asks for feet, obtaining from his tongue hands as well. Because of him the beds of the sick were emptied, because of him there is no difference between healthy and ill persons, because of him the lepers forgot their suffering completely, because of him there is no need of doctors, because of him pounded medicines are superfluous.'

8.   'This man does not stop discoursing against this holy place and against the Law (Acts 6:13). What kind of discourses are they then? We heard him saying that Jesus, this Nazarean, will destroy this place and will change the customs which Moses handed down to us (Acts 6:14).' It is with reason that you are called false witnesses and accusers, because you declare not true what is true, because you call blasphemies (cf. Acts 6:11) against God the prophecies which were made by him and about him, and you consider an abolition of the Law future events which he himself has threatened.[10]

9. Whose voice is it, whose prophecy, whose proclamation? Who has enjoined Isaiah, who has enjoined Micah, to speak like this? *'This is why, because of you, Sion will be ploughed as a field, and Jerusalem will become like a crop-watcher's hut'* (Mic 3:12). *'The daughter of Sion will be left like a tent in a vineyard, and like a crop-watcher's hut in a cucumber field'* (Isa 1:8). Who inspired David to make utterances like these? *'Remember, Lord, on the day of Jerusalem, the children of Edom who said: "Raze it, raze it, to its foundations"'* (Ps 136:7).

10. What, then, did Moses say? Wasn't he himself in agreement with Stephen's words? Didn't he write down those curses against you, which in your present experience have come to pass, and which allow everybody to see the causes from which they proceeded? Juxtapose Moses' words with the wounds which came upon the Jewish people. If you examine them literally, you will find that they have come to pass without any falsehood anywhere, small or great. *And if, after that, you walk in a crooked way* (Lev 26:21). I mean that they have never possessed a straight heart towards God, but it is much more in later times that they have made the call of Christ crooked. For this reason he added the words: *And if you don't want to obey me* (certainly they didn't obey Christ when he called them), *I will send you seven plagues, corresponding to your iniquities* (Lev 26:21). In fact, because they denied the seven gifts of the Spirit, the seven spirits of evil which entered and dwelt in them changed into seven plagues for them, and their *last state was worse than the first* (Matt 12:45; Luke 11:26).

11. *And I will let loose on you the wild beasts of the earth* (Lev 26:22). He means the nations – they were formerly wild animals on account of their ignorance, because it was under the guise of wild animals and quadrupeds and snakes (cf. Rom 1:23) that they were accustomed to worship their divinity. It was to them that David addressed his curses: *'May those who make these images and all those who put their trust in them become like wild animals'* (Ps 113:16). Now God has let loose on them these nations who do what the lawgiver subsequently said: *'And they will devour you, and destroy your cattle, and reduce your number, and your roads will be deserts'* (Lev 26:22). In fact, each of these disasters befell them, in the literal sense and in the spiritual sense, when they came under the domination of the nations.

12. Indeed, up to today God has not put a stop to Moses' threats to these senseless people, but [he made] threats more serious and more important than the ones uttered [by Moses]. For he said:

'You will take a wife, and another man will have her. You will build a house, and you won't live in it. You will plant a vine, and you won't harvest it. Your calf will be slaughtered before your eyes, and you won't eat any of it' (Deut 28:30–1). After making many other threats against them, he did not hide the cause of these disasters, but addressed it with a multitude of threats which are connected to the ones we just spoke about: *'Your life will be suspended before your eyes, and you will be in dread day and night, and have no assurance of your life. In the morning you will say: "If only it were evening!" And in the evening you will say: "If only it were morning!", both because of the dread which your heart will fear, and because of the sights which your eyes will see'* (Deut 28:66–7).

13. So listen to the accomplishment of these threats, listen too to their fulfilment, and don't blame Stephen for addressing to the people words which were in keeping with the Law and the prophets. *You will take a wife* (Deut 28:30), that is, the Old Testament; *and another will have her* (Deut 28:30) – in fact, the people descended from the nations acquired her. *You will build a house, and you won't live in it* (Deut 28:30). It's clear that this is the temple, for you see it's fallen down. *You will plant a vine, and you won't harvest it* (Deut 28:30): it hasn't produced grapes, but thorns (cf. Isa 5:2). Or else, let's think of the vine of Christ (cf. John 15:5): it's from the Jews that Christ came, the vine of our life, but we're the ones who harvest the grape, we're the ones who mix the wine, we're the ones who drink the sweet wine. *Your calf will be slaughtered before your eyes, and you won't eat any of it* (Deut 28:31): the sacrifice of Christ is in fact due to them; they're the ones who led up to the altar the calf from heaven, but we're the ones who have the meal, we're the ones who have the table.

14. And why is this? Precisely because they were sick from disbelief, because they preferred ignorance to knowledge, because, at the moment of acknowledging God, they slipped into blasphemy. They went into the nuptial canopy, but did not welcome the bridegroom; they decorated the bridal chamber with crowns, but refused marriage. And while the crucifixion was taking place, the elements shook (cf. Matt 27:51), but they did not change. That's in fact what [Moses] added subsequently: *Your life will be suspended before your eyes* (Deut 28:66). Who is life? It's Christ, who says: *'I am the way and the life and the truth'* (John 14:6). And where is it suspended? On the wood of the cross. In fact, the one who suspended the earth by his word is suspended on the cross,

carrying while he is carried, suspending while he is suspended, lifting while he is lifted up. *'For when I am lifted'*, he says, *'I will draw all people to myself'* (John 12:32). *And you will be in dread day and night, and have no assurance of your life* (Deut 28:66). So then disbelief became the reason for dread.

15.   *You will be in dread day and night* (Deut 28:66) – the same day was actually day and night, according to the saying: *Over all the earth there was darkness from the sixth hour* (Matt 27:45). This is why Zechariah didn't know how it was preferable to designate it, what it was appropriate to call it, whether to designate the moment of the crucifixion as a result of the darkness which had occurred or as a result of the practice of measuring daylight. So then he said: *'And it will happen on that day that there is no light; and there will be cold and ice. It is a continuous day; it will be known to the Lord. There will be neither day nor night, and towards evening there will be light. And on that day living water will come forth from Jerusalem, half of it to the eastern sea, half of it to the western sea'* (Zech 14:6–8). These events took place literally and spiritually.

16.   *It will happen on that day that there is no light* (Zech 14:6), for the sun set at midday, while darkness and ignorance filled the Jews' hearts. *There will be cold and ice* (Zech 14:6). Peter is witness to this as he warms himself by the brazier because of the extreme of the winter season (cf. John 14:6–8). But in addition to this there was *cold and ice* because the Jews' love of God, especially at that moment, had become cold – otherwise they wouldn't have crucified the Saviour and Redeemer who came from him. *It is a continuous day* (Zech 14:6). How, in fact, wouldn't it be a continuous day, on which Adam was remodelled, sin was abolished, death destroyed, the potter recovered his vase (cf. Rom 9:21), the shepherd his sheep (cf. John 10:16), the merchant his pearl (cf. Matt 13:45)? *It will be known to God* (Zech 14:7). How, in fact, does the one who knows everything not recognise especially the day on which he delivered his only-begotten son to be sacrificed? *There will be neither day nor night*, because it is the course of a day that has passed, not that of a night. *Towards evening there will be light* (Zech 14:7), when after the ninth hour darkness ceased (cf. Matt 27:45 etc.). So then the same day became both one night and one day.

17.   *And living water will come forth from Jerusalem* (Zech 14:8). From where? From the side of the [one who is] life, for it is with reason that the church was modelled in the same place as Eve was remodelled. *Half of it into the eastern sea* (Zech 14:8), obviously that of

baptism. *And half of it into the western sea* (Zech 14:8), obviously that of repentance. For the tears of repentance are left over from the gift of baptism: the proof is clear. The person who is not baptised repents in vain if they have not hastened to be baptised. In vain do they offer a prayer of sacrifice, in vain do they ask for forgiveness, in vain do they shed tears. The point is that without baptism the forgiveness of sins is not effected. But the person who has been baptised has acquired an effective repentance: they weep and are delivered, they groan and are in mourning and pray, and immediately are purified.

18. But hear how also the rest of the prediction of the Law came to pass: *In the morning you say: 'If only it were evening!' In the evening you say: 'If only it were morning!'* Why? *Because of the dread in your heart which it fears, and because of the sights of your eyes which you have seen* (Deut 28:67). Since on account of the signs and wonders which were effected at the moment of the crucifixion – earthquake, flight of the sun, covering of the sky, breaking of rocks, tearing of the curtain, opening of graves – being fearful and troubled they were forced with reason to say to each other: *'If only it were evening!'* (Deut 28:67), so that we might seize life from the cross, so that we might hide on earth the one from heaven, so that we might shroud in a tomb the immortal one, so that we might rid ourselves of the wonder which has caused us so much dread.

19. But even after having done this, they did not achieve their goal: what they attempted to do turned out the opposite way for them. And this is why they said in the evening: *'If only it were morning!'* (Deut 28:67). Because once again the wonders accomplished in the night of the resurrection were full of dread, because they perceived the tomb as a bridal chamber, the monument sealed (cf. Matt 27:66), and the corpse emerging alive, the soldiers like dead men (cf. Matt 28:4), the women carrying unguents (cf. Mark 16:1–2; Luke 24:1), the angels guarding the bandages (cf. Luke 24:12; John 20:5, 7, 12), another sitting on the stone proclaiming the resurrection (cf. Matt 28:2), then they said: *'If only it were morning!'* (Deut 28:67), so that we would supply the soldiers with money, so that we would ruin Pilate, so that we would steal the truth by deceit, so that we would make it public *that his disciples came by night and stole him while we were asleep* (Matt 28:13).

20. These events the Law [foretold] and Moses through it, but in each case it is rather God who testifies that this people is senseless. In accusing them, Stephen the theologian was called by them

a blasphemer (cf. Acts 6:11). And the chief priest said: '*How is this so?*' (Acts 7:1). Don't you know that this is how it is? Wasn't it you who prepared the trap? Wasn't it you who engaged the services of the false accusers? Wasn't it you to whom the witnesses of deceit owed their wages? 'But there is a need', he says, 'of falsehood and dissembling, and we need guile to cast forth the net. In this way we sold Joseph (cf. Gen 37:28), killed Naboth (cf. 1 Kings 21), crucified Christ.'

21.   Having found the right moment for teaching, Stephen poured out into the people's ears many words concerning salvation, but he brought his public address to a conclusion, profitable both for himself to utter as a witness to the truth and for them to hear, because they had been incited to fight against God and they were suffering from their opposition to the Spirit. *Hard of heart and uncircumcised in heart and ears, you always resist the Holy Spirit. You are like your fathers, you too* (Acts 7:51).

22.   And how did you express it at the beginning? '*Brothers and fathers, listen to me*' (Acts 7:2). 'These words', it says, 'belong to the noble race of Abraham, but those belong to their badness. These words belong to the good root, those to bad branches (cf. Rom 11:16). These display the mark of the flesh, those disorder, dryness and unbridledness.' To this end the opening of Isaiah urges us:[11] '*Speak, those who are our brothers, to those who hate and abominate us, so that the name of the Lord may be glorified*' (Isa 66:5). They force the speech to this conclusion even against expectation: 'I called them brothers, I addressed them as fathers, lest anyone should think that I accused them as enemies, that I denounced them as opponents. But the same people I addressed as *hard of heart* and *uncircumcised* (Acts 7:51), because one ought to prefer the truth to ancestry and spare neither friends nor brothers nor fathers nor other relatives, when they transgress the law.'

23.   Of course the children of the Jews did not tolerate these words, but *ground their teeth* (Acts 7:54) like wild beasts, surging to devour Stephen while he was still addressing them. *They ground their teeth.* In fact, it had been said about them: '*Sons of men, their teeth are arms and darts, and their tongue is a sharp sword*' (Ps 56:5). Stephen directed his gaze not towards them, but towards God, and leaving earth surged towards the heavenly court, and with a loud voice proclaimed: '*Look, I see the heavens open*' (Acts 7:56). That is, the gain is a common one, the road has been made easy for everyone, the gate is open for those who want to go in. Let

the brave man combat intensely, let the real foot soldier now use his arms, let him demonstrate now the extent of his might. For the President of the games is looking on: he presides over the distribution of crowns and prizes.

24.   *Look, I see the heavens open* (Acts 7:56). And who is the one who, on opening them, did not permit to remain in ignorance the person who wished to know? And this is why he cried out: '*And the Son of Man standing at the right hand of God*' (Acts 7:56), meaning that the one who is incarnate is God the Word. For from the time that the Son of God became the Son of Man, from the time that the same one, from Father and virgin, was established as the meeting point between earth and heaven, the dividing wall of enmity was abolished (cf. Eph 2:14), the partition was out of the way (cf. Eph 2:14), what pertained to lifestyle was common to angels and human beings, if the human beings wished. It is possible for those on earth to do military service in heaven, to be below in the flesh, to be above in spirit, to be through mud with mud, but through the mind with God.

25.   So Stephen made this speech about God, but disorderly shouts followed his orderly speech about God, and shouts followed shouts, and barrages of stones succeeded his teachings on the divine laws. Lacking arms, they armed themselves from the ground, in the absence of swords they improvised with stones in their right hands, and, when they had taken him outside the city, they sacrificed him (cf. Acts 7:58). It wasn't in fact Old Jerusalem that was appropriate for this sacrifice, but this lamb too had to be slaughtered near the lamb who is the shepherd; the soldier had to receive the pledges of victory in the same place as the king fixed the trophy of his universal triumph.

26.   But what provisions did he receive for his end? Prayer and the perfume which came from it, and when he put off his flesh, he put on prayer. But what was this prayer? '*Lord Jesus, receive my spirit*' (Acts 7:59), that is, 'take what is yours, take back what you entrusted to me; collect the pearl which you put in my safe-keeping; I am sending you what I possess, which is in your image (cf. Gen 1:26–7). *Receive my spirit* (Acts 7:59), for the souls of the just no longer go into a weeping Hades (cf. Ps 83:7), the gloomy regions of death no longer accept the spirits of the living. After you became the first fruits of the living and of the dead (cf. 1 Cor 15:20) at the same time, to become lord of both dead and living (cf. Rom 14:9), it is not beside the point to say that the dough of

all the dead became confident (cf. Rom 11:16). *Receive my spirit* (Acts 7:59). Don't allow hunters to lie in wait for your ostrich (cf. Lam 3:52), nor enemies who meet at gates (cf. Prov 12:13) to spoil my migration from earth, nor trouble my ascent into heaven.'

27.   But while he offered this prayer on his own behalf, he offered again another on behalf of the Jewish people. *'Lord, don't hold this sin against them'* (Acts 7:60). And this is what he meant, for he didn't say: 'Don't charge them', but *'Don't hold against them'*, most certainly so that you would learn that your Judge weighs scrupulously, balancing the actions of each person (cf. Matt 16:27) at the moment of judgement. In fact, *if he weighed the mountains in a scale and the hills in a balance* (Isa 40:12), how much more wouldn't he weigh our actions, whether they are faulty or good? *Don't hold this sin against them.* Don't submit it to the scale of judgement, don't charge on my account those who are charged by themselves. May my blessing to them not become the occasion of a curse, may my gain (cf. Phil 1:21) not cause damage to the Jews.

28.   I don't want my sacrifice to harm those who sacrifice me. I mean that even if they are sacrificing me out of an evil design, nonetheless I respect them, those who have, contrary to expectation, become the occasion of my appearing before you, of the kingdom of heaven, of my release from mud, of my transfer above, of the victory of my witness, of confessing you and being confessed by you. In fact, the voice which addresses us is yours, at the instigation of which I have given myself up readily to be sacrificed, and by my confession I have poured my blood into your hands, as into a mixing bowl. *Everyone who confesses me before human beings I too will confess them before my Father in heaven* (Matt 10:32). To him be the glory forever and ever. Amen.

An encomium of Hesychius on St Stephen.

A homily in praise of Saint Procopius

Introduction

In his *editio princeps* of this homily in 1905 Hippolyte Delehaye expressed doubt about the authenticity of the text and about the martyr Procopius the Persian (Delehaye 1905). The doubt about authenticity was overturned in 1968 by Paul Devos (Devos 1968), and Michel Aubineau has since established that the title of the

homily is not the work of Hesychius but of a copyist who transformed Procopius of Caesarea, originally of Jerusalem, into the
unknown Procopius the Persian.[12]

The end of the homily, with its references to the 'linen cloths
in this spot', indicates that it was preached in the church of the
Resurrection (Anastasis), which was built on the Holy Sepulchre
(Coüasnon 1974: 21–36). Because the Armenian lectionary of the
church of Jerusalem, which reflects liturgical practice between 417
and 439, does not mention the feast of Procopius (Tarchnischvili
1959–60), it is probable that Hesychius delivered the homily around
the middle of the fifth century, towards the end of his life. Aubineau
speculates that the recently introduced feast of Procopius was
celebrated either on 23 June or 8 July (Aubineau 1978: 541). The
homily which Severus of Antioch delivered on the deposition of
the relics of the martyrs Procopius and Phocas in the church of the
angel Michael in Antioch sometime between November 514 and
November 515 does not help us to date the feast.[13]

The death of Procopius of Caesarea, who was martyred under
Diocletian in 303, is reported in Eusebius' *Martyrs of Palestine*
(1.1–2), where he is said to have died with a Homeric verse on his
lips. Procopius is variously represented in hagiographical literature
as a lector, exorcist, and ascetic, and as a pagan soldier who converts
to Christianity (see Aubineau 1978: 538–9). In one legend, whose
anonymous author is indebted to Eusebius' account, long discourses
against idolatry are put into the martyr's mouth. While Hesychius
does not tell us exactly who Procopius was, in paragraphs 4 and 5 we
read a fictitious speech from the martyr on the subject of idolatry.

Translated from the edition by M. Aubineau; Aubineau 1978:
546–64.

Text

1.   In Procopius Christ crowned sacrifice, when he saw that he was
an exceedingly handsome bull and very courageous with his horns
gilded by a multitude of virtues, taking first place in the herd of
martyrs which is dear to him, while by virtue of this authority
butting the enemies of the flock, with a single glance and roar
stunning the savage and murderous lions, with faith and ardour
putting to flight the many-spotted demonic leopards, with
bravery and sanctity scattering the various species of wild beasts
which belch out our death, making rise for us a brilliant spring

after the dim winter of error, being shown by his deeds to be the disciple of Paul, while propagating everywhere the theology of John, imitating the ardent sentiments of Elias of Thebes (cf. 1 Kings 17:10), practising his vocation from childhood as Samuel did (cf. 1 Sam 3:4), stronger than Samson – he didn't destroy his hair in the spiritual sense (cf. Judg 16:14, 19), comparable to David because he decapitated the many-headed Goliath (cf. 1 Sam 17:51), but also imitating Noah's ark by his cargo of virtues (cf. Gen 6:14), like Abraham disowning affection for home, race and country (cf. Gen 12:21), like Isaac becoming a burnt-offering before a martyr's death (cf. Gen 22:1–14) by means of mortification of his body.

2.   Jacob wrestled with God (cf. Gen 32:25–33), but Procopius wrestled on behalf of God, and set up his revered trophy before the whole world. It is true that Moses smashed a single idol, the golden calf, and he put to death many thousands of Jews, who were blasphemers against the law (cf. Exod 32:4, 20–6). Procopius for his part did not act like that, but on the one hand he trans-fixed all the statues of wood without an axe, while on the other hand he offered to Christ many nations and cities and lands after he had fished them in with his prophetic-sounding language. He was pure like Enoch, in the manner of Job *blameless, upright like him and just and God-fearing and turning away from all evil* (Job 1:1). I mean that the frankness of his confession showed that he was *upright*, his way of life demonstrated that he was *just*, the length of his trials proclaimed him *God-fearing*; abstention from pleasures, mastery of the belly, rejection of luxury, frugality of diet, mortification of the body – asceticism of many kinds, forms and varieties made him *turn away from all evil* (Job 1:1, 8).

3.   So he was pure like Enoch (cf. Gen 5:24), in the manner of Job *blameless* (Job 1:1, 8; 2:3); the one who feeds on accusations against sinners and belches forth calumnies against the just was unable to denounce him or blame him in any regard; he did not dare to say about him: 'Does Procopius revere the Lord for nothing?' (cf. Job 1:9). Procopius neither saw flocks of sheep prospering for him, nor did he acquire herds of camels (cf. Job 1:3) for transport. From where would grazing she-asses (cf. Job 1:3) have come to the martyr? From where would have come pairs of oxen (cf. Job 7:5) working the land to the one who had not even kept for himself a lump of earth (cf. Job 7:5)? But not even this did the common calumniator dare to allege, and, having reviled

the patience of the martyr, [said]: *'Skin for skin, all that a human being possesses they will give in payment for their life'* (Job 2:4).

Didn't the martyr have about him in his possession a band of sons or a crown of daughters (cf. Job 1:2)? Didn't he have his slaves' children, the offspring of his concubines, a robust body? Didn't he have bread to eat and water to drink? Didn't he have a continual fast? Didn't he have a dinner that was more frugal than abstinence? In the same way Abel in dying was passing judgement on Cain (cf. Gen 4:8, 10): the earth possessed his body; heaven, his mouth; Hades, his tongue; the judge, his voice (cf. Gen 4:10); the clay, his clay; the merchant, his pearl (cf. Matt 13:45); save in dying he was passing judgement on Cain. It was not the same with Procopius, but he interceded with God on behalf of his enemies and pleaded for them, negotiated on behalf of the pagans, appealed on behalf of the Jews, was eager to mediate on behalf of the Samaritans, and showed kindness to his enemies after his death, and reforged the ears of those of them who were deaf, he made a new sun for the blind, he straightened the feet of the lame, and those who previously were unable to move their toes were seen to run. I mean that the lepers did not come near the tombs, but before approaching they stripped off their scales and presented themselves purified, like dancers for the wedding-chamber, like the escorts for the bridegroom (cf. Matt 9:15 etc.).[14]

4.   But who would be capable of singing the praises of Procopius one after the other? Which of his struggles shall we take up first? Which shall we rank second? Which shall we put third? Where will the fourth be situated? What fitting spot will the fifth find? What sixth crown shall we fit on him? What seventh prize shall we devise for him? To what eighth step of praise shall we ascend? What ninth tower of encomia shall we forge? Which of the stories shall we be able to run through as the last?

Error was holding the human race prisoner. Adam had been deceived but had not realised the deception; God was not God in his eyes, but stones were gods; the creator was not the creator, but the creators were the works of human hands (cf. Acts 7:41), objects engraved by his fingers, figures of metal which the smith had blown and the furnace had purified, whose anvil had hollowed out the stomach, whose hammer had spread out the back, put into relief the shoulder and raised the neck, had forged the head and superimposed the skull, whose engraving tool had dug out the ears and curved the nostrils, delineated the lips, carved the eyes on the surface, formed the pupils, wreathed curls, circled eyebrows and added eyelids. This is why the enemy showed contempt for human life: the words *you shall not kill* (Exod 20:15) were made sport of; the words *you shall not commit adultery* (Exod 20:13) were ridiculed; the words *you shall not steal* (Exod 20:14) were suspended; the words *you shall not bear false witness* (Exod 20:16) were considered trash and a fable; the words *you shall not covet your neighbour's goods* (Exod 20:17) were a commandment hostile to human life; and the Law became foreign to their lifestyle.

5.   Procopius came forward in public and began to exhort all the drunks: '*Men, you are brothers. To what purpose do you do each other wrong?* (Acts 7:26). Why do you take no notice of the fact that you are killing each other with your swords? Why don't you take account of the fact that each of you is wounding themselves with their own arrows or with those of their neighbour? Give me your eyes, you who are blind with regard to intelligence – I should say, entrust to me first of all your feet, you who are lame with regard to understanding. To what purpose do you compare the divine to idols, equate the creator of all with animals, and compare the one who animates creation to inanimate beings, rank the one who planted reason with beings without reason? To what purpose, abandoning virtue too, do you get drunk on pleasures? Gold which does not belong to us, but to the earth which we have received, we should trample underfoot. Silver is a gift from clay: what good can clay do for a soul endowed with reason? Expensive clothes feed moths (cf. Jas 5:2) and deceive eyes, beguiling and cheating the human being. Wasn't it linen that the well-known rich man was wearing (cf. Luke 16:19)? But the fireplace and the furnace of limbs and the incandescent saucepan of the tongue (cf. Acts 12:23) replaced the linen. Wasn't Herod attired in a royal robe (cf. Acts 12:21)? But worms ate his clothes, along with his flesh. How many tunics of gold and purple did the Pharaoh possess? But it's in a state of nakedness that he's buried in the Red Sea (cf. Exod 15:4).'

If you, on the other hand, desire purple tunics, exercise moderation. If you are concerned about linen, bring about justice. Train yourself in patience; it's a royal necklace. Work on almsgiving: its cloth is woven on earth, but it's cut in heaven. If you are keen to put a lofty crown around your head, pursue humility, for as far as God is concerned nothing is ranked more gloriously than that.

For this crown, don't resile from trials, nor avoid dangerous situations, nor demand exemption from sweaty exertions, nor be timid in the face of death.

6.   Don't resile from trials, for *happy is the man who endures trial* (Jas 1:12). Don't demand exemptions from persecutions, *since blessed are those who are persecuted for justice's sake, because theirs is the kingdom of heaven* (Matt 5:10). Don't avoid danger, for *the dangers of Hades have found me, and I have called on the name of the Lord* (Ps 114:3–4), says David, and like an ally he has come from heaven to meet me. Don't be timid in the face of death, for just now you heard the church singing: *'Precious before the Lord is the death of his saints'* (Ps 115:6), and this is quite proper. The grain before the harvest – in no way can the farmer permit himself to rely on it, because he both suspects the locust and fears the grasshopper, he is afraid of mildew, he does not stop mistrusting the showers of hail, he is anxious about the damage caused by gusts of wind. But once the grain has been taken by the sickle, and has come into the hands of the harvester, and has been put in sheaves, and carried on the wagons with the straw, and taken over the threshing-floor, and been thrown up by the fan, and after winnowing is kept sealed in the barn, then the farmer has confidence and rejoices because he has become rich, he is proud because he has not toiled in vain. At one time he opens up his barns and loosens the bolts and throws open the doors [and] welcomes people; at another, when he has displayed his grain in public in the midst of the merchants, he prides himself on the labours of his own hands. In the same manner indeed the sower of our race, the farmer of our dough, is not confident about Adam before he has seen him taken away from the earth, before he has embarked on trials, before he has ridden on horseback through the dangers of the stadium for the sake of the Christian way of life.[15]

7.   When Adam passed away from earth, then [the sower of our race] was happy and confident and proud and said to him: *'Well done, good and faithful servant'* (Matt 25:23). Then he added: *'Enter into the joy of your lord'* (Matt 25:23). Then he addressed him: *'Come, you blessed of my father'* (Matt 25:34). Then, through the experience of good things, he showed that *for those who love God all things work together for good* (Rom 8:28). Whether tribulation lays siege to the human being,[16] whether distress constrains the believer, whether nudity possesses him, whether dangers encircle him, whether the sword has been sharpened, none of these things

could separate the believer from Christ, none could set the soldier apart from his king. I mean that if tribulation lays siege to them, on seeing Christ, the prince of joy, they rejoice; if distress constrains them, on looking at the teacher they relax; if persecution dogs them, on looking forward to heaven they take no thought for earth, but steady their feet in order not to stumble; if famine threatens them, in groping for *the bread of life* (John 6:35, 48) they eat their fill; if nudity possesses them, they put on the spirit, they become enveloped in grace and are right to take no thought for clothes; if danger menaces them, they know who the general is, they recognise the one who fights with them and are right not to countenance curbing their frank talking; if the sword has been sharpened, the tongue does not put up with being silent, even if it has been sacrificed; for each of the events which ensue, they are ready, like guileless sheep and pure flocks and lambs, receiving with pleasure the injunction of the shepherd: '*Look, I am sending you like flocks into the midst of wolves*' (Matt 10:16), that is, have confidence and go forth, hurry off immediately, gather the nations, cause the herds to increase, throw the wolves confusion, prove the power of the shepherd.

8. You are not of less account than Moses, nor yet are you second to Jeremiah, nor have you been entrusted with a grace inferior to that of Ezekiel. With you is the one who sent Elijah: he sends you forth too, like each of the prophets. Look, then, who Moses was and to whom he was sent, and what kind of trophy he raised up and established (cf. Num 21:8–9). Unarmed was the legislator, and he was sent to people who were *respecters of persons* (Acts 10:34 etc.), but the rod of the unarmed man subjected and tamed camps of men-at-arms. You, on the other hand, instead of armour must put on as breastplate the following command: '*Therefore become as cunning as serpents and as pure as doves*' (Matt 10:16). Cunning is good, and purity is similarly admirable, but when they are combined with each other they acquire what is helpful and advantageous: neither sheer cunning nor mere purity can justify and save a human being, and this is why it is necessary to acquire together the cunning of serpents and the purity of doves. I mean that the serpent is cunning (cf. Matt 10:16), but not pure, and you rightly regard the animal as beyond the pale because it is venomous. The dove is just pure, and because of this is easy prey for everybody's schemes. You, therefore, must mingle cunning with purity and become pure in worldly affairs, cunning

in spiritual affairs. If you are buying a field, or selling, or exchanging something else among worldly goods, pursue purity, because to endure injustice is more munificent than to commit it, to be a victim of fraud is more advantageous than to perpetrate it, in the eyes of those who wish to achieve heavenly gains rather than earthly ones. If you study Law, then disgorge your cunning and search for the meaning of what is written, how this is written, why that, what the letter of the law means, what the spirit of prophecy has enjoined, whether the passage is straight-forward, whether the learned pen is making suggestions in parables. With these considerations pay attention to what other military and strategic signs you receive on behalf of the one who is sending you.

9. *They will deliver you to sanhedrins* (Matt 10:17), but be confi-dent, the Father is not separated from you, the Son is not far away, the Spirit is not aloof, angels are your bodyguards. *And in their synagogues they will flog you* (Matt 10:17). But rejoice greatly, for the stripes from the enemy as a result of the floggings [which are endured] for the sake of piety are more glorious than the sun's rays. *And you will be dragged before governors and kings for my sake, to bear testimony to them and to the Gentiles* (Matt 10:18). Don't become paralysed on this account: it's on my account that you appear before governors, it's for my glory that you are brought before kings. With you, therefore, is the one who has anointed kings, in you is the one who has assigned boundaries to gover-nors, the one who has allotted the tribunal to the latter and bestowed the sceptre on the former. But consider further this too: it is not so much as defendants that you will appear before kings and governors, but to give witness before them, obviously before the children of the Jews, but moreover before the Gentiles, so that they may know the power of the one to whom you are testifying, because the poor are bridling the rulers, country people are fright-ening the council of consuls and despising the illustrious senate, ordinary people are shaming tyrants and confounding kings. *When they deliver you up, do not be anxious how you are to speak or what you are to say* (Matt 10:19). I mean that you are tongues of the word, and flutes of wisdom, and heralds of life, and orators of the one who does not need orators, and because of this fact it is for you that the following ensues: *For what you are to say will be given in that hour* (Matt 10:20). Before that hour the speech of grace will not be accorded to you, lest you think that the expressions which

come from you are your own. *For it is not you who speak, but the spirit of your father who speaks in you* (Matt 10:20). The contest, in fact, is about him, the struggle is on his account. I mean that the race in the stadium is in his favour. Therefore you must await grace from him, look for the word, receive the grace of confessing him, hope for a suit of armour against which the enemy will be powerless, because it has been forged by God.

10. *Brother will deliver up brother to death, and the father his child, and children will rise against parents and put them to death* (Matt 10:21). Nature divides and grace brings together. Mud campaigns against itself, but the creator does not put up with abandoning the mud. The pots come into collision with each other, such that they need the potter's wheel and thus of necessity retain the memory of the potter. *And you will be hated by all for my name's sake* (Matt 10:22). It is enough for your glory, it is sufficient for your reputation, it is not a small thing to make you confident, the fact that you will be hated by all.

The one who is over all does not put up with abandoning you, but continues to cherish you and makes his love ever warmer. *For you will be hated by all for my name's sake. But the one who endures to the end will be saved* (Matt 10:22).

11. Listen to the word, believer, and keep the commandment, and cultivate patience with zeal, and reap with great joy the ear of corn which comes from it. Gather the bunch of grapes, tread the cluster. There are many things you must not say: 'The dangers are varied, the troubles are difficult, the constraints are sombre. What comes from the native land gives joy, but what happens abroad is hateful. Those who console are few, but those who trip up are many. The Christian way of life is insulted and virtue is mocked. Fear takes hold of me regarding my household slaves, my parents' struggle falls on me, the worry of my personal affairs takes me by siege.' Don't say this, don't think it, nor relax the reins of your patience, nor cultivate in yourself the seeds of negligence, but direct your gaze with zeal toward this royal cross, contemplate it and, after it, consider this holy temple, the Resurrection.[17] Draw for yourself the king hanging on a tree, a master wrongly beaten by slaves (cf. Matt 26:67 etc.), a lawgiver shamelessly spat on by subordinates (cf. Matt 26:67 etc.), the one who is opulent in all his clothes impudently stripped of his tunic (cf. Matt 26:28). But look, do you see the resurrection in these events? In this spot, the linen cloths of the one who was stripped prove

his wealth, angels will demonstrate the power of the one who was beaten, the voices of those who came down from heaven reveal the glory of the one who was slapped. To him be the glory now and always and forever and ever. Amen.

Notes

1 See Aubineau 1978: XV. *Editio princeps* by Devos 1968.
2 *Itinerarium* 27, Corpus Christianorum Series Latina 175, 143.
3 Homily 17, *On the Holy Martyrs* (CPG 6588), Aubineau 1980: 706–14, surviving in a fragment, is of dubious authenticity; homily 13, *On saints Peter and Paul* (CPG 6577), Aubineau 1978: 499–509 treats its subjects as apostles, not as martyrs.
4 Homily 10, *On saints Jacob and David* (CPG 6574), Aubineau 1978: 351–68.
5 For a survey of the churches in Jerusalem and its vicinity see Baldovin 1987: 46–55.
6 For the evidence of place and date of delivery see Aubineau 1978: 319–26.
7 This is a pun on the Greek *stefanos*, which is both a proper name and means 'crown'. Cf. Asterius, *Hom. on Stephen* 7.4.
8 We take these references to be to the various churches in Jerusalem where the 'numerous feasts' of Stephen were celebrated.
9 That is, the sanctuary.
10 On the eight threats against Jerusalem see Aubineau 1978: 296–7.
11 In fact this quotation occurs towards the end of the book of Isaiah. Aubineau 1978: 345, sidesteps the problem by translating 'A cet exorde poussaient les paroles d'Isaïe'.
12 Aubineau 1978: 536–41. The title reads: 'Hesychius, presbyter of Jerusalem, an encomium on the holy martyr Procopius <the Persian>; and on the response to the Psalm: *Precious before the Lord is the death of his holy ones* (Ps 115:6); and on the saying of the Apostle: *For those who love God everything works together for good* (Rom 8:28); and on the commission to the apostles: *See, I am sending you like sheep into the midst of wolves* (Matt 10:16) etc.' It is reasonable to assume that the verses cited in the title were the readings for the liturgy on the feast of Procopius. The verse from Ps 115:6 is taken up again at the beginning of par. 6.
13 Homily LXXII, ed. M. Brière, PO 12/1 (1973) 71–89.
14 In his Homily 72, *On the Deposition of the Sacred Bodies of the Holy Martyrs Procopius and Phocas* (PO 12 [1985] 87), Severus of Antioch speaks of the power of the martyrs' limbs, which effect cures and chase demons away.
15 This is the Greek word *filosofia*. Regarding the semantic range of this term in martyrial homilies see above John Chrysostom (n. 34) and Asterius of Amasea (n. 90).

16 From this line to the citation from Matt 10:16 at the end of the paragraph, Hesychius uses echoes from Rom 8:35.

17 This makes it clear that the homily was delivered in the church of the Resurrection (Anastasis).

BIBLIOGRAPHY

Primary sources: editions and translations

Editions of texts included in this volume

Aubineau, M. (1978) *Les homélies festales d'Hésychius de Jérusalem. I. Les homélies I–XV*, Brussels: Société des Bollandistes (Subsidia Hagiographica 59/1) [*On Stephen*: 328–50; *On Procopius*: 546–64].

Datema, C. (1970) *Asterius of Amasea. Homilies I–XIV: Text, Introduction and Notes*, Leiden: Brill. [*On Phocas*: 114–27; *On Stephen*: 165–73].

Delehaye, H. (1905) 'Hesychii Hierosolymorum presbyteri laudatio S. Procopii Persae', *Analecta Bollandiana* 24: 473–82.

Devos, P. (1968) 'Le panégyrique de saint Étienne par Hésychius de Jérusalem', *Analecta Bollandiana* 86: 151–72.

Halkin, F. (1965) *Euphémie de Chalcédoine. Légendes Byzantines*, Brussels: Société des Bollandistes (Subsidia Hagiographica 41) [*Ecphrasis on Euphemia*: 4–8].

Heil, G., Cavarnos, J., Lendle, O. and Mann, F. (1990) *Gregorii Nysseni Sermones. Pars II*, Leiden: Brill (GNO, X, 1/2) [*On Theodore*: 61–71; *On the Forty Martyrs of Sebaste Ia and Ib*: 137–56].

Sancti patris nostri Basilii, Caesareae Cappadociae archiepiscopi, Opera omnia quae exstant vel quae sub ejus nomine circumferuntur (PG 31), Paris: Migne, 1857 [*On Gordius*: cols 489–508; *On the Forty Martyrs of Sebaste*: cols 508–26].

Sancti patris nostri Joannis Chrysostomi, archiepiscopi constantinopolitani, Opera omnia quae exstant vel quae sub ejus nomine circumferuntur (PG 50), Paris: Migne, 1859 [*On the Holy Martyrs*: cols 645–54; *On Julian*: cols 665–76; *On Pelagia*: cols 579–84].

Schatkin, M.A., Blanc, C., Grillet, B. and Guinot, J.-N. (1990) *Jean Chrysostome. Discours sur Babylas* suivi de l'*Homélie sur Babylas*, Paris: Cerf (SC 362) [*On Babylas*: 294–312].

Translations of texts in this volume prior to our own

Aubineau, M. (1978) *Les homélies festales d'Hésychius de Jérusalem. I. Les homélies I–XV*, Brussels: Société des Bollandistes (Subsidia Hagiographica 59/1) [French translations of *On Stephen*: 328–50; *On Procopius*: 546–64].

Brandram, T.P. (1889) 'On the Holy Martyr s. Babylas', in P. Schaff (ed.), *A Select Library of the Nicene and Post Nicene Fathers of the Christian Church*, New York: The Christian Literature Company, IX, 141–3.

Castelli, E. (2000) 'Asterius of Amasea; Ekphrasis on the Holy Martyr Euphemia', ch. 39 in R. Valantasis (ed.), *Religions of Late Antiquity in Practice*, Princeton: Princeton University Press (Princeton Readings in Religions) [*Ecphrasis on Euphemia*: 462–8].

Mango, C. (1972) *The Art of the Byzantine Empire 312–1453: Sources and Documents*, Englewood Cliffs: Prentice Hall (Sources and Documents in the History of Art) [*Ecphrasis on Euphemia*: 37–9].

Schatkin, M.A., Blanc, C., Grillet, B. and Guinot, J.-N. (1990) *Jean Chrysostome. Discours sur Babylas* suivi de l'*Homélie sur Babylas*, Paris: Cerf (SC 362) [French translation of *On Babylas*: 294–312].

van der Meer, F. and Bartelink, G. (1976) *Zestien preken van Asterius*, Nijmegen: Dekker & van de Vegt [Dutch translations of *On Phocas*: 170–80; *Ecphrasis on Euphemia*: 199–203; *On Stephen*: 203–15].

Other editions

Amsler, F. (1999) *Apocrypha Novi Testamenti: Acta Philippi: commentarius*, Turnhout: Brepols (Corpus Christianorum. Series Apocryphorum 12).

Aubineau, M. (1980) *Les homélies festales d'Hésychius de Jérusalem. II. Les homélies XVI–XXI*, Brussels: Société des Bollandistes (Subsidia Hagiographica 59/2).

—— (1989) 'Ps-Chrysostome, *In S. Stephanum* (PG 63,933–4): Proclus de Constantinople, l'impératrice Pulchérie et saint Etienne', in A.A.R. Bastiaensen, A. Hilhorst and C. Kneepkens (eds), *Fructus centesimus: mélanges offerts a Gérard J.M. Bartelink*, Steenbrugge: in Abbatia S. Petri (Instrumenta Patristica 19), 1–16.

Bernardi, J. (1983) *Grégoire de Nazianze. Discours 4–5: contre Julien*, Paris: Cerf (SC 309).

Bidez, J. and Hansen, G.C. (1995) *Sozomenus. Kirchengeschichte* (2nd rev. edn), Berlin: Akademie Verlag (GCS N.F. Bd 4).

Borret, M. (1969) *Origène. Contre Celse. IV: Livres VII et VIII*, Paris: Cerf (SC 150).

Bretz, A. (1914) *Studien und Texte zu Asterios von Amasea*, Leipzig: Hinrichs'sche Buchhandlung (Texte und Untersuchungen zur Geschichte der altchristlichen Literatur 40.1).

Brooks, E.W. (1911) *The Hymns of Severus*, Turnhout: Brepols (PO 6).

Canivet, P. (1958) *Theodorète de Cyr. Thérapeutique des maladies helléniques*, Paris: Cerf (SC 57).

Canivet, P. and Leroy-Molinghen, A. (1977, 1979) *Théodoret de Cyr. Histoire des moines de Syrie*. Sources Chrétiennes, vols 234 and 257, Paris: Cert.

Courtonne, Y. (1957–66) *Saint Basile. Lettres*, Paris: Société des éditions 'Les Belles Lettres' (Collection des Universités de France).

Datema, C. (1978–9) 'Les homélies XV–XVI d'Astérius d'Amasée', *Sacris Erudiri* 23: 63–93.

Eusebii Pamphili, Caesareae Palaestinae episcopi, Opera omnia quae exstant, Paris: Migne (PG 23).

Featherstone, J.M. (1997) *Nicephori Patriarchae Constantinopolitani Refutatio et Eversio Definitionis Synodalis Anni 815*, Turnhout: Brepols (Corpus Christianorum. Series Graeca 33).

Gallay, P. (1964–7) *Saint Grégoire de Nazianze. Lettres*, Paris: Société des éditions 'Les Belles Lettres' (Collection des Universités de France).

Galletier, É. *et al.* (1978–96) *Ammien Marcellin. Histoire*, 3 vols, Paris: Société des éditions 'Les Belles Lettres' (Collection des Universités de France).

Gebhardt, O. (1902) *Acta martyrum selecta. Ausgewählte Märtyreracten und andere Urkunden aus der Verfolgungszeit der Christlichen Kirche*, Berlin: Alexander Duncker.

Geyer, P. (1965) *Itineraria et alia geographica*, Turnhout: Brepols (Corpus Christianorum. Series Latina 175).

Giet, S. (1968) *Basile de Césarée. Homélies sur l'Hexaéméron* (2nd rev. edn), Paris: Cerf (SC 26bis).

Hansen, G.C. with Sirinjan, M. (1995) *Sokrates. Kirchengeschichte*, Berlin: Akademie Verlag (GCS N.F. Bd 1).

Heil, G. (1967) *Gregorii Nysseni Sermones, Pars I*, Leiden: Brill (GNO IX).

Henry, P. (1977) *Photius: Bibliothèque Tome VIII ('codices' 257–280)*, Paris: Les Belles Lettres (Collection Byzantine).

Hill, D.E. (1985) *Ovid. Metamorphoses I–IV*, Warminster: Aris & Phillips Publishers.

Klostermann, E. and Benz, E. (1935) *Origenes. Matthäuserklärung*, Leipzig: Hinrichs (GCS 40.1).

Koetschau, P. (1899) *Origenes. Die Schrift vom Martyrium; Buch I–IV gegen Celsus*, Leipzig: Hinrichs (GCS 2).

Krüger, G. (1965) *Ausgewählte Märtyrerakten: Neubearbeitung der Knopfschen Ausgabe* (4th rev. edn), mit einem Nachtrag von G. Ruhbach, Tübingen: Mohr.

Malingrey, A.-M. (1980) *Jean Chrysostome. Sur le sacerdoce (Dialogue et Homélie)*, Paris: Cerf (SC 272).

—— with Leclercq, P. (1988) *Palladios. Dialogue sur la vie de Jean Chrysostome*, Paris: Cerf (SC 341–2).

Maraval, P. (1971) *Grégoire de Nysse. Vie de Sainte Macrine*, Paris: Cerf (SC 178).

—— (1990a) *Grégoire de Nysse. Lettres*, Paris: Cerf (SC 363).

—— (1990b) *La Passion inédite de S. Athénogène de Pédachthoé en Cappadoce (BHG 197b). Introduction, édition, traduction. Appendice: Passion épique de S. Athénogène de Pédachthoé. Edition et traduction*, Brussels: Société des Bollandistes (Subsidia Hagiographica 75).

—— (1997 [1982]) *Egérie. Journal de voyage (Itineraire)*, Paris: Cerf (SC 296).

Metzger, M. (1985–87) *Les constitutions apostoliques*, 3 vols, Paris: Cerf (SC 320, 329, 336).

Mossay, J. and Lafontaine, G. (1981) *Grégoire de Nazianze. Discours 24–26*, Paris: Cerf (SC 284).

Musurillo, H. (1972) *The Acts of the Christian Martyrs*, Oxford: Clarendon Press (Oxford Early Christian Texts).

Parmentier, L. and Hansen, G.C. (1998) *Theodoret. Kirchengeschichte* (2nd rev. edn), Berlin: Akademie Verlag (GCS, N.F. Bd 5).

Petitmengin, P. *et al.* (1981, 1984) *Pélagie la pénitente. Métamorphoses d'une légende*, 2 vols, Paris: Études augustiniennes [Greek *vitae*: I, 77–131].

Piédagnel, A. (1982) *Jean Chrysostom. Panégyriques de S. Paul*, Paris: Cerf (SC 300).

Prieur, J.-M. (1989) *Apocrypha Novi Testamenti: Acta Andreae*, Turnhout: Brepols (Corpus Christianorum. Series apocryphorum 5–6).

Tarchnischvili, M. (1959–60) *Le Grand Lectionnaire de l'Eglise de Jérusalem (v^e–viiie siècle)*, Leuven: Secrétariat du Corpus SCO (Corpus Scriptorum Christianorum Orientalium 188, 189, 204, 205).

Thümmel, H.G. (1992) *Die Frühgeschichte der ostkirchlichen Bilderlehre*, Berlin: Akademie Verlag (Texte und Untersuchungen zur Geschichte der altchristlichen Literatur 139).

Wenger, A. (1970) *Jean Chrysostome: Huit catéchèses baptismales inédites*, Paris: Cerf (SC 50bis).

Zelzer, M. (1982) *Sancti Ambrosii Opera. X. Epistula et acta. III. Epistularium liber decimus, Epistulae extra collectionem; Gesta concili Aquileiensis*, Vienna: Hoelder-Pichler-Tempsky (Corpus Scriptorum Ecclesiasticorum Latinorum 82/3).

Secondary literature

Reference works

Berardino, A. di (ed.) (1992) *Encyclopedia of the Early Church = Dizionario patristico e di Antichità Cristiana*, 2 vols, translated from the Italian, Cambridge: James Clarke & Co. (Institutum Patristicum Augustinianum).

Geerard, M. (1974) *Clavis Patrum Graecorum. II. Ab Athanasio ad Chrysostomum*, Turnhout: Brepols.

—— and Noret, J. (1998) *Clavis Patrum Graecorum. Supplementum*, Turnhout: Brepols.

Lampe, G. (2000 = 1961) *A Patristic Greek Lexicon*, Oxford: Clarendon Press.

Liddell, H., Scott, R. and Jones, H. (eds) (1996) *Greek–English Lexicon with a Revised Supplement*, Oxford: Clarendon Press.

Books and articles

Adkin, N. (1992) 'The Date of St. John Chrysostom's Treatises on "subintroductae"', *Revue Bénédictine* 102: 255–66.

—— (1994) 'The Date of John Chrysostom's *De virginitate*', *Orientalia Christiana Periodica* 60: 611–17.

Aigrain, R. (1953) *L'Hagiographie. Ses sources, ses méthodes, son histoire*, Poitiers: Bloud & Gay; (2000) Brussels. Société des Bollandistes (Subsida hagiographica).

Alexander, P. (1958) *The Patriarch Nicephoros of Constantinople. Ecclesiastical Policy and Image Worship in the Byzantine Empire*, Oxford: Clarendon Press.

Alexandre, M. (1984) 'Les nouveaux martyrs. Motifs martyrologiques dans la vie des saints et thèmes hagiographiques dans l'Éloge des martyrs chez Grégoire de Nysse', in A. Spira (ed.), *The Biographical Works of Gregory of Nyssa. Proceedings of the Fifth International Colloquium on Gregory of Nyssa (Mainz, 6–10 September 1982)*, Cambridge MA–Philadelphia PA: Philadelphia Patristic Foundation (Patristic Monograph Series 12), 33–70.

—— (1986) 'L'épée de flamme (Gen 3,24): textes chrétiens et traditions juives', in A. Caquot, M. Hadas-Lebel and J. Riaud (eds), *Hellenica et Judaica. Hommages à V. Nikiprowetsky*, Leuven–Paris: Peeters, 403–41.

Allen, P. (1996) 'The Homilist and the Congregation. A Case Study of Chrysostom's Homilies on Hebrews', *Augustinianum* 36: 397–421.

—— (1997) 'John Chrysostom's Homilies on I and II Thessalonians: The Preacher and His Audience', *Studia Patristica* 31: 3–21.

—— and Cunningham, M. (eds) (1998), *Preacher and Audience. Studies in Early Christian and Byzantine Homiletics*, Leiden: Brill (A New History of the Sermon, 1).

—— and Mayer, W. (1993) 'Computer and Homily: Accessing the Everyday Life of Early Christians', *Vigiliae Christianae* 47: 260–80.

—— and —— (2000), 'John Chrysostom', in P. Esler (ed.), *The Early Christian World*, London: Routledge, II, 1128–50.

Amat, J. (1985) *Songes et visions: l'au-delà dans la littérature latine tardive*, Paris: Institut des études augustiniennes (Études augustiniennes. Série Antiquité 109).

Ameringer, T.E. (1921) *The Stylistic Influence of the Second Sophistic on the Panegyrical Sermons of St. John Chrysostom*, Washington: Catholic University of America (Catholic University of America Patristic Studies 5).

Amore, A. (1968) 'Sebastia, XL martiri di', *Bibliotheca Sanctorum* 11: 768–71.

—— (1969) 'Teodoro', *Bibliotheca Sanctorum* 12: 238–41.

Balas, D.L. (1985) 'Gregor von Nyssa', *Theologische Realenzyklopädie* 14: 173–81.

Baldovin, J.F. (1987) *The Urban Character of Christian Worship. The Origins, Development, and Meaning of Stational Liturgy*, Rome: Pontificium Institutum Studiorum Orientalium (Orientalia Christiana Analecta 228).

Barnes, T.D. (1997) 'The Collapse of the Homoeans in the East', *Studia Patristica* 29: 6–13.

Baumeister, T. (1988) 'Heiligenverehrung I', in *RAC* 14: 96–150.

Baumstark, A. (1954) 'Begleitfeste', in *RAC* 2: 78–92.

Baur, C. (1959–60) *John Chrysostom and His Time*, ET by Sr M. Gonzaga, 2 vols, Westminster MD: Md. Newman Press.

Bernardi, J. (1968) *La prédication des Pères Cappadociens: le prédicateur et son auditoire*, Marseille: Presses Universitaires de France (Publications de la Faculté des lettres et sciences humaines de l'Université de Montpellier 30).

Biddle, M.E. (1999) 'Redaction Criticism, Hebrew Bible', in J.H. Hayes (ed.), *Dictionary of Biblical Interpretation. II. K–Z*, Nashville TN: Abingdon, 373–6.

Bland-Simmons, M. (2000) 'Julian the Apostate', in P. Esler (ed.), *The Early Christian World*, London: Routledge, II, 1251–73.

Brändle, R. (1999) *Johannes Chrysostomus. Bischof–Reformer–Märtyrer*, Stuttgart–Berlin–Köln: Verlag W. Kohlhammer.

—— Pradels, W. and Heimgartner, M. (2001) 'Das bisher vermisste Textstück in Johannes Chrysostomus, Adversus Iudaeos, Oratio 2', *Zeitschrift für Antike und Christentum* 5: 23–49.

Brown, P. (1981) *The Cult of the Saints: Its Rise and Function in Latin Christianity*, Chicago–London: Chicago University Press & SCM.

—— (1983) 'The Saint as Exemplar in Late Antiquity', *Representations* 1: 1–21.

Cameron, A. (1998) 'Education and Literary Culture', in A. Cameron and P. Garnsey (eds), *The Late Empire: AD 337–425*, Cambridge: University Press (The Cambridge Ancient History 13), 665–708.

Campbell, J.M. (1922) *The Influence of the Second Sophistic on the Style of the Sermons of St. Basil the Great*, Washington: Catholic University of America (Catholic University of America Patristic Studies 5).

Christo, G.G. (1997) *Martyrdom According to John Chrysostom. 'To Live is Christ, To Die is Gain'*, Lewiston: Mellen University Press.

Coüasnon, C. (1974) *The Church of the Holy Sepulchre in Jerusalem*, London: Oxford University Press.

Daniélou, J. (1955) 'La chronologie des sermons de Grégoire de Nysse', *Revue des sciences religieuses* 29: 346–72.

Delehaye, H. (1921) *Les passions des martyrs et les genres littéraires*, Brussels: Société des Bollandistes.

—— (1923) 'Euchaïta et la légende de saint Théodore', in W.H. Buckler and W.M. Calder (eds), *Anatolian Studies Presented to Sir W.M. Ramsay*, Manchester: Manchester University Press, 129–34 [=(1966) *Mélanges d'hagiographie grecque et latine*, Brussels: Société des Bollandistes (Subsidia Hagiographica 42), 275–80].

—— (1933) *Les origines du culte des martyrs* (2nd rev. edn), Bruxelles: Société des Bollandistes (Subsidia Hagiographica 20).

De Ligt, L. (1993) *Fairs and Markets in the Roman Empire. Economic and Social Aspects of Periodic Trade in a Pre-Industrial Society*, Amsterdam: Gieben (Dutch Monographs on Ancient History and Archaeology 11).

—— and De Neeve, P. (1988) 'Ancient Periodic Markets: Festivals and Fairs', *Athenaeum* 67: 391–416.

Delmaire, R. (1997) 'Jean Chrysostome et ses "amis" d'après le nouveau classement de sa Correspondance', *Studia Patristica* 33: 302–13.

Den Boeft, J. (1988) 'Milaan 386: Protasius en Gervasius', in A. Hilhorst (ed.), *De heiligenverering in de eerste eeuwen van het christendom*, Nijmegen: Dekker & van de Vegt, 168–78.

Dihle, A. (1998) 'Theodorets Verteidigung des Kults der Märtyrer', in E. Dassmann, K. Thraede and J. Engemann (eds), *Chartulae: Festschrift für Wolfgang Speyer*, Münster: Aschendorff (Jahrbuch für Antike und Christentum. Erganzungsbände 28), 104–8.

Donahue, J.R. (1999) 'Redaction Criticism, New Testament', in J.H. Hayes (ed.), *Dictionary of Biblical Interpretation. II. K–Z*, Nashville TN: Abingdon, 376–9.

Dörrie, H. (1983) 'Gregor III (Gregor von Nyssa)', in *RAC* 12: 864–70.

Downey, G. (1938) 'The Shrines of St. Babylas at Antioch and Daphne', in R. Stilwell (ed.), *Antioch On-the-Orontes II. The Excavations 1933–1936*, Princeton: Princeton University Press, 45–8.

—— (1959) 'Ekphrasis', in *RAC* 4: 921–44.

Drobner, H. (1996) *Archaeologia Patristica. Die Schriften der Kirchenväter als Quellen der Archäologie und Kulturgeschichte: Gregor von Nyssa, Homiliae in Ecclesiasten*, Vatican City: Pontificio Istituto di Archeologia Cristiana (Sussidi allo studio delle antichità cristiane 10).

Duval, Y. (1988) *Auprès des saints, corps et âme. L'inhumation 'ad sanctos' dans la chrétienté d'Orient et d'Occident du IIIᵉ au VIIᵉ siècle*, Paris: Institut des études augustiniennes (Études augustiniennes. Série Antiquité 121).

Esbroeck, M. van (1976) 'La passion arménienne de s. Gordius de Césarée', *Analecta Bollandiana* 94: 357–86.

Eyice, S. and Noret, J. (1973) 'S. Lucien disciple de S. Lucien d'Antioche. A propos d'une inscription de Kirsehir (Turquie)', *Analecta Bollandiana* 91: 363–73.

Fedwick, P.J. (ed.) (1981) *Basil of Caesarea: Christian, Humanist, Ascetic. A Sixteen-hundredth Anniversary Symposium*, 2 vols, Toronto: Pontifical Institute of Mediaeval Studies.

Fowden, G. (1978) 'Bishops and Temples in the Eastern Roman Empire AD 320–435', *Journal of Theological Studies* 29: 53–79.

—— (1987) 'Pagan Versions of the Rain Miracle of AD 172', *Historia* 36: 83–95.

Fox, R.L. (1986) *Pagans and Christians in the Mediterranean World from the Second Century AD to the Conversion of Constantine*, San Francisco: Harper & Row.

Franchi de' Cavalieri, P. (ed.) (1901) *I martiri di S. Teodoto e di S. Ariadne con un' appendice sul testo originale del martirio di S. Eleuterio*, Vatican City: Tipografia Vaticana (Studi e Testi 6).

Gain, B. (1985) *L'Église de Cappadoce au IVᵉ siècle d'après la correspondance de Basile de Césarée*, Rome: Pontificium Institutum Orientale (Orientalia Christiana Analecta 225).

—— (2000) 'Kaisareia I (in Kappadokien)', in *RAC* 122: 992–1026.

Gavrilovic, Z.A. (1980) 'The Forty in Art', in S. Hackel (ed.), *The Byzantine Saint*, London: Fellowship of St Alban and St Sergius (Studies Supplementary to Sobornost 5), 190–4.

Girardi, M. (1988) 'Bibbia e agiografia nell'omiletica sui martiri di Basilio di Cesarea', *Vetera Christianorum* 25: 451–86.

—— (1990) *Basilio di Cesarea e il culto dei martiri nel IV secolo: scrittura e tradizione*, Bari: Università di Bari. Istituto di studi classici e cristiani (Quaderni di Vetera christianorum 21).

Grabar, A. (1972 = 1943–46) *Martyrium. Recherches sur le culte des reliques et l'art chrétien antique. I. Architecture. II Iconographie. III. Album*, Paris: Collège de France.

Greatrex, G. and Watt, J.W. (1999) 'One, Two or Three Feasts? The Brytae, the Maiuma and the May Festival at Edessa', *Oriens Christianus* 83: 1–21.

Gribomont, J. (1984) *Saint Basile: Évangile et église. Mélanges*, 2 vols, Bégrolles-en-Mauges: Abbaye de Bellefontaine (Spiritualité orientale et vie monastique 36–7).

Guinot, J.-N. (1995) 'L'Homélie sur Babylas de Jean Chrysostome: la victoire du martyr sur l'hellénisme', in S. Pricoco (ed.), *La narrativa cristiana antica. XXIII Incontro di studiosi dell'antichità cristiana*, Roma: Istituto Patristico Augustinianum (Studia Ephemeridis Augustinianum 50), 323–41.

Hagedorn, D. (1984) '*PUG I 41* und die Namen der vierzig Märtyrer von Sebaste', *Zeitschrift für Papyrologie und Epigraphik* 65: 146–53.

Hägg, T. and Rousseau, P. (2000) 'Introduction: Biography and Panegyric', in iid. (eds), *Greek Biography and Panegyric in Late Antiquity* Berkeley: University of California Press (Transformation of the Classical Heritage 31), 1–29.

Halkin, F. (1961) 'Un second saint Gordius?', *Analecta Bollandiana* 79: 5–15.

Hammerstaedt, J. and Terbuycken, P. (1996) 'Improvisation', in *RAC* 136: 1212–84.

Harvey, S. Ashbrook (2001) 'On Holy Stench: When the Odor of Sanctity Sickens', *Studia Patristica* 35: 90–101.

Haykin, M. (1994) *The Spirit of God: The Exegesis of 1 and 2 Corinthians in the Pneumatomachian Controversy of the Fourth Century*, Leiden: Brill (Supplements to Vigiliae Christianae 27).

Helgeland, J. (1979) 'Christians and the Roman Army from Marcus Aurelius to Constantine', in *ANRW* 23.1, Berlin–New York: De Gruyter, 724–834.

Hohlweg, A. (1967) 'Ekphrasis', in *Reallexikon zur Byzantinischen Kunst* 2: 33–75.

Honigmann, E. (1953) 'Basileus of Amasea', in id., *Patristic Studies*, Vatican City: Biblioteca Apostolica Vaticana (Studi e Testi 173), 6–27.

Hunt, E.D. (1984) *Holy Land Pilgrimage in the Later Roman Empire AD 312–460*, Oxford: Clarendon Press.

—— (1998a) 'Julian', in A. Cameron and P. Garnsey (eds), *The Late Empire: AD 337–425*, Cambridge: Cambridge University Press (The Cambridge Ancient History 13), 44–77.

—— (1998b) 'The Church as a Public Institution', in A. Cameron and P. Garnsey (eds), *The Late Empire: AD 337–425*, Cambridge: Cambridge University Press (The Cambridge Ancient History 13), 238–76.

Ireland, S., Ireland, H., Yüce, A. and Özdemir, C. (2000) *Greek, Roman and Byzantine Coins in the Museum at Amasya (Ancient Amaseia, Turkey)*, London: British Institute of Archaeology at Ankara (Royal Numismatic Society, Special Publications 33 – British Institute of Archaeology at Ankara Monographs 27).

Karlin-Hayter, P. (1991) 'Passio of the XL Martyrs of Sebaste. The Greek Tradition: the Earliest Accounts', *Analecta Bollandiana* 109: 249–305.

Kaster, K.G. (1976) 'Vierzig Martyrer von Sebaste', in *Lexikon der christlichen Ikonographie*, Rome: Herder, 8: 550–4.

Kelly, J.N.D. (1995) *Golden Mouth. The Story of John Chrysostom – Ascetic, Preacher, Bishop*, London: Gerald Duckworth & Co. Ltd.

Kinzig, W. (1990) *In Search of Asterius. Studies on the Authorship of the Homilies on the Psalms*, Göttingen: Vandenhoeck & Rupprecht (Forschungen zur Kirchen- und Dogmengeschichte 47).

—— (1997) 'The Greek Christian Writers', in S. Porter (ed.), *Handbook of Classical Rhetoric in the Hellenistic Period (330 BC–AD 400)*, Leiden: Brill, 633–70.

Kirchmeyer, J. (1968) 'Hésychius de Jérusalem', in *Dictionnaire de Spiritualité* 7: 399–408.

Klock, C. (1984) 'Architektur im Dienste der Heiligenverehrung. Gregor von Nyssa als Kirchenbauer (Ep. 25)', in A. Spira (ed.), The Biographical Works of Gregory of Nyssa. Proceedings of the fifth International Colloquium on Gregory of Nyssa (Mainz, 6–10 September 1982), Philadelphia: Patristic Foundation (Patristic Monograph Series 12), 161–81.

—— (1987) *Untersuchungen zu Stil und Rhythmus bei Gregor von Nyssa. Ein Beitrag zum Rhetorikverständnis der griechischen Väter*, Frankfurt am Main (Beiträge zur klassischen Philologie 173).

Koep, L. (1951) 'Biene', in *RAC* 2: 274–82.

Lackner, W. (1970) 'Eine verkappte Hesychios-Passio', *Analecta Bollandiana* 88: 5–12.

Leemans, J. (2000) 'Schoolrooms for Our Souls. Homilies and Visual Representations: The Cult of the Martyrs as a Locus for Religious Education in Late Antiquity', in M. Depaepe and B. Henkens (eds), *The Challenge of the Visual in the History of Education*, Gent: CSHP (Paedagogica Historica – Supplementary Series 6), 113–31.

—— (2001a) 'On the Date of Gregory of Nyssa's First Homilies on the Forty Martyrs of Sebaste (Mart Ia and Ib)', *Journal of Theological Studies* 53: 93–8.

—— (2001b) *Meer dan een herinnering. Een historisch-literaire studie van de martelaarsencomia van Gregorius van Nyssa, met een bijzondere aandacht voor de Lofrede op Theodorus*, unpub. PhD diss., Katholieke Universiteit Leuven.

—— (2001c) 'A Preacher-Audience Analysis of Gregory of Nyssa's Homily on Theodore the Recruit', *Studia Patristica* 37: 140–7.

—— (2001d) 'Celebrating the Martyrs. Early Christian Liturgy and the Martyr Cult in Fourth Century Cappadocia and Pontus', *Questions Liturgiques/Studies in Liturgy* 82: 247–61.

—— (forthcoming) 'Gregory of Nyssa and the Agonothetes: An Exploration of an Agonistic Image to Speak about God and Christ'.

Leyerle, B. (2001) *Theatrical Shows and Ascetic Lives. John Chrysostom's Attack on Spiritual Marriage*, Berkeley: University of California Press.

Liebeschuetz, J.H.W.G. (1990) *Barbarians and Bishops. Army, Church, and State in the Age of Arcadius and Chrysostom*, Oxford: Clarendon Press.

Lochbrunner, M. (1993) *Über das Priestertum. Historische und systematische Untersuchung zum Priesterbild des Johannes Chrysostomus*, Bonn: Verlag N.M. Borengässer (Hereditas: Studien zur Alten Kirchengeschichte 5).

Maguire, H. (1996) *The Icons of Their Bodies. Saints and Their Images in Byzantium*, Princeton: Princeton University Press.

Malingrey, A.-M. (1961) *'Philosophia'. Étude d'un groupe de mots dans la littérature grecque, des Présocratiques au IVe siècle après J.-C.*, Paris: Klincksiek.

Mango, C. and Sevçenko, I. (1972) 'Three Inscriptions of the Reigns of Anastasius I and Constantine V', *Byzantinische Zeitschrift* 65: 379–93.

Maraval, P. (1985) *Lieux saints et pélerinages d'Orient: histoire et géographie. Des origines à la conquête arabe*, Paris: Cerf.

—— (1988a) 'Grégoire, évêque de Nysse', in *DHGE* 22: 20–4.

—— (1988b) 'La date de la mort de Basile de Césarée', *Revue des Études Augustiniennes* 34: 25–38.

—— (1990) *Grégoire de Nysse. Lettres*, Paris: Cerf (SC 363).

—— (1997) 'Grégoire de Nysse, évêque et pasteur', in *Vescovi e pastori in epoca teodosiana. XXV Incontro di studiosi dell'antichità cristiana, Roma, 8–11 maggio 1996. II. Padri Greci e Latini*, Rome: Institutum Patristicum Augustinianum (Studia Ephemeridis Augustinianum 58), 383–93.

—— (1999) 'Les premiers développements du culte des XL Martyrs de Sébastée dans l'Orient byzantin et en Occident', *Vetera Christianorum* 36: 193–211.

Markus, R.A. (1990) *The End of Ancient Christianity*, Cambridge: University Press.

May, G. (1971) 'Die Chronologie des Lebens und der Werke des Gregor von Nyssa', in M. Harl (ed.), *Écriture et culture philosophique dans la pensée de Grégoire de Nysse. Actes du Colloque de Chevetogne (22–26 septembre 1969)*, Leiden: Brill, 51–68.

Mayer, W. (1997) 'The Dynamics of Liturgical Space. Aspects of the Interaction between John Chrysostom and His Audiences', *Ephemerides Liturgicae* 111: 104–15.

—— (1998) 'John Chrysostom: Extraordinary Preacher, Ordinary Audience', in M. Cunningham and P. Allen (eds), *Preacher and Audience. Studies in Early Christian and Byzantine Homiletics*, Leiden: Brill (A New History of the Sermon 1), 105–37.

—— (1999) 'Female Participation and the Late Fourth-Century Preacher's Audience', *Augustinianum* 39: 139–47.

—— (2000a) 'Cathedral Church or Cathedral Churches? The Situation at Constantinople (c. AD 360–404)', *Orientalia Christiana Periodica* 66: 49–68.

—— (2000b) 'Who Came to hear John Chrysostom Preach? Recovering a Late Fourth-Century Preacher's Audience', *Ephemerides Theologicae Lovanienses* 76: 73–87.

—— (2001a) 'Patronage, Pastoral Care and the Role of the Bishop at Antioch', *Vigiliae Christianae* 55: 58–70.

—— (2001b) 'At Constantinople, How Often did John Chrysostom Preach? Addressing Assumptions about the Workload of a Bishop', *Sacris Erudiri* 40: 83–105.

—— (2003) *The Homilies of St John Chrysostom: Provenance. Reshaping the Foundations*, Rome: Pontificium Institutum Studiorum Orientalium (Orientalia Christiana Analecta).

Mayer, W. and Allen, P. (2000) *John Chrysostom*, London: Routledge (The Early Church Fathers).

Meredith, A. (1995) *The Cappadocians*, London: Geoffrey Chapman.

—— (1999) *Gregory of Nyssa*, London: Routledge (The Early Church Fathers).

Méridier, L. (1906) *L'influence de la seconde sophistique sur l'œuvre de Grégoire de Nysse*, Paris: Hachette.

Merkelbach, R. (1975) 'Der griechische Wortschatz und die Christen', *Zeitschrift für Papyrologie und Epigraphik* 18: 101–48.

Michel, O. and Klauser, T. (1976) 'Gebet II', in *RAC* 9: 1–36.

Mitchell, M. (2000) *The Heavenly Trumpet: John Chrysostom and the Art of Pauline Interpretation*, Tübingen: Mohr Siebeck (Hermeneutische Untersuchungen zur Theologie 40).

Mitchell, S. (1982) 'The Life of S. Theodotus of Ancyra', *Anatolian Studies* 22: 93–113.

—— (1993) *Anatolia: Land, Men and Gods. II. The Rise of the Church*, Oxford: Clarendon Press.

Moshammer, A. (2001) 'Gregory of Nyssa as Homilist', *Studia Patristica* 37: 212–40.

Mossay, J. (1965) *Les fêtes de Noel et d'Epiphanie d'après les sources cappadociennes du IVe siècle*, Leuven: Abdij Keizersberg (Textes et études liturgiques 3).

Nardi, C. (1980) 'A proposito degli atti del martirio di Bernice, Prosdoce e Domnina', *Civilta Classica e Cristiana* 1: 243–57.

Nicholson, O. (1994) 'The "Pagan Churches" of Maximinus Daia and Julian the Apostate', *Journal of Ecclesiastical History* 45: 1–10.

Oikonomides, N. (1986) 'Le dédoublement de saint Théodore et les villes d'Euchaïta et d'Euchaneia', *Analecta Bollandiana* 104: 327–35.

Olivar, A. (1991) *La predicación cristiana antigua*, Barcelona: Herder (Biblioteca Herder. Sección de teología y filosofía 189)

Pasquato, O. (1998) *I laici in Giovanni Crisostomo. Tra Chiesa, famiglia e città*, Rome: LAS (Biblioteca di Scienze Religiose 144).

van de Paverd, F. (1970) *Zur Geschichte der Messliturgie in Antiocheia und Konstantinopel gegen Ende des vierten Jahrhunderts*, Rome: Pontificium Institutum Studiorum Orientalium (Orientalia Christiana Analecta 187).

Perrin, M.-Y. (1995) 'Le nouveau style missionaire: la conquête de l'espace et du temps', in C. Piétri and L. Piétri (eds), *Naissance d'une chrétienté*

(250–430), Paris: Desclée (Histoire du christianisme des origines à nos jours 2), 585–621.

Pouchet, R. (1992) 'La date de l'élection épiscopale de saint Basile et celle de sa mort', *Revue d'Histoire Ecclésiastique* 87: 5–33.

Quacquarelli, A. (1970) 'Ai margini dell' "actio": la "loquela digitorum"', *Vetera Christianorum* 7: 199–224.

Rice, D.T. (1963) 'Ivory of the Forty Martyrs at Berlin and the Art of the Twelfth Century', in F. Barisic (ed.), *Mélanges Georges Ostrogorsky*, Beograd: s.n. (Académie Serbe des Sciences et des Arts Beograd. Recueil de Travaux de l'Institut d'Études Byzantines 8), I, 275–9.

Rousseau, P. (1994) *Basil of Caesarea*, Berkeley: University of California Press (Transformations of the Classical Heritage 20).

Rowe, G.O. (1997) 'Style', in S. Porter (ed.), *Classical Rhetoric in the Hellenistic Period 330 BC–AD 400*, Leiden: Brill, 121–59.

Rylaarsdam, D. (1999) 'The Adaptability of Divine Pedagogy: *Sunkatabasis* in the Theology and Rhetoric of John Chrysostom', unpub. PhD diss., University of Notre Dame, Indiana.

Sage, M. (1987) 'Eusebius and the Rain Miracle: Some Observations', *Historia* 36: 96–111.

Sawhill, J.A. (1928) *The Use of Athletic Metaphors in the Biblical Homilies of St. John Chrysostom*, unpub. PhD diss., Princeton University.

Schneider, A.M. (1951) 'Sankt Euphemia und das Konzil von Chalkedon', in A. Grillmeier and H. Bacht (eds), *Das Konzil von Chalkedon. Geschichte und Gegenwart. I. Der Glaube von Chalkedon*, Würzburg: Echter Verlag, 291–302.

Schrier, O.J. (1984) 'A propos d'une donnée négligée sur la mort de Ste Euphémie', *Analecta Bollandiana* 102: 329–53.

Skedros, J. (1999) *St. Demetrios of Thessaloniki: Civic Patron and Divine Protector (4th–7th CE)*, Harrisburg PA: Trinity Press International.

—— (2001) 'The Cappadocian Fathers on the Veneration of Martyrs', *Studia Patristica* 37: 294–301.

Speyer, W. (1971) 'Die Euphemia-Reden des Asterios von Amaseia. Eine Missionsschrift für gebildete Heiden', *Jahrbuch für Antike und Christentum* 14: 39–47.

—— (1986) 'Asterios von Amaseia', *Reallexikon für Antike und Christentum. Supplementheft* 4: 626–39.

Steinbrink, B. (1992) 'Actio', in *Historisches Wörterbuch der Rhetorik* 1: 43–74.

Stephens, J. (2001) 'Ecclesiastical and Imperial Authority in the Writings of John Chrysostom: A Reinterpretation of his Political Philosophy', unpub. PhD diss., University of California Santa Barbara.

Stupperich, R. (1991) 'Eine Architekturbeschreibung Gregors von Nyssa. Zur Diskussion um die Rekonstruktion des Martyrions von Nyssa im 25. Brief', in *Studien zum Antiken Kleinasien, Friedrich Karl Doerner zum 80. Geburtstag gewidmet*, Bonn: Habelt (Asia Minor Studien 3), 111–25.

Treidler, H. (1967) 'Halys', in *Der Kleine Pauly* 2: 927.

Troiano, M.S. (1987) 'L'*omelia XXIII in Mamantem Martyrem* di Basilio di Cesarea', *Vetera Christianorum* 24: 147–57.

Trombley, F. (1985) 'The Decline of the Seventh-Century Town: The Exception of Euchaita', in S. Vryonis (ed.), *Byzantine Studies in Honour of M.V. Anastos*, Malibu CA: Undena (Byzantina kai Metabyzantina 4), 65–90.

Vaes, J. (1984–6) 'Christliche Wiederanwendung antiker Bauten: ein Forschungsbericht', *Ancient Society* 15–17: 305–443.

Vaggione, R.P. (2000) *Eunomius of Cyzicus and the Nicene Revolution*, Oxford: Oxford University Press (Oxford Early Christian Studies).

Vailhé, S (1912) 'Amasea', in DHGE 2: 964–70.

Van De Vorst, C. (1911) 'Saint Phocas', *Analecta Bollandiana* 30: 252–95.

Vasey, V. (1986) 'The Social Ideas of Asterius of Amaseia', *Augustinianum* 26: 413–36.

Vinel, F. (1997) 'Sainteté anonyme, sainteté collective? Les quarante martyrs de Sébastée dans quelques textes du IVe siècle', in G. Freyburger and L. Pernot (eds), *Du héros païen au saint chrétien. Actes du colloque organisé par le Centre d'Analyse des Rhétoriques Religieuses de l'Antiquité (C.A.R.R.A.), Strasbourg, 1er–2 décembre 1995*, Paris: Institut d'études augustiniennes (Études augustiniennes. Série Antiquité 154), 125–31.

Vinson, M. (1994) 'Gregory Nazianzen's Homily 15 and the Genesis of the Christian Cult of the Maccabean Martyrs', *Byzantion* 64: 166–92.

Vinzent, M. (1993) *Asterius von Kappadokien: Die Theologische Fragmente*, Leiden: Brill (Supplements to Vigiliae Christianae 20).

Wacht, M. (1997) 'Inkubation', in *RAC* 138: 179–265.

Wagner-Lux, U. and Brackmann, H. (1996), 'Jerusalem I', in *RAC* 17: 631–718.

Walter, C. (1999) 'Theodore, Archetype of the Warrior Saint', *Revue des Études Byzantines* 57: 163–210.

Wilmart, A. (1920) 'Le souvenir d'Eusèbe d'Émèse. Un discours en l'honneur des saintes d'Antioche Bernice, Prosdoce et Domnine', *Analecta Bollandiana* 38: 241–84.

Wilson, A. (1998) 'Biographical Models: The Constantinian Period and Beyond', in S. Lieu and D. Montserrat (eds), *Constantine: History, Historiography and Legend*, London: Routledge, 107–36.

Woods, D. (1991) 'The Date of the Translation of the Relics of SS. Luke and Andrew to Constantinople', *Vigiliae Christianae* 45: 286–92.

Wright, W. (1866) 'An Ancient Syrian Martyrology', *Journal of Sacred Literature* 8: 45–55, 423–33.

Zuckerman, C. (1991) 'The Cappadocians and the Goths', *Travaux et Mémoires* 11: 473–86.

SCRIPTURAL INDEX

THEMATIC INDEX

Jesus: crucifixion of 122; followers of 81; journeys of 118; as son of God 33; Stephen's preaching on 197; and the virgin martyrs 152

Jews/Jewish communities 170; at Antioch 115–16; shrines 116; synagogues 115–16

Job: and the Forty Martyrs 86, 93, 99, 105

Johannes, Alexandria 12

John Chrysostom *see* Chrysostom, John

John, son of Zebedee (apostle) 80, 179, 206; feast day (27 December) 166

John the Theologian 91

Joseph 59, 145, 153, 171

Judas 74, 170

judgement 65, 182, 204, 207; and punishment 122

Julian the Apostate (emperor) 9, 25, 34, 40, 83, 116, 140, 163; and disinterment of Babylas's body 144–7; homilies on 114; as a tyrant 143–4

Julian (of Cilicia) the Martyr 5, 13; death (drowning) 128; humiliation and torture of 131–40; John Chrysostom's homily on 16, 19–20, 29, 32, 39–40, *126–8*, **129–40**, 149; martyrium 128; relics 127–8

Julian the tax collector 21–2

Julitta of Caesarea 12, 17, 56

Juventinus (Roman soldier): homilies on 114

lamentation 65, 120, 122, 123

the Law 197, 199, 201, 206, 211

law: secular and divine 112

Lazurus, homilies on 141 (Chrysostom); 164 (Asterius)

Lent 3, 68, 165

Libanius (orator) 26, 165

Licinius (Roman Emperor) 56

literary genres: ecphrasis 8, 34–5, 41, 173, 174; hagiobiography 22–5; panegyrics viii, 4, 7, 15, 22–31, 33, 36

literature: Christian 34; Greek 34

liturgical services 15, 16, 17

Lives of the Sophists (Philostratus) 26

Longinus (Greek rhetorician) 26

Lucian (martyr) 6; homilies on 114

Luke (apostle) 164

Maccabees (Holy Martyrs) 23, 25, 43, 128; Antioch festival (1 August) 115; cult as Christian martyrs 115–17; homilies on 114; relics 116

Macedonius (ascetic) 13, 128

Macrina (sister of Gregory of Nyssa) 13

Maiuma (pagan festival) 127

Mamas (martyr) 5, 16; feast day (2 September) 56

Maraval, P. 83

Mars, cult of (at Caesarea) 40

martyr cult i, criticisms of 166–7; Old Testament background to 167

martyrdom 34, 42, 43, 86, 106, 166; analogies/metaphors of 29, 42, 91, 97, 129–30; and ascetism 128, 142, 149; in Greek writings 43; as panegyric element 27, 42, 116; as a public spectacle 57; as a reward/trophy 98, 182; and suicide 149, 150; theme of 38; theology of viii, 112

martyr festivals 4, 6–7, 14, 15–22, 24, 32, 45, 167; attendance 20–1, 116–17; commercial activities 19; and homilies 47; liturgical celebrations 15–17, 22; and non-Christians 21–2; and pleasure-making 19–20; social aspects 17–18; in Syria 117

martyria 5–14, 128, 174; designs
and building 7–9, 35; devotional
practices 85–6, 114; functions
and practices 14; and incubation
12–13; as places of comfort 121;
and relics 10
martyrology 115, 127, 148
martyrs 34; bodies of 84–5, 136,
137, 143, 147; burials of 117;
coffins of 121–2, 128, 137;
crowns of 96–7, 119, 129–31,
135, 143, 150; death of 134;
deeds (as voices) of 119–20;
female 149–51; as intercessors
and patron saints 11–12; and
miraculous happenings 89; in
panegyrics 31–2; and resurrection
120, 129; as role models 38;
sweet smell 59, 132, 147;
veneration of 4, 9, 15, 22, 169;
see also feast days; martyr cult
Martyrs of Palestine (Eusebius)
205
Matthias 74
mausoleums 114
Maximinus (Roman soldier) 114
Mayer, W. 38–9, 44
Meletius of Antioch 18, 23,
111–12, 141; and ascetism 142;
homilies on 114
Menander 26–7
menologia, Byzantine 57
Menologion (Metaphrastes) 167
metaphors 29–30, 42
Metaphrastes, Symeon 167
miracles: and Pelagia 149; rain 99
money: wordplay 126
monologues: as stylistic feature
33–4
Moses 58, 79, 145, 178, 180, 197,
201, 206, 210
mysteries 61, 175, 178, 196;
participation in 5, 122, 138; of
the Psalms 94; teaching/
knowledge of 170, 196

Nazianze 5, 6
Nectarius (bishop of
Constantinople) 112
Neocaesarea 81
Nero (Roman emperor) 166
Nicaea, second council of 163
Nicene Creed 55
Nicenes/Neo-Nicenes 18, 55,
78–9, 111, 140
Noah and the ark 135, 206
Nonnos (bishop) 148
numerarii 18
Numerian (Roman emperor) 149

Old Testament 167
On Epideictic Speech (Menander)
26–7
orators/orations: Greek 26; Pagan
26; subjects for 95–7; training
25–6

pagans/paganism: begetting of gods
87; and Christianity 15–16, 21,
25, 162; cults 12, 40, 83, 88;
education 164; festivals 127; and
incubation 12; and martyr cults
167; rejection of 82; and
religious terminology 174;
sacrifices of 89
paideia 25
Palladius (bishop of Amasea)
163
panègureis *see* martyr festivals
panegyrics 22, 23, 26–7, 28;
approach to 45–7; author sources
40, 41; classical models 165;
genesis reconstruction 40–1;
structure 27–8; stylistic features
29–35; use of comparisons 30
Paradise 102, 103; revolving sword
of 106–7
parallelisms: uses in panegyrics
32–3
parents: honouring and love 94–5,
103